SERMONS WITH INSIGHT

ROLAND ZIMANY, Ph.D.

Sermons With Insight
Copyright ©2015 Roland Zimany

ISBN 978-1622-879-10-6 PRINT
ISBN 978-1622-879-11-3 EBOOK

LCCN 2015940513

August 2015

Published and Distributed by
First Edition Design Publishing, Inc.
P.O. Box 20217, Sarasota, FL 34276-3217
www.firsteditiondesignpublishing.com

Cover by – Deborah E Gordon

Library of Congress Cataloging-in-Publication Data
Zimany, Roland
   Sermons with insight / written by Roland Zimany.
   p. cm.
   ISBN 978-1622-879-10-6 pbk, 978-1622-879-11-3 digital

1. Christian Ministry / Pastoral Resources. 2. Sermons / Christian. 3. Christian Life / Prayer.

S4864

Table of Contents
The Church Year

Other Important Topics

Sermons by Church Year Categories

SERMONS WITH INSIGHT

THE CHURCH YEAR

(Adv)

"Preparing for Christmas"

(John 12:24-26; Philippians 2:4-11)

In this vast universe is a tiny planet in parts of which, during this time of year, men and women prepare to commemorate the invasion of that planet by God. We call that event "Christmas."

What we want to consider here, for the next few minutes, is what kind of preparation for the celebration of Christmas on our part will be most meaningful.

Is it sufficient to prepare for the coming of Christ by developing the spirit of giving, feeling more friendly towards others, being more cheerful, being more pious, reaffirming our belief in the Incarnation, or developing a feeling of awe, or appreciation, or humility?

All of these have some value, but our Scripture readings suggest that they fall short of what is needed in order for Christ to come into our lives at Christmas -- or at any other time, for that matter.

Do you want Christ to come into your life? If so, listen to what Jesus said: "Unless a grain of wheat falls into the earth and dies, it remains just a single grain."

Jesus wasn't giving us a lesson in horticulture. What he was saying was that *we* must die. Not the kind of death where we end up in a coffin. Well, what kind of death?

Consider that grain of wheat. As long as it remained as it had been, as a grain-seed, it was alone and bore no fruit. It was only when it gave up being what it was in the past, when it stopped holding onto its former, unproductive qualities, that it became possible for it to be changed into an abundance of wheat. Or, in the words of our Gospel, it became possible for it to "bear much fruit."

The same principle is described in Paul's comments in the Epistle Lesson. Christ stopped being merely spiritual. He let go of his past condition.

He emptied himself and, as a result, became something different, a human being. In that form, he bore the fruits which Christians still enjoy today. That is, he lived the kind of life that showed what humanity at its best is like: a life characterized by a flexible willingness and commitment to doing God's will, in whatever way circumstances required; a givingness and generosity of spirit; love for the unlovely (in whatever form that unloveliness might take); acceptance of all kinds of people; concern for people in need and on the fringes of society; a no-nonsense attitude toward institutions and practices in society that needed to be changed; trust in God's power and goodness, and so: personal freedom, based on that faith and trust, and openness to the possibility of the unexpectedly good occurring.

Why is it that we, too, must die and empty ourselves? If Christ is to be reborn in our hearts -- and presumably that's what we want (we sing "O Holy Child... descend to us... Cast out our sin and enter in, be born in us... ") -- we have to ask, What keeps him out?

The answer is our self-centered wills; our rebellious nature, which causes us to insist on doing things our way instead of God's way; our extreme egocentricity, which makes us think we are as good as God, and which results in our refusing really to trust God, but instead, holding onto our lives and trying to save them and give them their fullest meaning and vitality, even though we know that, ultimately, we can't. It is this opposition of our will to God's which must be banished, before God can have His way with us and come into us; and it is to this preoccupation with self that we must die.

If we do so, then there becomes room for something or Someone else. Then if we commit ourselves to Christ, we are no longer alone. He does come in; and he *can* come in, even at Christmas time.

Having entrusted our life into God's Hands, we are freed to be concerned for others, to act without asking what we will get out of it, and to do what is needed, without asking whether we will get hurt. In short, by dying to self we are freed, for the first time, to bear much fruit.

4 Adv (C)

"Magnificat"

(Luke 1:39-55)

Before considering the important part of the sermon, let's take a look at today's Gospel lesson and ask, What's wrong with this picture? What takes place in our Gospel story that does not reflect the way things usually happen in the world?

If I were teaching a class, I would now stop talking, and there would be a long period of silence, while you look through the biblical text on your bulletin insert, to try to find something unusual. But to ensure that this sermon ends before it's time for Sunday School to begin, I'll save some time by pointing out that it is highly unusual for two pregnant women to meet and for one to say to the other, "You're going to be the mother of someone whom I'll be calling 'Lord.'" Normally, Elizabeth--or anyone else--would not know such a thing in advance. Right? The reference is to Jesus, of course. Elizabeth calls him "Lord," and that fact provides a clue to what is going on here that you, as an average person-in-the-pew, would not even begin to imagine. At least, I didn't, until I went to seminary.

You see, among the Jews of Jesus' day, Jesus was called "Master," or "Rabbi," or "Rabboni." He wasn't called "Lord." "Lord" was a title used by Greeks, and it was a popular title applied to Jesus when Christianity spread out of Palestine into Greek-speaking areas. But it wasn't a title that people who actually knew Jesus called him. So when you see Jesus being called "Lord" in the Gospels, that is a clue that that passage reflects the practices of the early Christian Church and does not come from Jesus's own time. (In case you didn't realize it, the Gospels were not written by people who took notes while the events of Jesus' life were taking place. For better or worse, the Bible was developed through a much more complicated process).

A second piece of the puzzle: Elizabeth was to be the mother of John the Baptist. After Jesus was baptized, he went on a mission baptizing people himself; and John's disciples got very jealous, because more people were following Jesus than John. How do we know? It says so right in the

Bible. In John 3:26, John the Baptist's disciples come running to him and say, "Teacher, you remember the man who was with you on the east side of the Jordan, the one you spoke about? Well, he is baptizing now, and everyone is going to him!" (TEV) Eventually, when both men were no longer on the scene, there were still a lot of followers of John, whom the disciples of Jesus wanted to win over to the new Jesus-movement.

A third piece of the puzzle: John the Baptist got arrested. This made him available to have his head cut off when the daughter of Herodias danced before Herod and made that request, in response to Herod's offer to give her anything she wanted (Mk. 6:17-27). But while John was still in prison he heard of Jesus' success, and he sent word to him asking, "Are you the one who is to come, or are we to wait for another?" (Mt. 11:3)

That question shows that John did not know who Jesus was. (Repeat question. Add citation.) But when the Gospels were written, a minimum of 40 years later, the early Christians were still trying to woo John the Baptist's followers over to their movement, so they did two things.

First, they provided a prominent place for John at the beginning of their new scriptures. And second, they depicted John as endorsing Jesus, by having him say about Jesus, "Behold, the Lamb of God, who takes away the sin of the world" (Jn. 1:29) and 'The one coming after me is greater than I am. I am not good enough even to untie his shoelaces' (Mk. 1:7). If John had really said those things, then he wouldn't have asked, from prison, whether Jesus was the one everyone was waiting for. Would he? Nor would you expect his disciples to have been jealous of Jesus.

As a clincher, Luke pushes the matter back before John was even born and has his mother profess allegiance to Jesus as Lord. Here were all sorts of reasons, then, for John's followers to become Jesus' followers, instead.

Now, it is sometimes said that preachers often answer questions that nobody is asking, and I may have given you a good example of that in what I've said so far. But the point is this: The Bible is the book of the Church, and right from the beginning, the Church was forming its holy scripture to reflect its basic belief that Jesus Christ is Lord. I've just pointed out ways in which it did that.

A second point is that it's not good enough to point to the Bible and say, "It says right here in the Bible" and consider the matter closed. There's much more that you have to know about what was going on both inside and outside the Bible, before you can start feeling comfortable with your interpretation.

We come now to Mary's response, known as the Magnificat, because of the first word in its Latin form. It is a beautiful piece of poetry. Could it really have come from a peasant girl? Interestingly, next to the name Mary, just before the poem, my Bible has a footnote that says, "Other ancient authorities read 'Elizabeth'." By "other ancient authorities" they mean "other very old manuscripts." In other words, the way some ancient versions of this story were recorded, the Magnificat was spoken by Elizabeth. It probably didn't come from either of them; but it could have been constructed by Luke or some other early Christian leader or poet to express how the New Testament Christians believed God was at work in the world. And what an exciting way that was!

If we have a passing familiarity with the Magnificat at all, we probably don't remember much more than the first one or two verses: "My soul magnifies the Lord, and my spirit rejoices in God my Savior, for he has looked with favor on the lowliness of his servant" or, in the King James Version, "he hath regarded the low estate of his handmaiden." Here Mary praises God and is content with being humble.

But if we read further, we see that when God is at work in the world, everything is turned upside down!

> "He has scattered the proud. . . .
> He has brought down the powerful from their
> thrones,
>   and lifted up the lowly;
> He has filled the hungry with good things
>   and sent the rich away empty."

When God comes to the world, inequalities are reversed! The foundations are shaken! Nothing is the same again. As Jürgen Moltmann, a theologian in Germany with whom I studied briefly and whom I saw again up in Chicago just before Thanksgiving ('94)--as Moltmann said, "No one who believes in Jesus Christ can be satisfied with the status quo." Of course not. We cannot be satisfied with things as they are, because as long as the Kingdom of God has not fully come, as long as we live in a sinful world, there are always improvements that can be made--in many areas, vast improvements!

In Japan and Germany, for example, the top executives of major corporations earn 9 or 15 times what the lowest-paid worker in their companies earn. In the United States, by contrast, top executives earn 200 times the lowest company wage! A former president of General Motors retired with a pension of a million dollars per year! Why is this a matter of concern? Well, in addition to the obvious inequality that it perpetuates, it so isolates the wealthy and powerful from the problems of the poor that those who are in a position to make changes that could make life more tolerable for the people at the bottom have not the slightest idea of what the people who are struggling--perhaps even some of us who are struggling--have to face day after day. The gap between rich and poor in this country has been growing noticeably for the past decade, and that does not bode well for maintaining a unified and harmonious country.

Would Jesus be concerned about this problem? Well, where did he spend his time? With the halt , the maimed, the blind, the prostitutes, outcasts, the people on the fringes of society, the people who didn't go to church.

And what about us, who are supposed to be his followers? Do we share his love for those who are needy and who are shunned by society? Perhaps we do--a little. But why only a little? Aren't we on fire for the Lord?

Has God come to us in such a way as to turn everything upside down? Have our lives been changed by the transforming power of the Holy Spirit, so that we can love, and give, and naturally want to do God's will at all times and in all situations? The God who can pull down the powerful and raise up the lowly can do that, you know. Radical transformation is God's specialty.

It's more evident in the case of the drunken bum, who can get up at a revival meeting and say, "I used to be a drunken bum. But one day I turned my life over to Christ, and God came into my heart and made me a new person; and now I have a good job and I'm an upstanding citizen." But what about those of us who have always been upstanding citizens? Are we experiencing the abundant spiritual life that Christ said he came to bring? Or are we content with three-quarters of a loaf--and figure that it doesn't get much better than that?

I know one thing. If Lutheran theology is true, then "we are in bondage to sin and cannot free ourselves." We say that every Sunday. We could be a conduit through which the Holy Spirit is flowing vigorously, but we are clogged by some sinful inclinations that we really don't want to let go of. Is that right? We are comfortable being the way we are.

Jesus talked about people like that by calling them "grains of wheat." He said, 'Unless a grain of wheat falls into the ground and dies, it remains alone. But when it dies, it bears much fruit. Those who would save their lives will lose them'--save our life by holding onto ourselves just the way we are, or trying to give meaning and purpose to our life apart from God's will, or insisting on having the satisfaction of having things done our way--'but,' Jesus continued, 'those who lose their life for my sake will find it.'

You can go on being 80 or 90% committed, if that's what you are. Or you can find new life in Christ by being 100% committed, by figuratively dying to your present self, by totally surrendering your life to God. Death and resurrection didn't occur only on Good Friday and Easter. You can know--in this life--the transforming power of Christ's resurrection, but only after you are willing to let go of your sinful self.

What a nice gift it would be if you were to give Jesus yourself for Christmas. In Advent we say that Christ is coming. Beat the Christmas rush! Open your heart to Christ and let him overwhelm you with his presence today!

Perhaps you have never fully committed yourself to God in this way. Now is your chance.

If you are in the Confirmation class or the prospective members' class, that's what you are being prepared for. You are being given information so that you can make an intelligent, free choice to follow Jesus. If you want to, you may jump the gun and invite Jesus into your heart today and become his disciple right now. Just say, "Yes, I want to do that."

If you are a teenager, you are probably being challenged practically every day. Whose side are you on? Are you on God's side? Be on God's side, not because your parents want you to be, not because I want you to be, not even because God wants you to be, but because you want to be. Recommit your life to Christ!

We can all stand to recommit our lives to Christ, so that we might be renewed and be given, perchance, the power and energy to bear much fruit. Do it today. Do it now!

Let us bow our heads to pray.

In the quiet of this moment, O God, come to us. As we think about this sermon later in the day and later in the week, come to us. Breathe on us, Breath of God, fill us with life anew, that we may love what you love and do what you would do. Now take our lives and let them be consecrated, O God, to you, in the spirit and power of Jesus Christ, our Lord. Amen.

Christmas Eve

"Why the Fuss about Jesus?"

(John 1:1-14)

Most of us have been celebrating Christmas for many years, many of you, possibly, right in this church on Christmas Eve. So as I began to prepare this sermon, I found myself asking myself, What can I say about Christmas that people haven't heard before?

Well, here's something: Happy Easter! Right? What clearer evidence is there that the spirit of Christ survived the grave than the fact that, 2,000 years later, we are still celebrating his birth?

Now, I know that a keen observer can raise at least one question about that conclusion. In fact, it was a question that I myself started pondering, when I noticed how many houses around here were decorated with lights even before Thanksgiving, not to mention Advent. I found myself wondering whether we in the Des Moines area are beginning to have a Japanese Christmas. The Christmas season in Japan is a major holiday season. Commercialism is fully flourishing. There are plenty of gifts to buy, and stores are decorated with lots of lights and bathed in Christmas music. But almost no one in Japan is Christian.

You may have seen my letter to the editor in the *Register* right after Thanksgiving weekend, in which I wondered what percentage of the people whose houses were already decorated for Christmas had been in church that weekend. What do you think? Were the people who decorated early reflecting an active Christian faith, or were they just anxious for another party, or yielding to the pressure of their neighbors to put something up, or deciding to put up a <u>bigger</u> display than their neighbors, or simply taking advantage of the warm weather, by decorating sooner than they otherwise would?

I do know that I could buy Christmas cards this year with the message, "May the spirit of nature bring you peace this holiday season." And the percentage of Americans who respond to polls by saying that they have no church preference has been steadily increasing. We may, indeed, be moving toward a Japanese Christmas.

This is a cause for concern, because, as someone has pointed out, every religion is one generation away from extinction. Right? If the Christian faith is not passed on to our children, then they won't have it to pass on to their children. There is one flaw in that argument, and that is that it ignores the role of grandparents. Grandparents did a remarkable job of keeping Christianity alive in the Soviet Union, under communism, when parents would have nothing to do with the Church, in order to obtain the best employment opportunities for themselves and the best educational opportunities for their children. Grandparents are doing the same thing here and elsewhere, as well. At the same time, when children see their parents go to church only on Christmas and Easter--and maybe on Mothers' Day--they get a pretty good idea of how important their religion is to them.

Actually, we find that religion never does disappear. People will believe in something. Martin Luther said, "Everyone has God or an idol," and very often the idol is ourselves. The question is whether what people believe in will be true, reliable, adequate, and effective in the long run. Will the spirit of nature finally save them? Will they be able to overcome their problems by thinking good thoughts, as some believe? Or, in the real world, is sacrifice needed to overcome evil, as the central symbol of Christianity indicates? And if such sacrifice is really needed, how insignificant must be the sacrifice of not sleeping late on Sunday mornings?

This evening we celebrate, quite solemnly, "the revelation of the mystery that was kept secret for long ages but is now disclosed," to quote Romans, chapter 16 (vv. 25b-26a). It is the basis for the Christian claim that what we have believed for 2,000 years is true. It is the awesome claim that God invaded the world.

Indeed, "it is what existed from the beginning that we announce; what we have heard, what we have seen with our own eyes, what we have beheld and touched with our hands. It is the very message of life. For life has been revealed, and we have seen it and testify to it and announce to you that eternal life that was with the Father and has been revealed to us," says the First Letter of John in the Goodspeed translation.

"It is what we have seen and heard that we announce to you also, so that you may share our fellowship, for our fellowship is with the Father and with his Son Jesus Christ."

In the words of the hymn, Love came down at Christmas, in the form first of a vulnerable baby but then of the man Jesus, who went where love was needed most--to outcasts, sinners, and scoundrels--giving people whom no one else cared about a sense of acceptance and self-worth, thereby expressing what God is like, how God acts, and what God is concerned about.

Here was one who, through associating with people on the fringes of society, through his healings, through his teachings about God's Kingdom, through his eager expectation of that New Age that was coming and that he also was bringing, and through his forgiveness of sinners, was overcoming the forces of death again and again during his lifetime.

Here was a person who made the love of God real and near, and who brought grace to those who thought they were so far beyond the reach of God that they were beyond hope. To them and to trillions of his subsequent followers, he brought hope: surely hope that the unexpectedly good could occur and that there was a power at work in the world that could transform lives and bring people into a right relationship with God the heavenly Father.

His personal freedom, which came from his faith in God, his willingness to oppose hypocrisy, and his profound ethical insights caused his followers to believe that the way he behaved and what he taught didn't just begin to be true when he taught it or when he was born but had always been true.

So John's Gospel begins, "In the beginning was the Word"--God's truth, God's Self-expression--"and the Word was with God, and the Word was God." And then, "the Word became flesh and lived among us, and we have seen his glory, the glory as of the Father's only Son, full of grace and truth." Forty years ago, at Catholic Mass, when the priest intoned "And the Word was made flesh," everyone would kneel. Of course. What better way to respond liturgically to the claim that God had come to earth, that the Spirit of God was fully present in the actions and teachings of Jesus?

Here, in Jesus, humanity was being given the clue to the mystery of God's very Being. Here, in Jesus, was the open secret of the divine intention (Eph. 1:9). Although "no one has ever seen God" (Jn. 1:18a), and although God dwelt largely in the realm of the unknown, Jesus said, "Follow me and you shall know."

In the words of the last paragraph of Albert Schweitzer's book, *The Quest of the Historical Jesus*, Christ "comes to us as One unknown..., as of old [in the manger and] by the lakeside he came to those people who knew him not. He speaks to us the same word: 'Follow me!' and sets us to the tasks which he has to fulfil for our time. He commands. And to those who obey him, whether they be wise or simple, he will reveal himself in the toils, the conflicts, the sufferings which they shall pass through in his fellowship, and, as an ineffable mystery, they shall learn in their own experience who he is." The claim is that we know who Christ is by following him.

We don't <u>have</u> to believe and follow Christ. There is no coercion. But we may, if we wish. It's a risky journey, trusting in Christ's way rather than in our wealth and in worldly power-structures, but it also can be radiant. It can, at times, be very uncomfortable; but it can also be filled with the most joyous surprise! It is the road of authentic love in action. In this faith many have traveled, over the centuries, and they found that in this faith they were saved.

It is not surprising, therefore, that the Letter to the Colossians says that Christ "is the image of the invisible God" (1:15) and that in him "the whole fullness of deity dwells bodily" (2:9). Nor is it surprising that the Church eventually should sing to the risen Christ, in the "Gloria in Excelsis," a hymn developed from the very day of his birth, "You only are holy; you only are the Lord; you only, O Christ, with the Holy Spirit, are most high in the glory of God the Father. Amen.

Epiph

"Themes of Epiphany"

(Isa. 60:1-3; Mt. 2:1-12; 3:13-17; Jn. 2:1-11)

If I were to ask you what the major Christian holidays are, you'd probably all say "Christmas and Easter." And that would certainly be true for the industrialized Christian world in the 21st century.

Even today, however, the peasants in Bolivia -- and probably in other parts of Latin America, as well -- consider Passion Week, the last week of Jesus' life, to be more important than Easter. They can identify with Jesus being arrested, being mistried, being beaten. They understand his sufferings. They know what suffering is. They are less able to find meaning in Easter. Easter represents victory, and victory is not what they usually experience. Easter is celebrated by the rich and by the landlords. For the peasants, Christianity's two main holidays are Christmas and Passion Week. (I wouldn't be surprised if migrant workers in this country, if they are religious at all, would feel the same way.)

So even today, our selection of Christmas and Easter as the major holidays does not apply worldwide. And if you would look into the history of Christianity, you'd find that Christmas hasn't always been listed among the top two, either. For the first three centuries, the major celebrations were Epiphany and Easter. Christmas, as a special commemoration of Christ's birth, developed only later.

The first Christians celebrated Easter, of course. They believed that Christ had risen from the dead, thereby destroying the power of death and making a new quality of life available -- even in this life -- to all of humanity. Today we would also say that the Resurrection means that Jesus' way of life continues to be God's way. Jesus' way of being human: his kind of love, his kind of faith and expectant openness to the future, his freedom to challenge the status quo, his concern for the oppressed and the infirm and for people on the fringes of society, his respect for the individual, his ability to bring people together and to give them a sense of worth -- these are still what it means to be fully human. They are still the things that bring abundant life. They didn't die out when Jesus was crucified.

And it is those characteristics that explain why the second big holy day that the early Christians celebrated was Epiphany. Epiphany means "showing forth" or "manifesting." The Christian claim was that God's glory had been shown forth or revealed in Jesus: in what he did and in what he taught. That's what was important. The fact that he had been born was considered incidental.

We are in the Epiphany season, which began on January 6th. Why was that date selected for Epiphany? Well, it was considered the birthday of the sun (S-U-N) in the ancient Egyptian calendar. It was the time when the people in that area celebrated the appearance of light. But Christians had found that Christ had brought light to their darkened and meaningless lives. "We were darkness, but now we are light in the Lord," they said. Their lives had been illumined by the spirit of Christ. God's glory had been manifested to them in Jesus. What better time to assert this claim than on the festival of the appearance of light?

Christ is the light of the world, and the early Church witnessed to this belief through four different scriptural passages which were appointed to be read during the Epiphany season. Let's take a look at them.

The first passage was the story of the three wise men bringing gifts. These men were not Jewish. And by means of them, the early Church said, "Look! Even the Gentiles are attracted to Jesus! God's glory has been revealed beyond the borders of Palestine!"

Now, we probably are not dealing with a historical event here. At least, you might expect that if three kings or even magicians went out of their way to find Jesus when he was born, they would have been interested enough to look in on him later on in his life. Where were they or their representatives when he needed them during Passion Week? But that wasn't a question that the early Christians were interested in. It wasn't a point of their story. They wanted to celebrate the fact that non-Jews were flocking to Jesus!

It becomes easier to accept the suggestion that the visit from the three wise men may never have occurred, after you've studied the other major religions. Because then you would see that, in almost all of them, all sorts of legends develop around their central figures -- especially in connection with their birth and death. For example, when the Buddha was born, wise fortunetellers -- so the story goes -- predicted that he would be either a great political leader or a religious savior of the world. And when he attained enlightenment, there was a great earthquake and the stars fell from the sky. That event -- when the Buddha attained enlightenment -- was awesome, from a Buddhist point of view, so it was depicted in that way in their scriptures, with earth-shattering events, to emphasize its importance.

Lao-tzu, the grand old man of Chinese Daoism, is said to have been so extraordinarily wise that he was conceived by a shooting star and born already an old man of 80.

Legends developed about Mohammed, too. The most popular one is that, at one point during his life, he was taken by a white stallion up to heaven from Jerusalem.

Of course, if you think about the direction you'd be moving, to get to heaven, it can get a bit confusing. If this circle that I'm making with my hand is a globe, going up perpendicularly from Jerusalem would shoot you off in this direction; whereas if you went to heaven from Australia, you'd head in the opposite direction; and it doesn't seem likely that the two people would ever get to the same place.

That's the problem with talking about heaven as a place. It's more likely to be a symbol for something more abstract, like "the best" or "the highest." Heaven is always up, because it stands for the highest, the morally superior, that is above the shabbiness of our normal existence. When we say that God is in heaven, we may well mean simply that God is where perfection occurs: indeed, maybe God is the potential for and the occurrence of the best or the extraordinarily good. But a more primitive mind that doesn't think in abstractions portrays those intuitions in concrete terms, as places (such as heaven) or personages (such as God the Father).

To realize all this, however, doesn't detract at all from the significance of Epiphany or even of Christianity. Because the question still remains, Why did they tell these stories about Jesus? Why not about someone else? What was it about him that made him so attractive? By raising reasonable challenges to the literal truth of some parts of the Bible, our attention simply is directed away from the fanciful and toward the essential, forcing us to consider afresh what it is that made Jesus unique.

But getting back to the three wise men, after the Bible was written the legend about them developed to broaden its racial base, so that one of the three wise men was considered to have been black. (They were all given names, as well.) Through the black representative, God's glory was depicted as being revealed equally to all the races (that they knew about). That was the point of the story, and it reflects the main purpose for celebrating Epiphany.

The story of the three wise men also includes a star that guides the Magi. Now, we're probably dealing with more legendary material here. Sure, ancient mariners used to follow the stars to be guided in the general direction that they wanted to go. But when a star directs you down a particular street and points out the house that you should stop at, we've moved out of the way nature operates and into another form of discourse, another way of telling a story.

But by including a star that guided the Magi, the New Testament Church was exclaiming that the heavens themselves point Christ out! Christians are attracted to the teachings, actions, and person of Jesus not, for the most part, as a result of straight-line logical reasoning but at a more intuitive level, at which, in moments of praise, it would seem that all of nature endorses our commitment.

The story of the star was often combined with one of Jesus calming the troubled waters at sea, to enable the Church to make another point, namely, that the Lord of the Universe had come. Here the sentimentality of Christmas is missing. Something much more important is being asserted. The God of the waves and of the stars and of the infinite variety of snowflakes -- the God of spontaneous remissions of cancer and of favorable mutations and of quantum physics -- this God is with us.

The third scriptural passage -- first was the three wise men, second was the star -- was the account of the baptism of Jesus. That passage is appropriate for Epiphany, because it includes a voice from heaven designating Jesus as God's beloved son. It depicts the Son of God coming to us in our weakness and sin, and doing what all people need to do. What we need to do is to be cleansed and to submit ourselves to doing God's will. That's what Jesus did at his baptism. There Jesus shows himself to be a true son -- not a rebellious one -- by submitting himself to God's will, as all true children of God do. In Jesus, also, God was present in the midst of sin. Here is the claim that in the very worst of conditions, there are forces for good that can come into play.

Finally, there was the story of Christ's first miracle, a story told only in John's Gospel, about Jesus changing water into wine at a wedding feast in Cana. Here, God's glory is revealed in the actions of Jesus. And that certainly must have been true. Otherwise, his followers wouldn't have considered him important enough to become his disciples in the first place. They saw in him a behavior and a being which they considered to be nothing less than extraordinary. And as they talked about him later, they expressed that assessment of him in the things they said that he could do. We miss that point somewhat if we think of the story of the wedding feast in Cana as being primarily about a supernatural transformation of water into wine. We miss it because the account, in some translations, uses units of measure that we're not familiar with. What the story says that Jesus did was to take six stone jars of water and create 180 gallons of wine! What a quantity! Isn't that amazing! And that's precisely the message that Jesus' followers wanted to convey. Where the spirit of Christ is at work, amazing things can happen, because Jesus was amazing! Faith in him provides not only what you need, but far more than it would even occur to you to ask for!

Another point of that story is that the new wine from Jesus' hand was the best that had been served all evening! That's because "new wine" is one of John's symbols for Christ himself. Faith in Christ and in his way can bring us and society a completely new life, and certainly the best kind of life that we could experience. And it isn't by chance that I relate wine to life. Wine was the Hebrew symbol for life. And the Christian claim is that Christ brings a transformed life to those who take the risk of following <u>his</u> way.

A further point of the story is that Christ does not come only in our moments of weakness and need. He is present also at our high points. He provides the best at a wedding feast, because he is lord of <u>all</u> of life. Indeed, if we do not experience his presence in our joy, we should not expect to find him in our sorrow. Faith in God is really a relationship <u>with</u> God, and meaningful relationships are not simply occasional ones.

For the first three centuries, in addition to Easter the early Christians celebrated Epiphany. And we join them in that celebration today. We celebrate the fact that God reveals Himself, that what is ultimate makes itself known.

So we are called to be watching for where God is at work. And since God has been at work in some very unlikely places, such as among a tribe of outsiders in Palestine, and in a homeless, unwed, pregnant, teenage girl in a stable, and at an execution, we would do well to be especially sensitive to watch for God to be at work where we least expect it: even in the part-time worker or uninteresting teacher, in the below average student, or in the insensitive spouse, boss, pastor, or administrator.

In addition, of course, God can be at work even through us. Which is why, if society is to improve, if laws are to be obeyed, if people are to be brought into the Church, if the world's economy is to be made more fair, if appropriate steps are to be taken to prevent global warming and the drowning of our coastal cities and towns, it must be done by people. And not necessarily only by <u>other</u> people. (There are people in this room who have given evidence that they know that.)

But the good news of the Gospel is that the burden does not rest ultimately on <u>our</u> shoulders. This is <u>good</u> news, rather than an escape from responsibility, <u>only</u> <u>after</u> we've done all we can. But when the times come when we are at the end of our rope, and it appears that nothing will work, and we are feeling helpless, then it becomes important whether or not you believe, as Epiphany claims, that God manifests God's glory. <u>Then</u>, after we've done all we can, and in the face of panic, anxiety, and despair, it becomes important, in other words, whether or not you believe that we are saved by the power and presence of God: by the extraordinarily good which <u>can</u> occur, even when we would not have anticipated it. It can become important, in other words, whether or not you accept the Christian Gospel that we are saved, ultimately, by grace.

"Jesus' Baptism and Ours"

(Matthew 3:13-17)

"Theology" means "reasoning about God." Why, over the centuries, have we kept doing theology? Why not get one correct answer and keep it?

The answer to that question is similar to the answer to the question my father asked me when I was in seminary. He asked, "Why are scholars still studying Bible? Haven't they decided what all the passages mean, yet?"

Well, the answer is that the world is constantly changing, in many ways, and our understanding of the Bible has to change to reflect our new knowledge. The Bible talks about the earth as being flat, but we know that it's round. So what had been understood literally must now be interpreted figuratively: We can no longer talk about the "ends of the earth" with the thought that we could actually get to a place where we could fall off the earth, because we had reached its end. We know, now, that disease comes from bacteria and viruses, not from demons. Sometimes, older manuscripts are discovered which show that more recent ones had been changed, in the process of being copied. New archaeological evidence shows what people were thinking back then. That evidence helps us to realize why certain things were done and what they meant to the people in biblical times.

The same process of re-shaping our understanding applies to the biblical accounts of Jesus' baptism. The first three Gospels offer three accounts of Jesus' baptism, each slightly different. John doesn't mention it at all. In the three accounts, a voice comes from heaven, but different words are used. That fact, by itself, shows that God didn't dictate the Bible. Surely God would not have been confused about which words were used. And was the voice heard as soon as Jesus came out of the water, or was it heard while Jesus was praying, as Luke 3:21 states?

Why was Jesus baptized at all? John the Baptizer was baptizing for repentance and forgiveness of sins. Did Jesus think that he, too, was sinful? Was it only later followers who treated him as holy? Two gospels don't deal with this question at all. Jesus' explanation in Matthew's Gospel is that he was being baptized "to fulfil all righteousness." What does that mean? Jesus said our righteousness had to exceed that of the Pharisees. Perhaps he was going the extra mile, in line with his call to be generous. Perhaps he saw himself as setting a good example (as baptismal sponsors are expected to do). Or perhaps he was placing himself in solidarity with all the rest of us sinners.

Later, when people responded to the Gospel by accepting Jesus as Lord, they were baptized for the forgiveness of sin. Baptism was by immersion, until Christianity expanded into colder climates, where a dunk in a river is not a pleasant experience. That's when theology went to work: Theologians reasoned that Baptism is only a symbolic washing. It isn't physical sin that is being washed away, so it's not important for your entire body to be covered by water. And it is God Who does the forgiving. The symbol "works" even if only a little water is used.

After the first generation of Christians, those children raised in Christian homes were considered to be part of the Christian community, as they are here in our church. We are kidding ourselves if we think that if we wait to baptize a person until that person can make a decision on his or her own, that decision will be unbiased. So theology was at work again, and from earliest times, people were baptized as infants. That fact is hinted at in the Bible, which reports that whole families became Christian at the same time. And the vast majority of Christians, today, were baptized as infants.

What is happening, according to a Lutheran understanding, when children are baptized? Let me present the answer in five parts.

First, infant baptism is a sign that Baptism is a gift from God. Baptism is something that God does. It's not a reward for something we decide to do.

Second, God reaches into the dark and sinful world and brings children into the safe community of Christ's followers. They are made part of the Body of Christ. They are made part of his Church, just like their parents. There, they can be nourished spiritually, and can learn the biblical story, and can grow in faith. They can develop Christian values, through the influence on them and their parents of Sunday School and other instruction, of the preached Word, and the Lord's Supper, and service projects, and wholesome friends.

Some might say, "God didn't bring the children into the Church; their parents did." Well, sure. But God works through people. That's a major point of the Christmas story. God came to us through Jesus, and we bring

Christ to our neighbors. So it's important how we treat one another. Our treatment of people is one way in which we bring Christ to our neighbors. God makes the world better through the actions of people.

Why did these parents bring their children for baptism now? If there was an outside influence, why did they respond the way they did? I want to say the Holy Spirit of God is at work, even if the people involved are unaware of it. It is God Who reaches into the world to bring children into the Church.

Come to think of it, this Lutheran view of Baptism is precisely like the way God deals with people throughout the Bible. Abram was minding his own business when God told him to go to a land that he would be shown. God came to the Hebrew slaves in Egypt, to rescue them. The Jews were called "God's Chosen People," not as a reward, but because God graciously decided to view them and use them that way. Certainly the Christmas story is about God taking the initiative.

If God didn't call us and come to us, we wouldn't know anything about God. Our only job is to respond. God showers us with love and hopes that we will respond graciously, givingly, generously -- just as God behaves -- and obediently. And if we don't, there is forgiveness for the penitent and a chance to start again.

My third answer: In Baptism, all of the bad things that the people being baptized ever did or were are washed away, and they start anew as children not only of their parents but as children of God.

That occurs because (fourth answer) Baptism is a sacrament. What is a sacrament? A sacrament is an outward and visible sign, established by Christ, of an inward and spiritual grace. Water is the visible sign in baptism. And the cleansing quality of water points to the spiritual cleansing through the presence of the Spirit of God that comes to the person being baptized.

So, fifth, we are symbolically buried, so we can rise to walk in newness of life as Christ's disciples. As the Apostle Paul says in Romans 6:4, "We were buried with [Christ] by baptism into death, so that as Christ was raised from the dead by the glory of the Father, we too might walk in newness of life." Even in our Lutheran practice, the baptized person is under water.

Luther said that all of us who have been baptized can remember that fact by dying daily to our sinful self and rising each morning to new life, through renewed commitment to Christ. In his own words, Baptism "signifies that the old Adam in us, together with all sins and evil lusts, should be drowned by daily sorrow and repentance and be put to death, and that [a] new [person] should come forth daily and rise up, cleansed and righteous, to live forever in God's presence."

Stated another way, at baptism we are "locked into" a power of renewal which is objectively inexhaustible.

Transfig. (A)

"Transfiguration and Transformation"

(Matthew 17:1-9)

I'd like to start, today, with congregational participation. Tell me, Who is the person that Christianity is built around? Who is the B-E-S-T best of all the R-E-S-T rest? Who is Christianity's "main man"? Who is the Son of God? It's very clear to you that the answer is "Jesus."

That answer was not quite so clear to Jesus' earliest followers and to their relatives and friends. They were all Jewish; and a central figure in their religion was Moses. Now Moses was quite impressive. You'd have to go some to be better than Moses. There were times when Moses got so close to God that his skin was dazzling. Did you know that? That's the way the story goes. Listen.

"As Moses came down from Mount Sinai with the two tablets of the covenant in his hand, Moses did not know that the skin of his face shone because he had been talking with God. When Aaron and all the Israelites saw Moses, the skin of his face was shining, and they were afraid to come near him. (Ex. 34:29-30)

Now, it's possible that one day Jesus was walking with a few of his close disciples on a mountain, when the bright 4 o'clock sun shone through the trees onto his white robe and his beatific face and made him look just as impressive as Moses.

Elijah was also supposed to have been on that mountain, but if you read the very next verse after our Gospel lesson, you see the disciples asking, 'Wasn't Elijah supposed to come first?'--implying that the disciples really hadn't just seen Elijah.

Well, when you come across biblical passages that don't seem to make complete common sense, the best thing to do is to ask what spiritual truth the passage might be teaching or symbolizing. In the Transfiguration story, that truth is quite clear.

Appearing with Jesus on the mountain were not just any two people but two pillars of the Jewish religion: Moses, the giver of the Law, and Elijah, the most famous early representative of the prophets, who called people back to obeying God's Law, when they went astray. Then, in a fragment of the baptismal account, there is a voice that says, "This is my beloved Son, with whom I am well pleased; listen to <u>him</u>!" There is a more complete and satisfying way than the way of Moses and the prophets. There is the way of Jesus. Listen to him! That's the point of the story.

Well, what do we need to hear from Jesus? What is the Word of God to us, today? The living Word of God, sharper than any two-edged sword, is what cuts through our present understandings and our present way of being and confronts us with the power of Truth, the Truth which we, with our sinful inclinations, are disinclined to make ourselves hear and are incapable of making ourselves become. The Word of God is God's personal address to us. The Word of God is the kingdom of heaven at hand. It is God having an impact on us, an impact that changes us and the way we think and the way we behave.

Do we need to be changed? Well, every Sunday we say, "We are in bondage to sin and cannot free ourselves." <u>Something</u> isn't right. If Jesus needed to be transfigured, we need to be transformed. Now technically, the two words mean about the same thing. But in the way that they're used, "transfigure" means a change of the <u>exterior</u>, while "transform" often refers to a change in the core or interior of a thing. When the face of Jesus shone like the sun, he just changed his exterior. His interior was solidly connected with God. <u>We</u> need a change in our <u>interior</u>. We need to be transformed.

How can that happen? Well, we could pray for it. As a matter of fact, we do, every time we say the Lord's Prayer. Did you realize that? "Thy Kingdom come" can be a plea not only for God to change the world but for the Kingdom to come to us, for God to transform us. Certainly, transformation is what would take place, if we were overwhelmed by the power of God. Wouldn't you say so? There is an ancient variation of the Lord's Prayer which, instead of saying "Thy Kingdom come," says, "Let Thy Holy Spirit come upon us and cleanse us." That is the way the Kingdom comes to us, and in that way, God's will <u>can</u> be done on earth.

I don't know how or when the Holy Spirit works, but I am fairly certain that when the transforming power of God comes to us, it stays with us only through 100% commitment on our part and only with a serious resolve to give up our previous way of life. Could it be that the reason why many of us don't feel the power of God within us is that we haven't fully given up our sinful life?

It's like a reverse version of the Dutch boy with his finger in the dike.

God is behind the dike, yet God has trickled through to have <u>some</u> beneficial effect on all of our lives. But the sinful tendencies we are holding onto are stopping the full power of God behind the dike from bursting the dike, sweeping over us, and fully transforming us. Our sinful inclinations are blocking God out.

We keep being devoted to things that don't fully satisfy but which we treat as gods, in our devotion to them and in our seeking after them, because we <u>think</u> they will make life meaningful and pleasureful in the long run. They won't.

We need, in the words of a hymn, to "lay in dust life's glory, dead" ("life's glory" being the symbols of power and success in the world), so there might blossom forth life with an eternal quality.

Jesus said, 'Unless a grain of wheat falls into the ground and dies, it remains alone. But when it dies, it bears much fruit.' (Jn. 12:24) We are like grains of wheat. We need to die to our sinful inclinations, in order to unclog our pipeline to God, so we can zoom out under the full power of the Holy Spirit. 'Those who would save their lives will lose them'--save our life by holding onto ourselves just the way we are, or trying to give meaning and purpose to our life apart from God's will, or insisting on having the satisfaction of having things done <u>our</u> way--'Those who would save their lives will lose them, but,' Jesus continued, 'those who lose their life for my sake will find it' (Mt. 16:25). <u>That's</u> what we need to hear from Jesus.

Jesus and Paul spoke more than once of dying to the old so that the new might come. Not that we <u>physically</u> die, but that we stop letting ourselves be attracted to, intrigued by, enticed by what we know is contrary to God's will. We give up that way of life. We let go of it. We stop trying to be nourished by it.

This dying to the old, sinful way of life and rising to new life by the power of God occurred symbolically in our baptism. Paul says in Rom. 6:4, "We were buried . . . <u>with</u> [Christ] by baptism into death, so that as Christ was raised from the dead by the glory of the Father, we too might walk in newness of life" Now <u>we</u> have to let that symbol become a reality for us. So, Ephesians chapter 4 (:22-24), "Put off your old nature which belongs to your former manner of life and is corrupt through deceitful lusts, and be renewed in the spirit of your minds, and put on the new nature, created after the likeness of God in true righteousness and holiness." The Holy Spirit is prompting each of us to do that. The question is, Will you respond in the affirmative? Will you say "Yes" to the Holy Spirit's promptings? Acquiring the new nature is like being created all over again. That's why it's called being born again. "If anyone is in Christ," Paul says, "that person is a new creation or a new creature. The old has passed away; behold, the new has come" (II Cor. 5:17).

If you have been content with an inner quality of life that is only half a loaf, I'm here to tell you that you don't have to be content with half a loaf. But you do have to give up resisting God. You do have to surrender yourself to God. You do have to risk entrusting your life completely to God and committing your will to doing God's will--only. Faith requires risk.

With such risky faith, we can belong to Christ and "evermore dwell in him and he in us." We can follow Martin Luther, who confessed his faith by saying, "I believe that Jesus Christ, true God, begotten of the Father from eternity, and also true man, born of the virgin Mary, is my Lord, who has redeemed me, a lost and condemned creature, delivered me and freed me from all sins, from death, and from the power of the devil, . . . in order that I may be his... "When you are his, you no longer belong to your sinful self. Don't be contented with half a loaf. Be his.

Only you and God know how much you need to recommit your life to Christ.

Perhaps the idea of dying to self and of turning yourself over completely to God is a new idea for you. You may have to give it some thought.

But others of you know that that's precisely what you need to do. Some are resisting the promptings of God's Spirit, right this minute. For others it has been a long time in coming. But that time has now arrived. You may delay, until you are in the quiet of your room this evening. But you dare not delay, if now is the hour of salvation. You may recommit yourself right now, or as soon as I stop speaking. Or you may stop singing in the middle of the next hymn and relinquish your life to Christ is a way that you have never done before, and be overwhelmed by the transforming power of the Holy Spirit.

We have the opportunity for the power of God to move mightily through this congregation this morning. Take this opportunity to open the door to God wider and to take your finger out of the dike, as we stand to sing Hymn No. 296, "Just as I Am, Without One Plea."

Transfig. (B)

"Beyond Law and Prophets"

(Mark 9:2-9)

As a former teacher, I may be permitted to begin my sermon by springing a quiz on you. Who in the congregation can tell me the first and great commandment? I don't mean the first of the Ten Commandments. But at one point during his ministry Jesus identified what he called "the first and great commandment," with the second being like unto it. Can anyone tell me what they are?

This is the first and great commandment: You shall love the Lord your God with all your heart, and all your soul, and all your strength, and all your mind. And the second is like it: "You shall love your neighbor as yourself." Then Jesus added, "On these two commandments hang all the Law and the prophets."

All of the laws of Moses and all of the teachings of the prophets can be summarized in the command to love God and your neighbor. It's really quite simple. At least, it's simple to summarize.

The Prophet Micah puts it another way. He asks, "What does the Lord require but to do justice, love mercy, and walk humbly with your God." A relationship with God and neighbor, again. What our religion boils down to is really very simple -- to state.

And there can be no question about who our neighbor is. Jesus made that very clear in the Parable of the Good Samaritan. Our neighbor is the person in need. And that applies even to people whom you can't see. So the need for love is greater than you might at first suspect. And if things are going well in our town, that doesn't mean that we have no one else to be concerned about.

But let's take a closer look at the Law and the prophets. Both of them are concerned with our relationship with God and with our neighbor. Take the Ten Commandments, for example. The first three, as we Lutherans count them, deal with our relationship with God. "I am the Lord your God. You shall have no other gods." "You shall not take the name of the Lord your God in vain." "Remember the Sabbath day, to keep it holy." But interestingly, the bulk of the Ten Commandments deal with how we behave toward people: "Honor your father and your mother." Don't kill. Don't steal, etc. All the rest deal with our behavior toward one another

Now, most people don't like to have rules imposed upon them. My students in ethics certainly didn't feel that they should have to follow someone else's rules. They wanted to be responsible for forming their own standards of ethics. They argued that if they were to follow someone else's rules, they wouldn't be genuinely moral, because they wouldn't be behaving in the way *they* think they should behave but would only be doing what someone else told them to do. And they were right. God wants us to be genuine and not phoney. But when we take responsibility for forming our own moral standards, we don't have to start from scratch. We have, in the Ten Commandments and other moral standards, guidelines for behavior that have held up for centuries. Generation after generation have found them worth following, as a means of fostering harmony in society. So it would be pretty foolish to overlook them, if you're thinking about how to act morally.

The biggest value of rules, of course, comes when you don't know *what* to do. In the presence of chaos, rules can be a source of salvation, because rules can provide order and direction, so that you can know where you stand. Unfortunately, dictators thrive precisely in chaotic situations, where people, in their confusion, turn to anybody who will speak forcefully enough and will appear to have all of the answers. We always need to be wary of that trap. Unfortunately, also, you can make a mistake by following rules, when you think that only *one* rule applies to a particular problem, when, in reality, the matter is much more complex, and *many* rules have to be considered and weighed. That's the kind of difficulty we're in on the abortion issue, for example. As a final problem, rules can be very stifling. And certainly the Christian Faith is not all about following rules.

But even with rules that they believed came directly from God, the Hebrew people were far from perfect. And their "imperfections," to understate the case, tended to follow the same pattern. The people in power took advantage of their power to mistreat the people who didn't have power. Things haven't changed very much since then.

Fortunately, a few individuals, over the course of Jewish history, were sensitive enough to the problems that arose when the Commandments and other laws of Moses were broken, that they spoke out against those multitudes who were breaking them. Those few individuals are identified in the Bible as prophets.

Some people think of the prophets as fortunetellers who predicted the future, but that isn't primarily what the prophets were doing. Primarily they felt impelled by God to say, "You guys had better shape us and stop breaking God's laws and mistreating the weak, or else, based on the way things are going, a neighboring enemy nation will overrun you, and that will be God's way of punishing you." Often enough the people did not listen to the prophets and the punishment that they threatened did take place. But that's not what the prophets wanted to happen. What they wanted to happen was for people to get back into harmony with God and, as a result, to treat their fellow human beings properly. In other words, what they wanted people to do was to follow what Jesus called "the first and great commandment," with the second being like it -- and to follow both parts, not just the part about loving God.

Listen to the way the prophet Amos, speaking on God's behalf, railed against the people of his day:

> You that turn justice upside down and bring
> righteousness to the ground,
> > you that hate a person who brings the wrong-
> doer to court
> > and loathe him who speaks the whole truth:
> You trample on the poor
> > and extort tributes of grain from them,
> > you persecute the guiltless, take bribes,
> > and throw the destitute out of court.
> Rather, you should hate evil, and love good, and
> establish justice.
> > I hate, I despise your feasts,
> > and I take no delight in your religious cere-
> monies.
> When you present your sacrifices and offerings
> > I will not accept them.
> Take away from me the noise of your songs;
> > to the melody of your harps I will not listen.
> Instead, let justice roll down like a river,
> > and righteousness like an ever-flowing stream.
> > (Amos 5)

We don't need more people "playing church" and going through religious motions. We need more people expressing love, in ways that move toward greater justice in the world.

But how do we get people to do that? Are we stuck with knowing the rules but still needing someone like the prophets to give us a kick in the pants before we actually follow them?

The Jews wondered about that question, too. One of them, Jeremiah, thought things could be different. He looked forward to a time when God would write His laws on our hearts, and when we would be in such harmony with God that we wouldn't have to learn about God because we already would be "in tune" with God and would just naturally do God's will. He looked, in other words, for a time when the law and the prophets would no longer be needed.

Have we reached that time? You answer. Do we always naturally do God's will?

But the writer of our Gospel lesson points us to one who has done so, showing what it is possible for people to be like, when they are in harmony with God. This is the one who not only saw that the law and the prophets were all about loving God and one's neighbor, but who actually lived that way. Here, in Jesus, was the embodiment of what the law and the prophets were getting at. And so, on the mount of Transfiguration, Moses, the giver of the law, and Elijah, the representative of the prophets, disappear, and only Jesus was seen.

If we think of the booths in the story as altars, the temptation may have been to worship this paragon of virtue, these standards of excellence. But the voice said, "Listen to him," with the implication that after you have heard him you are not to ignore him but are to follow him. Indeed, as the Apostle Paul said, you are to grow up into him who is your Lord and head: You are to become like him. He himself said, "Not everyone who calls me 'Lord' will enter the Kingdom of Heaven, but he who does the will of my Father."

Well, where are we on this journey? Are we like him? Are we even following him? Well, we're in church. That should mean something. But the question is, Where is he? The Bible records him spending much more time with the poor and the outcasts than in the Temple or synagogue. Maybe we should be with the coal miners or migrant workers.

And how easy do you think it is to follow Christ? When someone promised to follow Jesus wherever he would go, Jesus replied, 'You don't know what you're getting into. Foxes have holes, and birds of the air have nests, but the Son of Man has no place to lay his head.' The perfect Jesus doesn't have a home in this sinful world. When it really begins to matter, goodness doesn't fit in.

Let me suggest that it's either impossible to follow Jesus or it's very easy. It's impossible if you disagree with him, if you resist following, if you follow grudgingly, or if you have to work at it. It's easy if you are "in tune" with him, if you want to follow -- really want to -- if you have yielded your will to him, if you have his spirit. Paul said, "If a person does not have the spirit of Christ, that person does not belong to him." So we belong to Christ when we have his spirit, and that spirit *enables* us to follow him. Of course. We can't do it on our own. Did you think you could? And that spirit comes to those who come to Jesus, as he bids us: "Come unto me, all ye." And those who truly come, those who surrender their lives to him, find that his burden indeed is light. Because their will is yielded to him, so they are not struggling against him. As a result they have his spirit, his love, his generosity.

Would you say that you have his spirit? Let's look at a test case. Do you remember Jesus' parable of the "Laborers in the Vineyard"? The owner of a vineyard goes out at the beginning of the day and hires some migrant workers and agrees to pay them the usual day's wage. And two or three times during the day he goes back out and gets more workers; and finally, an hour before sunset he hires his final work gang. Then when it comes time to pay them, he pays them all the same. And the people who were hired first object, saying that they should get paid more. But the owner replies, "I choose to give to this last group as I give to you. Am I not allowed to do what I choose with what belongs to me? Can't I be generous if I want to be?" (Matthew 20:1-15)

Here, against our conventional standards of fairness, is the loving God at work. Here is the spirit of Christ, who goes the extra mile, seeks out the lost, and gives to those in need. Migrant workers, from all that *I* know about them, are always in need.

Now the question is, Do *we* have that spirit of generosity? In a very wealthy country such as ours, the test case is the Federal welfare budget. Many people, who would *never* want to trade places with people on welfare, *resent*, at a very visceral level, the efforts of the Government to provide funds for a minimally acceptable standard of living for a comparative handful of our citizens. And in their zeal to save themselves a few dollars of income tax, they advocate cutting the welfare budget for the working poor -- for those people who, despite the fact that they are working, are just barely able to get by *with* Government assistance, and who, without it, could possibly do better by going on welfare. And before we get caught up with arguing about whether or not the people on welfare are really lazy and just won't work -- although the statistics show that only 10% of them are able-bodied men -- or before we start telling the stories of welfare abuse that we've all heard -- let's not overlook the basic question, which is, Where is the spirit of generosity here? How, with this attitude, is the spirit of Christ being reflected, the spirit of the God Who gives even when we don't deserve it? It is impossible to love without also giving.

Or is there a need, in this case or in one that would be more appropriate for you, for more yielding of the will, more walking in the kind of places where Christ walked, more recognition of God's own generous love toward you, more trusting in that gracious Love, and more fervent prayer for the transforming power of the Holy Spirit? How else will God's laws become written on our hearts? How else will we be able to follow Jesus naturally? How else will the peace of God, which passes all understanding, keep our hearts and minds through Christ Jesus?

2 Lent (B)

"The Bondage of the Will"

(Mark 8:33-34)

Jesus was talking about having to suffer and to die. But Peter, like us, would have none of it. Peter knew, he thought, what God's will for Jesus was, and it certainly didn't include suffering.

Peter was exemplifying what Martin Luther called "the bondage of the will." And it is a bondage that applies not only to Peter but to everybody. Our wills are in bondage to sin. We want to do things our way, whether or not it's God's way. That is because sin is separation from God. Being separated from God, we can't even see what God's will is. Yet we assume that we know what it is. And so, as with Peter, we insist on our way, without even realizing that our way may not be God's way.

Our wills are in bondage to sin, and yet we act as though we don't even know it. Oh, we acknowledge that we fall short; we admit that we make mistakes; we know that we're not perfect. But we tend to assume--don't we?--that we're pretty much on the right track and only slip off from time to time. Luther and this morning's Gospel want to warn us that that is a very dangerous assumption. Because it keeps us from being open to the possibility that our way is not God's way.

Even God complicates the problem. Because the Holy Spirit _is_ at work in us from time to time, so that we are enabled to do God's will. We do not walk in complete darkness. We have been given light, and God continues to give us light from time to time. But we have a way of distorting that light and of _not_ _realizing_ _that_ _we're_ _distorting_ _it_. We don't realize it, because our wills are in bondage to sin.

One form that this bondage takes is a refusal to be inclusive: a refusal to see all aspects of the matter, and--very often--a refusal to consider a problem from differing points of view. Our government's approach to the Viet Nam war was an excellent example. And that applies especially to the Secretary of Defense, Robert Mac Namara--a brilliant man, with an incredible mental capacity, such that he could be looking at slides of statistics connected with the war and, when he got to slide 40, could say, "Wait a minute. Go back to slide 8. The data on slide 40 contradicts the data on slide 8." Here was a brilliant mind who, unfortunately, understood the war only in terms of logistics. Winning the war, he said, simply required getting so many more men and so much more equipment, bombs, and firepower to where the enemy was that you wipe out the enemy. He didn't want to hear intelligence reports on how corrupt the South Vietnamese government was and therefore how low the morale was in the South Vietnamese army. He didn't want to consider <u>all</u> of the factors involved in the war, rather than mostly only those that he could control? I suggest that the answer is bondage of the will — a bondage that reveals itself even in the most well-intentioned projects, such as urban renewal. What could be wrong with knocking down slum neighborhoods and replacing them with new housing, free of rats and of plumbing that doesn't work and of pealing ceilings? Well, only that you destroy the cohesiveness of a small neighborhood, one with people that knew how to handle the one or two problem people in their tenement building or on their block. Instead, you crowd them into a huge apartment complex, with many problem families, and with everything too large for the old neighborhood group to feel that they can do anything about. It isn't that urban renewal is all bad. But one suspects that more adequate answers could be found, if all of the facets of the problem were given more careful consideration, rather than relying overly heavily on the newness of the housing to transform the old evils that the new tenants brought with them.

The bondage of the will, reflected in our disinclination to be inclusive. Every group seems to be concerned only with its own members. Even revolutionary groups, dedicated to improving society radically, most often turn out to be interested only in replacing the people currently at the top of society with members of their own group. And those in more conservative groups — well, don't look to them for justice. They're quite content with benefits from the way things are. They would have to <u>give up</u> some of <u>their</u> comfort and power in order that <u>others</u> might benefit, and among sinners, that's not likely to happen.

In a word, we are trapped in the bondage of our will. We all have blind spots, and as Christians with a vision of the ultimate unity and harmony of humanity, we desperately need each other to help us to see what we, by ourselves, cannot see.

Jesus would have us be perfect. And the Greek word for "perfect" that the Gospel uses implies not so much sinlessness as inclusiveness, as in a perfect circle, which doesn't leave anything out of it by being imperfectly drawn.

Now, in our own spheres of authority, where we are boss, do we let our own opinions be modified by opposing points of view? Or are we in a bondage that we don't even see, because we have the authority to do things our way?

At other times the bondage of the will takes the form of not being able to see the forest for the trees. This bondage takes the form of being so caught up in our own way of looking at something that we can't see the big picture.

Walter Rauschenbusch learned about this form of bondage way back in 1890, and yet some of us still haven't benefited from his lesson. Rausch-enbusch was a Baptist minister who had a church at the edge of the worst slum in New York City, called "Hell's Kitchen," in the garment district. He went there to win souls for Christ, one at a time. But he found that for every person that he converted, 1000 people were won over to alcohol or prostitution, were overcome by exhaustion from work, or were stabbed in a gang fight. And how could it be otherwise? This was a time before child labor laws or unions, when people didn't have any time off for lunch — that was still true in some textile mills in North Carolina in 1979 — when they worked 14 hours a day, crowded into rooms with no air and little light: into "sweat shops" with no ventilation, where people literally sweat-ed, even though all they were doing was sewing, and for which they were paid, of course, almost nothing and couldn't be sure there would be work for themselves the next day. Then they would go home to their rat-infested, sixth-floor walk-up, where a family of six would live in two rooms, where the sinks and the toilets were in the hall, for everyone to use, and where you didn't have your own kitchen but shared one with every-one else in the building or on your floor. Under such conditions, we can understand why a person might not enjoy being sober and why others might try to get money by whatever means they could, in order to buy themselves out of there, which is what our economic system seems to re-quire.

To Rauschenbusch, it became abundantly clear that the only meaning-ful help for these people would come only by changing the structures of their society, and that meant only by legislation that would change the rules under which businesses and landlords could operate. It became clear to him that seeking to change legislation and procedures and social pat-terns that oppress people--and especially people at the bottom rung of the economic ladder, who usually are powerless to make the changes them-selves--is the 20th century version of Jesus walking among the poor and the outcasts and healing the lepers.

What were the churches doing at that time? Well, unlike Jesus, they preferred not to have anything to do with those people. But when they could muster a moment of mercy, they would come with baskets of food at Christmastime--a nice gesture, but really not touching at all the kind of help that the people needed. By and large, the church people, who, of course, were glad to get the inexpensive clothing made in the "sweat shops" (just as we are glad to get inexpensive fruit grown by cheap labor in Central America), just didn't see that there was anything else that could be done. That's called "bondage of the will."

Or take the liberal theologians in Germany prior to World War I. Eve-ry one of them endorsed Kaiser Wilhelm's military aggressiveness. With-out once considering the horror or destruction caused by war, they unan-imously endorsed their country, right or wrong. That's bondage of the will.

It wasn't much different twenty years later, when the majority of the German Christians endorsed Hitler and his efforts to purify the race. Oh, they still believed in Christ. But belief in Christ dealt only with spiritual matters, they said, so there was plenty of room for leadership from Hitler, too.

Which reminds me of a comment that someone made about a Sunday School class in one of the churches in North Carolina, when Barb and I were living there. This person was a member of that church, and he said, "The Men's Bible Class--why, that's the Ku Klux Klan!" It would appear that for them, too, belief in Christ had to do only with spiritual matters. More bondage of the will.

Now that desegregation is several decades behind us, especially our young people sometimes look back and marvel at how slow the pace of integration was during earlier parts of the last century. "How could people have been so callous?" we might ask. Answer: Bondage of the will.

Here's an example that demonstrates how deep the problem is. In Germany, Lutherans preach grace to one another until it comes out of their ears. You can't hear a German sermon without hearing about the grace of God, and God's love, and God's acceptance of us. Barb and I be-came particularly aware of this, after a year in Germany, when we visited England for a week and heard a sermon that said, in effect, "Try a little harder." You would <u>never</u> hear such a sermon in Lutheran Germany. That sounds too much like justification by works, and Lutherans will have none of it. And yet, in spite of all of their talk about grace, the Germans are the most driven, purposeful, try-harder, works-oriented people that I know. Pressures to achieve, to succeed, are tremendous, there. Which could explain a fairly high incidence of alcoholism and an even higher rate of wife-beating. At one level, Germans know that they need to be more relaxed, that they need to trust God more, that they need to live by grace. They preach that all the time. But they don't hear it as addressing their basic patterns of life. They can't seem to make it apply to the way they raise and educate their children or to the demands they make on themselves and others. At a very basic level, they are trapped in the bondage of their will.

As we all are. We all are trapped in bondage to our kind of people--which is sin, because it separates us from God and God's kind of people, which is all of humanity. We are trapped in a social, an economic, a nationalistic, and a racial bondage so thoroughly that we do not hear the cries of outsiders--or if we do, we tell each other, in some indirect but clear way, that those cries don't need our serious attention. As a result, we, like the Germans, cannot see the very things we need to change most.

Perhaps now we can understand what Jesus meant when he said, "Apart from me, you can do nothing." We can, of course, do all sorts of things apart from Jesus, except what is most necessary for our own salvation, i.e., except what will free us from bondage: except what will bring the Kingdom into our own lives and into our city and our nation.

What is the way out of our bondage? The way out comes from God, but Jesus tells us at the end of this morning's Gospel what <u>we</u> can do. We can deny ourselves. (We can? Make no mistake about it, when the point comes when we are able to lose our lives for Christ's sake, that will be a sure sign that the Holy Spirit is already at work in us.) The way out of our bondage, the only way out, is to die to our self-interest and to follow Christ, wherever he leads. We can get out, only if we are led out. "Make me a captive, Lord, and then I will be free."

The need to be led out explains the Lutheran emphasis on faith. (Sometimes, Lutherans are so concerned about faith that they forget to let their faith lead them into good works.) But doing what we already know we should do is not at the cutting edge of the advancement of God's Kingdom. God is always moving in new directions. The Risen Christ goes before us and is always a few steps ahead of us. He wants to <u>advance</u> his Kingdom, and until the world becomes perfect, he will never be content with the status quo, with things as they are. So having faith to follow

Christ means being willing to risk being led in new directions. It means being open to new ways of looking at things and watching for clues that God is at work in places where we don't normally expect God to be at work. Dying to ourselves means acknowledging the possibility of unexpected inputs into our lives and then not doing our best to block them out.

In what ways is your will in bondage? Well, at one level, you can't say. That's the frustrating and demonic part of the bondage of the will.

But we must never underestimate the slow, patient efforts of the Holy Spirit to break down the separation between us and God. So maybe you do know what changes you need to make. You won't know all of them. But maybe there is one change that you have felt under a gentle pressure to make and that you suspect really might be for the better, if only you would be willing to yield to that pressure. Now may be the right time. Or later, when you find yourself thinking again about this sermon. But if the change is in accord with what Jesus said and did, now is the hour of salvation. Amen.

5 Lent (A)

"Thriving or Not?"

(Psalm 130:1; Ezekiel 37:1-14; John 11:1-45; Romans 8:5-9)

Lent is a season of preparation for Easter, but today's scripture readings don't seem to be able to wait for Easter to come. The lessons overflow with the message of life coming to the dead.

Life comes to "dem dry bones" in Ezekiel, and to Lazarus in our Gospel lesson, and to believers who set their mind on the Spirit, in our epistle lesson. "To set the mind on the Spirit is life" (Romans 8:6).

Ezekiel presents a vision of dry bones being connected and coming alive. They stand for the whole house of Israel. They could easily stand for our congregation, because "They say, 'Our bones are dried up [--which even could be literally true, here--] and our hope is lost." (37:11) "We're tired. We've done all that before. Get someone else to do it."

Now the good news is that God says, "I am going to open your graves, and bring you up from your graves, O my people." (v. 12) Actual graves did not open up, when the Israelites returned from Exile to Jerusalem. But the people had become spiritually dead and dispirited, and God did revive them. "I will put my spirit within you, and you shall live," said the Lord. (v. 14)

Now, God has been at work among us for the past six months, at least, and we are not thriving yet. Why is that?

Last Saturday I attended a workshop so that I could be told the most successful way to reach out to the unchurched. And do you know what I was told? I was told that members of the congregation should invite friends, relatives, neighbors, and other people they know to come to church, because those are the kinds of people who are most likely to respond to an invitation of that kind. In case you don't remember, I said that very same thing at the reception you held for me, even before you elected me your new pastor. And you've heard it more than once since that time, too.

Perhaps we're not thriving because we're not desperate enough. Maybe not every one of you can think of a person who can be invited to church, but those of you who can may feel that you don't really have to take the step of actually speaking to someone about coming to church, because the new associate pastor will come and he'll solve all of our problems. Let me assure you that he won't. Let me assure you that he will have to work through you and rely on your efforts just as any pastor would, in this priesthood of all believers.

The writer of today's psalm called to the Lord only out of the depths, that is, only when things got bad enough. Someone named Mike Leavitt has said, "There is a time in the life of every problem when it is big enough to see, yet small enough to solve." We have reached that time, and we simply may not continue to defer action.

Perhaps we are not thriving yet, because we expect God to do it all. After all, didn't Ezekiel's God say, "I will bring you up from your graves"?

But if we examine John's Gospel, we will notice that God does not do what people *can* do. God does what we *cannot* do.

In today's story, when Jesus came to the tomb of Lazarus, he did not take away the stone. He told others to do that. After he raised Lazarus, he told others to unwrap him. The blind man, in last week's Gospel reading, had to take action himself: He had to wash in the pool, before he was cured.

We can do the inviting, and we must. That doesn't guarantee that the person invited will respond favorably, or become committed to Christ, or join the church. If those things occur, that would be a sign that the Holy Spirit is at work. Making the conversion is God's job. Our job is to do the reaching out and the inviting.

And according to our Gospel lesson, God is doing God's job. It seemed a little odd, in verse 27, for Martha to say to Jesus, "I believe that you are... the one who is coming into the world" (RSV) "Is coming"? Was Jesus there or not? But that language is theologian John's way of asserting that Christ is continuously making his power and person -- that is, making himself -- known. Be assured that we have a strong partner in our evangelism efforts.

But perhaps we are not thriving yet, because of the most serious reason of all. Perhaps, in the words of our epistle lesson today, we have set our mind on the flesh. Listen to what Paul writes, starting with verse 5 of the 8th chapter of Romans:

"Those who live according to the flesh set their minds on the things of the flesh, but those who live according to the spirit set their minds on the things of the Spirit. To set the mind on the flesh is death. For the mind that is set on the flesh is hostile to God; it does not submit to God's law, indeed it cannot; and those who are in the flesh cannot please God. But you are not in the flesh, you are in the Spirit, if the Spirit of God dwells in you." (RSV)

When Paul talks about being "in the flesh," he doesn't mean "having a body." He is not saying that people living in the world cannot please God. That's clear because he says to the Roman Christians, all of whom had bodies, "you are not in the flesh, you are in the Spirit." For him, "flesh" stands for following our sinful human nature and being turned away from God, while "Spirit" means being oriented toward God, committed to at least trying to do God's will. So the mind that is set on the flesh is hostile to God, does not submit to God's law, and cannot please God. Of course not; it is turned away from God. That's why "to set the mind on the flesh is death." A person oriented away from God is cut off from the source of life at its best, which God is.

Then Paul writes the very important next sentence in verse 9. Listen to it carefully. "Anyone who does not have the Spirit of Christ does not belong to him." Say that out loud with me. [Speak] This time everybody say it again. [Speak] O.K. "Anyone who does not have the Spirit of Christ does not belong to him."

And the Spirit of Christ is the spirit of Jesus, who was concerned about the lost, because lost people matter to God. In Luke's Gospel he told the parable of the lost sheep (15:3-7) ... and then, in case we didn't get it, he immediately followed up with the parable of the lost coin (15:8-10) ... and topped them all off with the parable of the lost -- or prodigal -- son (15:11-32). Jesus was saying, "I'm here because the lost matter to God." And "[a]s the Father has sent me, so I send you." (John 20:21) And while it would be nice if you could state why faith in Christ is important, all you have to do is to say what Philip said to Nathanael: "Come and see" (John 1:46).

Easter is coming, and people are predisposed to the idea of going to church on Easter -- at least, they would understand why you would be inviting them to go on that particular day. Next Sunday, our Palm Sunday service will offer contemporary music. That, too, can be a feature that non-churchgoers are likely to find attractive.

So here are opportunities to be known by your fruits -- to use Jesus' own criterion. Later (v. 15) in chapter 8 of Romans, Paul says, "you did not receive a spirit of *slavery* to fall back into *fear*." So set your mind on the Spirit, and then let God work through you, as you realize that.

"[I]f God is for us, who can be against us?" (v. 31, TEV). It can be like walking on air, when you let the Spirit of Christ take over and you finally decide to do what you know God has wanted you to do for a long time. And if you agree that God has wanted you to reach out to someone for a long time, then you probably *have* had the Spirit of Christ, and you are in a position to have a front row seat, as you watch God open a heart and change a life of someone who, apart from your effort, would still be spiritually in the grave.

Maund Thur

"A Communion Meditation"

(I Corinthians 11:23-26; Mark 14:22-25; Matthew 26:26-29; Luke 22:14-23)

Jesus proclaimed the coming of the new. He proclaimed the coming of God's new way of life and of the possibility of God's will actually being done here on earth. That's why he called for repentance: not simply for being sorry for the wrongs we have done, but for actually turning away from that way of life and letting go of the old, so that we might be open to God's newness.

But Jesus didn't just *talk* about the coming of God's Kingdom. He was so sure that it was about to break through to us that he behaved as though it had *already* broken through. And as a result, the Kingdom of God or the rule of God was present in his life. That was the secret of his success: He behaved as though the Kingdom of God were already here. And apart from our own lack of faith, and the mysterious workings of the Holy Spirit, there's no reason why God shouldn't be ruling in us and directing our lives, too

Jesus so trusted in God and in the correctness of God's will that he simply went ahead and did God's will in an evil world. And when he spoke about the Kingdom of God, in his parables and in his preaching, his disciples knew exactly what he meant, because they were witnessing the Kingdom of God in action in Jesus' own behavior. When they saw his openness to all sorts of people and his willingness to accept them; when they saw his continuing ability to love others and to extend himself on behalf of others; when they saw his refusal to be hemmed in by laws that disregarded the just needs of particular individuals; when they saw that his confidence in God kept him from having to worry about himself and seemed to provide him continually with all the energy that he needed -- then they were left with no questions about what God's will was or about what the coming Kingdom would be like. They were seeing it in Jesus.

They were caught up, with him, in their expectation of the coming

Kingdom, and when they ate with him, they started to view their meals as banquets of the new Kingdom. Mealtime with Jesus was the feast of the coming Kingdom!

And Jesus took his feast of the coming Kingdom, his feast of God's new reality, to those who needed it most: to the poor and the outcast, immigrants and those on the fringes of society; and it was a scandal. Of course. That's the way an evil world reacts to God's love. That's what God's love causes in an evil world. "Look, he's eating with tax collectors and sinners!" Those individuals and churches that participate in "Meals on Wheels," where hot lunches are brought to the poor who are old and shut in, offer for us to see and surpass just a small example of Jesus at work.

So when it came to the Last Supper, the apostles were not participating in an isolated event. This was one more banquet of the new Kingdom -- although (granted) under more solemn circumstances. But they had seen how the Kingdom comes. They had seen the band of Jesus' followers grow, and more importantly, they had seen changes in their lives and in the lives of that little community of followers of Jesus, as they experienced living in the presence of love, and of kindness, and of grace that gave even when it wasn't deserved. They experienced standards that were kept high because they were directed to motives and not just to appearances. They showed concern not just for their own group but for people outside their group. And they experienced freedom, because they were accepted by the highest authority in the universe, namely, God! They hadn't been transformed overnight, nor had they been completely transformed at all. But they saw -- they experienced -- how God's way works. And there was no doubt in their minds that the Kingdom of God was at hand.

For what is the Kingdom of God, if it isn't God's will being done? If everyone in the world were doing God's will, what more could reasonable people ask for? Oh, that's not spectacular enough, you might say. But I wonder whether we can even imagine what it would be like! People actually loving their enemies! People not ethnically cleansing whole communities. Oil prices not being raised arbitrarily. Money not spent for armaments but being used to improve the quality of life all around the world. Enough doctors, working in Appalachia, and even in Harlem, to say nothing of Calcutta. Food being shared! Resources being shared, so that 8% of the world's population -- that's us -- would *not* own 80% of the world's wealth -- or whatever the figures are of that incredible imbalance! People sacrificing luxuries -- even comforts -- on behalf of millions who are destitute, following the pattern of Jesus, whom some call their Lord. Can we imagine what that world would be like? If not, it would probably be quite spectacular!

Doing God's will is the way Jesus brought the Kingdom in his day. And it can come the same way in our day. All we need to do -- this may be a "tall order," but all we need to do is to take Jesus' faith seriously and let our behavior show that we are letting God's way be our way -- and that we expect the Kingdom to come.

Because that's what the disciples did. The Lord's Supper continued after Jesus' death. Those who had had the first taste of the coming Kingdom, in faith that their Lord was risen, continued to meet to celebrate the banquet of the new age, looking expectantly for the Kingdom, just as they had done when Jesus was sitting there with them. And by doing that, they were bringing the Kingdom in. Because what were they doing? They were lovingly sharing food with one another. And in that action, they were reflecting what the new world would be like. In that action, lovingly sharing food, God's will was being done on earth, as it is in heaven. God is present, where God's will is done. Evil is done when God is absent. God's will cannot be done, unless God be present. That's an old, basic doctrine of the Church, and it applies here, today. God is present, when God's will is done. And God's will is done when people share and when people recommit themselves to God.

But communion isn't only about God in general. It's about the person who made God present on earth and who lives to make God present for us and for all people. And as we expect him to come in his Kingdom, as we do his will, so, too, we look to the past, to recall him. If we didn't remember him, we wouldn't know what to expect from him in the future. But in remembering him, we don't keep him in the past. Instead, we recall him, in the way that a lawyer recalls a witness at a trial. We bring him back. We believe that our Lord is not confined to the past but is present to be with us. Because he promised to be. At the Last Supper, he promised that when two or more are gathered together with bread and wine in his name, he would be present: "This is my body. This is my blood. Do this to recall me."

The Lord's Supper was the Passover meal, a meal overflowing with symbolism. It was the symbol of freedom. It celebrated elimination of bondage to the old ways. A lamb was eaten for strength for the difficult journey ahead. The blood of an animal was poured, to save from death.

As the apostles looked forward to God's Kingdom coming and to the rule and power of God taking hold of their lives, more fully, at any moment, in the presence of him in whom God's will had been perfectly done, they heard, "Take and eat; take and drink." Jesus was offering them nourishment. He offers us the same thing. The journey into freedom required a source of strength for the Hebrews. The struggle for universal freedom from all forms of evil requires no less for Jesus' followers. In a setting that dealt with strength for freedom and with salvation from death and its causes, Jesus presented food that he called meat and drink, identified them with himself, and said, in effect, "Take me into you."

The elements of Communion are symbols. But, as in the traditional medieval definition of that word, a symbol is the sign of the presence of the thing. A symbol means that the thing that it symbolizes is present. The Risen Christ is present at the Lord's Supper. The elements of Communion are vehicles for enabling us to take Christ in, so that he can become part of us, and change us, so that we will be *able* to show, by our faith in him and by our actions that flow from that faith, that we believe that the Kingdom of God is at hand.

Good Fri.

"Jesus Before Pilate and Herod"

(John 18:37)

"To this end was I born… that I should bear witness to the truth."

The trial of Jesus occurred in connection with the most fully developed religion of his time and under the most sophisticated legal system to have been devised to that date by human beings. Yet both of those arbiters of the Good and the True could not do justice to the Truth incarnate. The best systems that humanity could devise could not protect Jesus from the sin of the world but could only condemn him to be executed. Light had come into the world, but people loved darkness rather than light, because there deeds were evil.

Nowadays, are our religion and our judicial system so much more advanced that the same thing could not happen again? We might like to think so, but the answer really is "No." Goodness and truth in their pure form are always rejected or misunderstood by fallen humanity. It isn't only Jewish leaders of old and Roman governors who prefer darkness rather than light.

What we do, in our darkness, is to decide the way *we* would like things to be and then become so committed to what *we* think would be best that we don't notice the light even when it is present. "We've always done it this way," they said. "It's part of our heritage." "He's perverting the nation! He's changing things! He's behaving differently!"

What could Jesus say? They didn't understand. The profound things of life are not explained in five minutes. They may *never* be explained. "Hurry up! Give us an answer so we can make a decision. There's a good TV program coming on!" Or, "at least reply to us so that we'll have an opportunity to show that we're right at least in part!" By not answering, Jesus just made the people more furious. But they were not seeking the Good and the True; they just wanted to justify their own position. So he answered never a word. Total calmness at the center of the storm. Suffering love: loving us because of what we *might* be, suffering because we cut ourselves off from understanding.

This is always the role of the Messiah, because the Messiah turns things upside down and makes them truly right. But when the Messiah comes, the lion eats straw with the lamb: the truly right is very different from what we're accustomed to. And we'll never recognize it as long as we cling to "the way we've always done it," and as long as we think that we can decide in advance what form the really True and the really Good will take. The Jewish leaders thought they knew what was best, so they weren't looking for God in someone like Jesus. As a result, they crucified the Lord of glory.

Are *we* crucifying anyone because he or she is different enough from us or wants to *do* things so differently that we feel justified in participating in persecution? Where may we be turning our back on God, when God comes to us in someone we know -- at work, or in school, or in church, or even in our family -- and that's not where we expect God to be at work? How can our deeds be less evil, so that we might see the Good? Even more basically, how can *we* be less evil? May we die to the way of life that causes the cross, so that we may be raised to the way of Life that the Cross causes. Amen.

Good Fri.

"An Appropriate Death on Good Friday"

(Mark 8:35)

Every Sunday we confess that we are in bondage to sin. Sin is separation from God. When we are separated from God, we tend to become concerned for ourselves. Of course. We figure, who else is going to take care of us? The temptation to be preoccupied with preserving ourselves wins out. And that preoccupation leads to death. Jesus said, "Those who would save their lives will lose them." That's a bad kind of death.

In the Garden of Eden story, Adam stopped trusting God and tried, instead, to enhance his own life by eating the fruit that would let him know everything. At least, that's one interpretation of his wanting to eat from the tree of the knowledge of good and evil. The way that the people in biblical times would express the notion of "everything" was to identify two extremes, thereby implying everything in between. So in order to say that a ruler ruled everything, they would say that he ruled from the River to the Great Sea, meaning the Euphrates River and the Mediterranean Sea, which was all of the land mass that they knew about. But that was a digression. My main point was that Adam stopped trusting God.

The New Testament depicts Jesus as the second Adam. He was the first person since Adam-before-the-Fall to live the proper way, the way a person ought to live, trusting in God and not trying to save his own life (or to "save his neck," as we might say).

Being preoccupied with preserving ourselves leads to a fear of death. And fear of death leads to bondage. It is a bondage that yields to the temptation to do everything we can to keep ourselves from death, since death is seen as the end. But if death were not really the end, then we wouldn't have to fear it so much, and we wouldn't be trapped into taking moral short-cuts to save our own life.

Besides, such efforts to prolong life or to give ourselves a higher quality of life are really losing battles, because we fear death even when we are at our best. Even when we are at our most superior, we can have the realization that "this won't last." Why live with that kind of fear, based on having to rely on your own ability to save yourself? Jesus tells us that in order to gain life at its best we have to lose our life, i.e., we have to surrender our entire life to God. "Those who would save their life will lost it, but those who lose their life for my sake and the gospel's will find it." (Mk. 8:35; Mt. 16:25) That's a good kind of death. That kind of death can lead to new life.

Obediently trusting in God, Jesus "stuck to his guns" in challenging the Jewish religious leaders, and he ended up on the Cross. Well, Easter tells us that "ended up" isn't quite the right phrase. His trust in God had an impact that could not be snuffed out.

But many people didn't understand Jesus' message. They hadn't experienced the new life that faith in the gospel can bring. And so they scorned Jesus on the Cross. "He trusted in God, and this is what happened!" "Look at the results of being good!" To which Jesus answered, "Father, forgive them, for they don't know what they're doing."

You see, love of self (preoccupation with giving life significance by yourself) nullifies community harmony. It can keep congregations from working together smoothly. And it can keep any large group of people from functioning cooperatively. Come to think of it, love of self potentially breaks all of the Ten Commandments. It certainly doesn't put God first. It can work against keeping the Sabbath and against honoring parents. And it is the driving force behind murder, stealing, lying, committing adultery, and covetousness -- all the result of living a life separated from God, the old life, for the elimination of which Christ died.

I say "old life," because we have been baptized, and that means that our old, sinful life has, at least symbolically, been buried with Christ and has died, "so that as Christ was raised from the dead by the glory of the Father, we, too, might walk in newness of life." And sometimes we do. But then the forces that want to keep us in bondage re-emerge, so that Luther said we have to die daily to sin. Every morning we can figuratively drown our old, sinful inclinations, so that the new person that Christ wants us to be and can help us to become can have a chance to flourish.

God let Himself be attacked on the Cross, but God still loves us anyway. That's what faith in the Cross of Christ enables us to realize.

What's the least we can do in response? Well, it was our type of old, sinful life that caused Christ to be nailed to the Cross in the first place. And it is that type of life that keeps us separated from God and from new life at its best that God can provide, when we aren't afraid to die to the old ways. So on a day when we remember the death of the innocent

Christ on the Cross, it would be most appropriate for us to nail our old, sinful life to that same cross.

May we die to the way of life that causes the cross, that we may rise to the Way of Life that faith in the Cross causes. Amen.

Easter Vigil

"Now We Are Free!"

Ma nishtanah ha-laylah ha-ze mi kol ha-leylot? "Why is *this* night different from all other nights?" That is the question that, traditionally, the youngest son asks at the beginning of the Passover Seder, that ritual meal which Jewish families celebrate, in commemoration of God's mighty act of liberating their ancestors from slavery in Egypt.

It is a question that we, too, could ask, this evening. Why is *this* night different from all others? For surely it is. The vigil that we are keeping is on the eve of the central feast-day of Christianity. So important is that day that our primary day for weekly worship was moved from Saturday to Sunday, to coincide with it.

And yet, it wasn't very long, in the history of Christianity, before the leaders of the Church saw a very close connection between *our* unique day and the Passover night celebrated by the Jews. We were reminded of that connection earlier this evening, in the scripture reading about the Exodus and in the entry procession behind the Paschal candle, reminding us of the biblical story of the pillar of fire by which God led the people of Israel out of bondage and through the wilderness toward the promised land.

A Jew might summarize that event by saying, "We were in bondage; but then something happened that we can't quite account for, and now we're free!" And a Christian, summarizing the meaning of Easter, might say something quite similar: "We were in bondage to sin and death; but then something happened that we can't quite account for, and now we're free!"

"We were in bondage." The Jewish version would appear to be more widely applicable; and it is no wonder that the slaves in this country found a lot of meaning in the story of the Exodus, as a symbol through which the power of God could free their spirits, even though their bodies were in chains. Faith in a God Who had once made physical freedom possible provided hope that something similar would occur again. And it did. But, just as in the case of the first Exodus, not without many deaths and much misery.

And again, at the beginning of the civil rights movement, back in the

'60s, the heirs of the slaves rallied around the story of the Exodus, as a source of hope that they could be freed from the bondage of a segregated society. And many forms of freedom emerged; but then, too, not without much effort, much misery, and more than a few deaths. And that battle still has not been fully won, as housing patterns in many cities and reluctance to bring industry into some towns fully attest.

The ancient Israelites had a valid claim to being God's people. The evidence for that claim lies in the fact that they didn't just *believe* some things about a God of freedom; they took action to give concrete form to their faith. They started the practice of freeing their Hebrew slaves every seven years. For their culture and their time, that was an amazing feat! For any slaveholders at any time it would be an amazing feat! And it shows that genuine faith in God results in concrete works of love. And not just in individual good works, but in efforts to change the structures and rules of society and of the economy, so that large numbers of people who are in bondage -- in whatever form -- may be given freedom. As Jürgen Moltmann, a theologian in Germany, has said, "No one who believes in Jesus Christ can be content with the status quo." To the extent that the world does not match the vision of perfection that Christ offers us, there is still much work to be done.

"We were in bondage." Many, many people know what those words mean. For many of *us*, they may not strike home quite so forcefully. If that's the case, it might be appropriate to ask, Are you here with the solution, or are you part of the problem? Certainly as consumers, if we are pleased with the comparatively low price of bananas and are not complaining about the low wages that monopolistic banana growers are paying their workers in Central America, then we must, in some sense, be counted as part of the problem. But we are beginning to get a taste of our own medicine, as citizens of foreign countries buy up property and businesses in the United States and take our wealth out of our country. Some Americans who are perceptive are beginning to feel the sense of helplessness in the wake of that activity that millions of people in third world countries have felt, as a result of similar actions taken by American business and the U.S. government. Some are beginning to realize, in a new way, that we are indeed in bondage, if not simply to sheer greed, then at least to insensitivity to the impact of our corporate and individual actions on other people -- sometimes on millions of people.

And being insensitive, we have devised and maintain economic indicators, for example, that disguise problems that we don't want to see. So our

Government tells us that when poor people in hospitals receive income from the government to pay hospital bills, those people are no longer living below the poverty level, although they certainly would be if they were not sick. Our economists take comfort from the fact that the Gross National Product of many third world countries is rising, because the GNP does not reveal that it is only a handful of wealthy families in those countries that are getting richer, while the vast majority of people is actually becoming poorer. These economic yardsticks can be changed, of course, so that they can be more sensitive and comprehensive, including reflecting the economic impact on the environment. Perhaps there is someone here this evening who will want to work on the problem. If so, such a person might well be free, because that person has prayed, more than once, "deliver us from evil." And God does answer prayer.

But what about the rest of us? Any of us who is in a position of authority in some area of our life can be part of the problem, can be a squelcher of freedom. We might not want that to be the case, but we would do well to ask what our secretary would say about the matter, or what a subordinate would say, or even a colleague, or our spouse. And why might you have a need to be a tyrant? "Something has happened that we can't quite account for." The ultimate reality of the universe *already* considers you important and significant and of infinite worth. You don't have to prove that. But perhaps there is some part of your life that needs to relinquish itself to God, so that God can make you free. "Make me a *captive*, Lord, and *then* I will be *free*," is the way the hymn goes.

To the extent that we are normal, materialistic Americans, many of us are in bondage to our possessions. I remember discovering myself moving in that direction, a few years after being graduated from college. I had been working long enough -- this was before a major career change to the academic world -- so that I had an adequate bank account and even enough money to buy some stocks. Shortly thereafter, a bill was introduced in Congress to raise the tax on profits from the sale of stocks. Well, I had always believed in the rationale behind the income tax, which is that the government takes a little money from everybody and especially from people who have more than they need and makes it available both to help those who have been hurt by the inequities of our economic system and to provide services, such as highways and Amtrack, for the public in general. But suddenly I found myself hoping that the bill would not pass, because if it did pass, I would not be permitted to keep as much of my profits. Then I realized, "This is what it's like to be in bondage to my possessions." I didn't need that money. If I did, it wouldn't have been available to be invested in stocks. At the time, I wasn't concerned about saving for retirement or for the children's education. But that's just as well, because it makes the point even more clearly. Since I had money, I wanted it to make even more money for me. The fact that other people needed the money more had stopped being a concern of mine. Jesus said, "Where your treasure is, there will your heart be also." I was treasuring my wealth and ignoring other people's needs, and I almost was stuck there. I certainly had forgotten what St. Paul said about possessions. He said, "Have these things as though you had them not." Hang loose with your possessions. Be so unconcerned about them that if you were to lose them, it wouldn't make any difference, as long as you still had what was most important, namely, faith in God; since with faith in God, you can get back on your feet again. Because otherwise, you can become a slave to your possessions, as I was starting to become. They can affect your thinking, so that you simply assume that holding onto them is the only reasonable course of action. They also can become barriers between you and other people. Treat them as being almost unimportant, or you will not be free to do God's will.

"We were in bondage; but then something happened that we can't quite account for, and now we're free!" In what other ways are you in bondage? Earlier I suggested that some people need to stop rebelling against God and to yield their lives to God. Other people need to step out into the freedom that God has already given. Are you one of those, who is too timid to take hold of the freedom you already have? The point of the Exodus is that God is on the side of freedom. (Not unlimited freedom, of course. In order for us to live harmoniously together, society places limits on us as individuals, and we need to recognize those limitations.) But it is for freedom that Christ has set us free (Galatians 5:1)! There are probably many fewer limitations than we assume. Besides, to believe in God at all is to be free; because to believe in God is to believe that the world is not ruled by hard determinism: the world is not ruled by the mechanistic forces of nature that do not allow for free will. To take belief in God seriously is to trust in a Power and a Truth that can overcome all other powers, even the power of sin. So the good news is that, through faith, we are free already! And with all due respect to Martin Luther King, Jr., if we are not free already, we never will be free at last.

In that connection, let me tell you another story. It took place in the early '60s, at the very beginning of the civil rights movement. One Monday morning my boss came to work looking very dejected, because over the weekend he had been going through the black neighborhood in his town, as a member of the Urban League, trying to get a petition signed that would have helped the people in that neighborhood. But time and again a person would come to the door and refuse to sign the petition, saying, "No, we don't want to make trouble. It would probably be safer if we don't do anything." Those people didn't feel that they were free already to take action. But without feeling free to take action, they would never be more free in the future. Without being free already, they might never be free at last.

Sisters and brothers, the good news is that we are free already! So if you think you'd like to do something that you're afraid to do, or to be some way that you're afraid to be, even though you know it would be good for you and not hurt anyone else, it's OK to take the risk of doing it. If it also seems to be in accordance with God's will, the full power of the Holy Spirit of freedom will endorse you, if you will take a chance and act. Some of you know that that's easier said than done. The Exodus, too, did not occur without effort. But it also would not have occurred without faith that God wanted it and faith that God would lead the Israelites out. There *are* forms of bondage that faith in God will enable you to step out of.

Christians also say, "We were in bondage to sin and death; but then something happened that we can't quite account for, and now we're free!" Sin and death, of course, are essentially the same thing. Both of them separate us from God. Both of them make life less than what it could fully be. I am speaking of death in its figurative sense, which may be the more important sense, for purposes of seeing the application of Christianity to our daily lives. Death in its figurative sense means anything that prevents us from being fully alive -- anything from fear of the dark to malnutrition to excessive eating to an unheated house in cold weather. I am also speaking of death in the ancient Hebrew understanding, where when you die, you are cut off from God. For the ancient Hebrews, life with God was life in *this* world. All of the forms of bondage that we have considered this evening, indeed, *all forms of bondage* are manifestations of sin and death. From these, Christ frees us -- if not already, then potentially.

Because "something happened that we can't quite account for." What happened? Jesus lived among us. He taught us how to live harmoniously in community with one another (especially as recorded in the Gospel according to Matthew, chapters 5, 6, and 7). Through his parables, he astonished us with word of a God Who is very close and not far off, Who loves us no matter what we do, Who continually reaches out to us for our response, Who lifts heavy burdens, and Who lets the oppressed go free. Jesus excited us with the possibility that God was breaking into this drab old world and transforming people's lives, and he called us to turn away from what holds us in bondage and to be open to the newness that God can bring. Through his actions he demonstrated the possibility of uniting divine and human love and directing it to where it was needed most, namely, toward people on the fringes of society, people who are not good at being religious, and women, who had been treated as second class citizens. So throughout his faith-filled life, Jesus was overcoming the forces of death at every turn. He demonstrated the ability to channel healing power to those who are broken and hurting; and he demonstrated the courage to stand up to hypocrisy and to oppose evil systems, a courage that comes when we are free, because we have faith in God as the fully reliable source of our security. In short, Jesus showed us what it means to be fully human, rather than being the incomplete, tarnished versions of children of God which we in fact are. And the good news is that the truths that he taught, the life that he brought, and the power that he embodied are still available to us today! They were not destroyed when Jesus was crucified. They are still present to make us free.

"We were in bondage to sin and death; but then something happened that we can't quite account for, and now we're free!" What happened? The power of death was destroyed! Some would say that God took the ultimate weapon that could be used against us to punish us, namely, death, and destroyed it. In what clearer way could God show that God loves us and forgives us, and therefore paves the way to a new life for us?

Now think for a moment. If you had no reason to be afraid of death -- if death had no power over you -- and if you were endorsed by the most ultimate force in the universe, wouldn't you have every reason to feel free?

Martin Luther thought you would (and this is my last point). He said that the Christian is the freest person of all and a slave to no one. Of course! When you're living in harmony with God, nothing else can dominate you!

Luther then said that the Christian is the most dutiful servant of all and slave to everyone. Is that a paradox? Not really. Because if you have given your life to God and have been freed by God's love, then you don't have to be preoccupied with saving yourself, and God's love can flow through you so that you automatically want to help other people. That's what it means to be perfectly free, when serving God, whose service is perfect freedom.

So when you leave this sanctuary tonight and when you re-enter the workaday world, leave to have fun and to be of service, because you're really free! Amen.

Easter

"Easter with St. John Chrysostom"

Shortly after midnight on Easter Sunday in all of the Greek and Russian Orthodox churches around the world -- and in the Bulgarian, Serbian, Rumanian, and Syrian ones, as well -- the parish priest -- or a person of higher rank in larger churches -- walks halfway down the center aisle (in those few churches that have aisles: most of them have no pews but just open space where you stand during the service) and then stands on a small stool and reads the Easter sermon of St. John Chrysostom. It takes 4-1/2 minutes, and it goes like this:

"If anyone loves God, let him enjoy this fair and radiant triumphal feast. If anyone is a wise servant, let him enter into the joy of his Lord rejoicing. If any have labored long in fasting, let him now receive his recompense: If any have worked from the first hour, let him today receive his just reward. If any have come at the third hour, let him with thankfulness keep the feast. If any have arrived at the sixth hour, let him have no misgivings, because he shall in no way be deprived. If any have delayed until the ninth hour, let him draw near, fearing nothing. If any have tarried even until the eleventh hour, let him, also, not be alarmed at his tardiness; for the Lord, who is jealous of his honor, will accept the last even as the first. He gives rest to him who comes at the eleventh hour, even as to him who has worked from the first hour. And he shows mercy on the last and cares for the first; and to the one he gives, and upon the other he bestows gifts. And he both accepts the deeds and welcomes the intention and honors the acts and praises the offering. So enter, all of you, into the joy of your Lord, and receive your reward, both the first and likewise the second.

"You rich and poor together, have a great festival! You who are sober and you who are heedless, honor the day. Rejoice today, both you who have fasted and you who have disregarded the fast. The table is fully laden; let everyone feast sumptuously. The calf is fatted; let no one go away hungry. Let everyone enjoy the feast of faith: let everyone receive the riches of loving-kindness. Let no one bewail his poverty, for the universal kingdom has been revealed. Let no one weep for his iniquities, for pardon has shone forth from the grave.

"Let no one fear death, for the Savior's death has set us free. He that was held prisoner of death has annihilated it. By descending into Hell, he made Hell captive. He angered it when it tasted his flesh. And Isaiah, fore-telling this, said: Hell was angered, when it encountered you in the lower regions. It was angered, for it was abolished. It was angered, for it was mocked. It was angered, for it was slain. It was angered, for it was over-thrown. It was angered, for it was fettered in chains. It took a body and met God face to face. It took earth and encountered Heaven. It took that which was seen and fell upon the unseen.

"O Death, where is your sting? O Hell, where is your victory? Christ is risen, and you are overthrown. Christ is risen, and the demons are fallen. Christ is risen, and the angels rejoice! Christ is risen, and life reigns! Christ is risen, and not one dead remains in the grave! For Christ, being risen from the dead, has become the firstfruits of those who have fallen asleep. To him be glory and dominion unto ages of ages. Amen."

That was a sermon preached in the 4th century, practically at the be-ginning of Christianity, by the golden-tongued orator named John Chrys-ostom, who was one of the most famous preachers and church leaders of his time.

He begins his sermon by pointing out that it is never too late to start again. Not all of us need to hear this message. But some of us may feel that we're kind of trapped in the sort of life that we're currently living: one that's not too bad, but one that's not especially good, either. We think we're trapped, because we don't really believe in the Resurrection. We don't believe that God can bring new life to situations of living death.

But if there are things that have been going wrong in your life that you could change, now is the time to make that change. If you are getting into habits that you know are not good for you, or if you have gotten into those habits so long ago that they seem to have been bound to you forev-er, it's never too late to give them up. You may appear to be a quite proper person, but if *you* are aware of ways in which you have been resisting God's will or if you have been doing things or wanting to do things *your* way rather than God's way, then it still is not too late to enter into the joy of your Lord, i.e., it still is not too late to turn your life over to God, to surrender yourself to the Lord, finally, so that God can make you the full, complete, abundantly alive person that you were meant to be. Because the God of life can overcome the living death that you're currently experienc-ing.

That's why our St. John, in his sermon, uses words that remind us of

Jesus' parable of the workers in the vineyard, who were hired at different times during the day--the 1st, the 3rd, the 6th, the 9th hours--but who all got paid the same at the end. That's so different from what we're accustomed to that we say it's unfair! But precisely the point of the parable is that God *is* different from what we're accustomed to! God is so good that we can't even imagine what it would be like if we didn't insist on God conforming to *our* standards and practices! But we do insist that God conform to our standards and practices. So we are not open to the different reality that God is.

Jesus was so different that even the most ethical religion and the most highly developed legal system of his time could not tolerate him! And because God *is* different, we Christians can expect the extraordinarily good to occur. Because God *is* different, we might expect that death would not have the last word. God in Christ was overcoming the forces of death all during Jesus' lifetime, as he resisted oppression, and associated with the halt and maimed and blind, i.e., with people on the fringes of society, social outcasts, the low life, giving them a sense of meaning and worth that they never had before, because at least *he* loved them, even if we don't. He healed their infirmities, and simply by his love he brought light to lives that had been in darkness and hope where hope had not existed. What a change that is, moving from hopelessness to hope! It's like moving from night to day! It's like moving out of death into life! And the power of the risen Christ, who brings life out of death, is present even today, even here, to do the same thing. If only we would believe that God *is* different! If only we could stop insisting on having things *our* way! If only we could let go and follow the vision of a better world that God has already given us in Jesus Christ.

But to follow such a vision means to take risks, because God's ways are not our ways and because the better world that we see through the eyes of Christ does not function the way our present world does. Rather than selling more armaments abroad, for example, those who see through the eyes of the Prince of Peace may need to work toward reducing the manufacture and sale of armaments worldwide.

We whom God holds responsible for caring for the world need to stop polluting the environment and stop losing our topsoil, even if it means taking the risk of making less money as a result.

We who follow Jesus in the twenty-first century cannot be indifferent to the distinction between rich and poor, as Chrysostom was in the 300s. Because we have seen that Jesus was not indifferent, and because we have seen that power structures can change. As Jesus taught us that love of our neighbor means love of people in need, we have come to ask how people in need got that way. Are they really all lazy, or is it at least part of the problem that the laws of the land and the customs of society work against them, while favoring those who already are well off? And as servants of Christ, what can we and our congregation do, by the way we vote and by what we discuss and even by what actions we take, to remedy the injustices in our society?

And what about you and your own family? Are there steps that you should be taking that would move you closer to God's will? Are we not even considering some possibilities because of the risks involved? Are we open to the new possibilities that the risen Christ may bring, the Christ who goes before us into the Galilees of our lives, where we live? Or are we afraid?

Fear certainly can result in the death of action. If we are afraid to try something new, perhaps we are already in the grave. But that's where the Christian message of Easter can be so powerful! Because as we said in the Easter Greeting that began this service, if we are already in the grave, Christ gives us life! We may not have to wait until we die for the Easter message to be meaningful. If we're afraid to do something--especially something good -- because we might get hurt, that's a mild version of being afraid of death. If we are afraid to take risks on behalf of what is good because of what people will say, we are already partly in the grave. If our fears stifle us and inhibit us, we might as well be dead!

But "let no one fear death," Chrysostom says, "for the Savior's death has set us free." We're already free because God loves us! We're free already when our faith lets God be with us. We're free because the power that overcame death *continues* to overcome death, continues to break the chains that bind us to sin and to fear and to unbelief. That God is able to do far more with the power already at work in us than all that we ask or think! If only we would believe! If only we would take the risk of believing! If only we would trust the God Who brought again from the dead our Lord and Savior Jesus Christ! If only we trusted that God, instead of our military power and our short-sighted business judgments and our social contacts. Then we'd really be free! What would you be like, if you were free?

The last part of Chrysostom's sermon talks about capturing Hell and making Hell angry. When that part is read in Greek Orthodox churches -- but not in Russian Orthodox ones (for some reason, the practice that I'm about to describe didn't develop there) -- the people in the congregation growl every time the word "anger" is mentioned. So in this part of the sermon, you hear a dull roar throughout the church.

In order to understand this part of the sermon, you need to know the myth that the Orthodox developed to depict the meaning of Christ's crucifixion and resurrection. They start with the Devil (who is referred to as "Hell" in the sermon) and say that the basic problem with the world was that the Devil was going around gobbling people up and corrupting their actions and dragging them off to Hell, and he was getting away with it because people are sinful and deserve to go to Hell. So the sinful human race was quite helpless in its efforts to combat the Devil. But God sent His Son into the world, as a perfect human being. And that's when the Devil overstepped his bounds. When he saw Christ on the Cross, he thought, "Ah, one more juicy morsel for me to gobble up!" But Christ was like the bait on a fishhook, and when the Devil tried to swallow him by taking him to the grave, the Devil was caught, like a fish on a hook, and the ultimate power of death was destroyed, and Hell was abolished, and the Devil was defeated; because he thought he was just gobbling up another sinful body (which he had a right to do), but he wasn't. He was attacking the sinless Son of God, and *he* ended up getting demolished. He judged just by appearances, and he didn't see the unseen power of God to overcome the death and evil that the Devil represents in society and in your life. But now we know the end result. Now we know where the ultimate power lies. Now we don't have to live in bondage to fear or to death or to self-centeredness. Now we're free, because God's love is victorious! The forces of life do win out, we believe, over the forces of death -- even in this lifetime! Good *will* triumph over evil, because in the paradigmatic event which we celebrate today and which God lives out through us, good *has* triumphed over evil.

So [repeat Chrysostom's Easter sermon, but replace the last two sentences with the following:] For Christ is risen from the dead, by death trampling out death, and to us in our graves giving life!

Easter

"What Are We Celebrating on Easter?"

What are we celebrating on Easter? Each of us will have his or her own answer to that question, and for most of us it will be the traditional answer. We are celebrating the fact that Jesus rose from the dead.

For some people, that will mean that "our man won," a view that may lead even further to the thought that we are better than they. 'They killed him, but God raised him.' Just who this "they" is isn't as clear as some may think. Both the Jews and the Romans wanted Jesus out of the way. The Jews -- or at least, the Jewish leaders -- wanted him out of the way because he was challenging some of their religious practices. The Romans wanted to get rid of him because he might become a rallying point for an insurrection against themselves as the occupying colonialist power. Scholars find signs that, as Christianity spread through the Roman Empire, the Christians wanted to "get on the good side" of Rome and, consequently, worded their scriptures to shift the blame for Jesus' death to the Jews.

But with Christ risen, his spirit was literally available to enter into people -- although when you talk about spirit, it isn't too easy to be sure that you are talking about a literal thing. When we hear, "He got his spirit of justice from his father," do we really envision something leaving the father and entering the son? Isn't that transfer of spirit more like the influence the father had on the son's own ideas, by what the father said and how he behaved?

Nowadays, more and more people are realizing that religious language is metaphorical -- or figurative or symbolic. We can't talk *literally* about God. Axel Kildegaard had an article in *Church and Life* not long ago, emphasizing the metaphorical nature of religious language. Metaphors take words from one subject-matter and use them in a totally different context. We use sports metaphors all the time. "You really hit a home run that time!" -- but he wasn't playing baseball. "Bull's eye!" we say, but she wasn't literally shooting at a literal, round target.

So when we talk about a physical body leaving a grave, we could really be celebrating our belief that Jesus' way is the best way, and that his way of life continues. It couldn't be destroyed by his death.

For those fully participating in that life, Easter can be a joyful celebration, as they recall their own experiences of being brought from darkness to light, in their own life.

Am I saying that Jesus did not rise from the dead? No. I don't know that. But I *am* saying that the symbol of Resurrection can apply to this lifetime. We don't have to wait until we die, in order to experience it.

Easter is the celebration of the power of God to overcome the forces of death, in whatever form they may take, from depression, to political (or some other kind of) oppression, to an unheated house in cold weather, to anxiety about some uncertainty in our life. Easter is the celebration of the power of God to bring us from death to life -- and often in very unexpected ways. So it can be in part, at least, a celebration of our own resurrection.

For people who haven't had experiences like this but who sense what they could be like and who want them, Easter can be a celebration of hope. "Hope springs eternal in the human breast," and the resurrection hope may underlie all other such inclinations to hopefulness.

We also may be expressing the hope that Jesus' way of peace does, indeed, foreshadow the ultimate way of the world; that freedom with responsibility will eventually be the condition of all people; that Jesus' openness to others will be reflected in the openness of all people to other races, and cultures, and new ideas; and that the powerless will, one day, be empowered.

Some might think that Easter might <u>not</u> be a cause for celebration, because it implicitly makes demands on us. If Jesus' way continues to be the best way, then it calls for us to sacrifice, as he did, on behalf of what is worthwhile. He didn't speak of preserving the environment and ending global warming. Today, we must. He did speak of turning the other cheek. And he did exhibit the openness that I mentioned, along with concern for the powerless. But the good news is that the Resurrection symbolizes the power of God to enable us to be that way. We are the body of Christ on earth, and we can bring Christ to our neighbors -- and beyond -- through the power of the Spirit of Christ to overcome our lethargy and fill our hearts with divine love.

Perhaps the most profound meaning of Easter exists for those who are following Jesus' way in the face of opposition. They are still choosing life at its best, which means life in the spirit in which he lived it, when all around there is nothing but death. They are still being moral, in the face of pressures to the contrary. They are still affirming freedom, especially in countries where freedom is politically restricted. And they are still affirming the right to be different, in the face of pressures to conform.

For them, the celebration of Easter is not jubilant, but it is an occasion for reaffirming their faith that what they are doing is what should be done. For them -- hopefully for many of us -- Easter is a time to say, quietly but firmly, albeit figuratively, "He lives!" Amen.

Easter (B)

"Open to God's Newness"

(Mark 16:7)

I.

We will probably all agree that life is characterized by change. There isn't anything alive that isn't also changing. Even a potted plant, which seems to be just sitting there, has leaves that move in the direction of the sun's rays, as the sunlight shines on them. And even as you sit here this morning, there is change taking place, if only in the form of the blood moving in your veins and your lungs breathing in and out.

Change isn't always for the better, of course. And we know that there is certainly nothing automatically wrong with stability. But when we see people or organizations falling into very fixed and rigid patterns, we often can notice a slowing down of activity, and we can suspect that a literal or figurative hardening of the arteries is setting in. Our natural interest in avoiding death provides reason enough to want to <u>change</u> such situations.

But it is especially when <u>we</u> are <u>benefiting</u> from those fixed patterns that we, as Christians, do well to sit up and take notice. For then the love of Christ impels us to ask whether anyone is being <u>hurt</u> by the very tried and true practices that are benefiting us. Because our Scripture reading says not only that Jesus does not endorse practices that are dead (because they're unchanging), but that he also does not endorse practices that <u>bring</u> death to <u>other</u> people -- even if that death is only in the form of less than a full life.

You see, Jesus is not <u>in</u> conditions of death. He is not here, in the tomb of our rigidities. At least, he is not giving <u>support</u> to organizations, or structures, or the spiritual lives of people where *rigor mortis* has set in. In fact, as the Son of God -- i.e., as the extraordinary human being -- he is <u>never</u> where our ordinary, sin-tainted, self-centered concerns are focused. <u>They</u> all lead to death. But Christ is risen from the dead.

So he doesn't coddle us in our comfortable status quo or in our efforts to return to it. Rather crassly he says, "Let the dead bury their own dead" (Lk. 9:59-60). Let those who aren't changing and developing bury those who aren't changing and developing. I've got more important things to do. There's still too much that needs to be improved. 'I'm going before you into Galilee' (Mk. 16:7).

II.

Christ is risen, and he's going before us, precisely because he <u>is</u> the Christ, who turns everything <u>upside down</u> -- when the Messiah comes, things don't get just a <u>little</u> better -- and makes them unexpectedly new. And he calls us, as disciples, to follow: <u>Not</u> to be content with <u>small</u> improvements -- for ourselves, or our family, or our Church, or our city, or our country -- but to be willing to risk and to sacrifice in ways which we haven't even dreamed of!

Well, that's easy to say. But it <u>is</u> the pattern set by him whose disciples we claim to be. And the only way that Christ and his Kingdom are going to return to earth is if <u>we</u> <u>follow</u> where he leads. And <u>he's</u> got <u>big</u> plans.

When talking about how God acts -- for example: when talking about <u>how</u> God expresses love -- we often note that God doesn't just "zap" people from out of the blue, and we often end up saying that God works through <u>human</u> means, that <u>we</u> are God's <u>instruments</u>. Well, you'd better believe it! We're talking about <u>our</u> <u>doing</u> things that we've never done before. We're talking about our trying things that we've never tried before. And all because we <u>believe</u> that he <u>is</u> going before us.

And that means that the risks we are called to take are not on our <u>own</u> behalf: They are not necessarily aimed at doing something that <u>we</u> would consider good for us -- such as building a bigger church building; rather, they are to be in accordance with <u>his</u> will, which we as sinful disciples might not automatically be in agreement with. <u>There</u> is the test of what condition our faith is in: to be willing to do <u>his</u> will, and not just <u>ours</u>.

Daring to follow One who goes before is not unknown in the history of the people of the Bible. In fact, it's what that history is all about! And it goes all the way back to the almost legendary patriarch of our Faith.

What were the first words that the Lord said to Abraham? They're recorded at the beginning of chapter 12 of Genesis: "Go from your country and your kindred and your father's house to the land that I will show you. And I will make of you a great nation, and I will bless you." It was the forerunner of Jesus saying to his disciples, 'Leave all, and follow me.' <u>We</u> tend to miss the <u>drama</u> of this call to Abraham, because we assume that if God spoke to <u>us</u> in the <u>same way</u>, we, too, would leave everything and strike out on an unchartered course, in obedience to God's command. At least, we would hope that we would. But God doesn't speak to people in a loud, booming voice nowadays, so we really can't put ourselves into Abraham's shoes. Well, I'd like to suggest that it didn't happen that way to Abraham, either. What we have in the Bible is not an <u>historical</u> account, but it's the way <u>primitive</u> people record history: namely, by telling a story. And in the story they have God talking to Abraham. But Abraham is great not because he simply followed orders, but because his situation was very much like ours, except that it differed in that <u>he</u> <u>followed</u> the impulse he had to break away and begin again. He acted on his vision, and in retrospect we say that the Lord was with him.

'But,' you may say, 'didn't <u>God</u> <u>give</u> him that vision or that impulse?' The answer is, We don't <u>know</u> where impulses, and visions, and ideas come from. God certainly <u>may</u> have been their source. But then what is the source of some of <u>our</u> better ideas and impulses? And if <u>they</u> may come from God, why don't we always follow them? Well, we answer, because following them is scary; they would require a lot of effort or major changes; there are risks involved. Besides, we're not even sure that they're <u>really</u> what God wants us to do. Was Abraham <u>sure</u>, as he left his homeland, that he would become the father of a great nation? I want to suggest to you that he was <u>not</u> sure, and that <u>we</u> can <u>never</u> be <u>sure</u> that we are doing God's will, and indeed, that we may never <u>be</u> doing it <u>100%</u>.

People who can take <u>that</u> seriously begin to know what it means to live by faith. They come to realize that faith is essentially <u>not</u> about agreeing with doctrines or accepting particular statements in the Bible, but is about a continuously risky relationship of trust in a God whom they can neither see nor hear. It is these kinds of risks to make these kinds of changes that we are called to take, because the risen Christ is going before us and is bidding us to seek him and to follow.

III.

But if he's ahead of us, we've got to be open to meet him; and we've got to be looking expectantly for him. Otherwise, we may be near him and not even know it. God reveals Godself in surprising ways and often in quite humble ways. Are we open to those surprises?

Jesus told a one-verse parable -- which I guess is the biblical version of a "one-liner" -- about a farmer plowing a field who hits into a treasure which had been hidden there (Mt. 13:44). If you were that farmer, would you have thought that your plow-blade might have hit into something good? Or would you just have gotten irritated at what you would have assumed to be just another rock in this lousy field that you're supposed to make a living from?

Openness to the new is a hallmark of faith in the risen Christ. The <u>original</u> disciples certainly weren't <u>expecting</u> his resurrection, and when they began to consider that possibility, as the story of the women at the tomb tells it, "they said nothing to anyone, for they were afraid" (Mk. 16:8b). And well they might have been! Because it took a lot of courage to say to the Romans and to the leaders of the Temple that the man whom <u>they</u> had crucified had, in fact, <u>not</u> been obliterated. Nevertheless, it is clear that the conviction grew among Jesus' followers that his power, his way, his presence were not limited by the tomb. And if <u>he</u> could do such an unusual thing as overcome death, then he could do lots of new and unusual things. And the disciples rejoiced in the power and expectation of being part of it!

In view of that dynamic resurrection faith, it is exceedingly strange that the followers of the Resurrection, the Christian churches, are among society's most conservative institutions. In contrast to the <u>courage</u> of the <u>early</u> Church, so many of <u>today's</u> churchpeople seem to prefer to say 'the time is not yet ripe' for the ordination of women, for example, in some denominations. Or the time is not yet ripe for new church structures, or new forms of worship, or even for new hymn tunes. And, of course, for most churches, the time is never ripe for political action. The trouble is, if we wait for the time to be fully ripe, when everyone is ready for change and when no one will be disturbed, we will remain in the tomb.

Faith in the Resurrection, however, brings us out of the tomb, daring to follow the new, right thing that we think God wants us to do. <u>Such</u> faith enables us to dare even to make mistakes. Indeed, the only way to insure that we won't make mistakes is to remain in the tomb! In view of that fact, we always have to test and question our programs, to see whether they are still meeting <u>current</u> needs, rather than past needs that no longer exist or that exist to a far lesser extent, while much greater needs have arisen that are being ignored.

The Bible itself is clear in its warning <u>against</u> holding onto past practices simply because they once were good. In the book of Numbers, chapter 21, you can read about how, when the Israelites were wandering in the Wilderness, after their remarkable escape into freedom from slavery in Egypt, they were beset by poisonous snakes that started biting and killing them. The people repented of past sins and turned to Moses, who turned to God, Who told Moses to make a serpent of bronze and put it on a pole, and if anyone bitten by a snake would look at that bronze serpent, that person would live. It was God's will that that bronze serpent be made and used.

Now you can read in the same Bible, in II Kings 18:4, that a couple of generations later, a king named Hezekiah "did what was right in the eyes of the Lord. He broke in pieces the bronze serpent that Moses had made," because the people of Israel had started burning incense to it. It had been so helpful to them that they were beginning to worship it, instead of worshipping God alone. Isn't there a danger that some things that we cherish most might fall into the same category -- and prevent us from being open to the _new_ things that God is trying to do in our time?

James Russell Lowell was on the right track, I think, when he wrote, "New occasions teach new duties; time makes ancient good uncouth." What worked in the past doesn't always work anymore. It may be that economic systems geared to growth, for example, won't continue to work -- or shouldn't be permitted to continue to work -- when the planet is running out of resources.

Which brings us back to the real world and to the many little, concrete ways in which God's will is or is not done, because we are or are not open to the promptings of the Christ who goes before us. At work, for example, how many times is the first response to a proposed _change_ something like, 'But we've _never_ done it that way; we've _always_ done it _this_ way!'? Is the person who says that any more likely to be inclined to follow _Christ_ in a new direction? And if that example sounded a little too pro-management, how often can you also hear, 'No one takes any suggestions around here. If only the bosses would listen to the people who are actually on the job _doing_ the work!'? We _like_ being in control of as much of our life as we _can_ be in control of, usually. But we dare not forget that other people feel the same way. And if our place in the power structure enables us to squelch other people, we shouldn't be surprised if the resulting resentment expresses itself in some other form. When that happens, of course, we can never understand why, because we don't want to look carefully enough at our _own_ version of closed-mindedness. We don't want to have to be open to the _possibility_ that it's the Lord who is coming to us in a new proposal or in a person who is different from us.

IV.

Our final question is short, but crucial. Since Christ is going before us, even if we are open and expectantly watching for the <u>newness</u> that he brings, how will we recognize him when we encounter him? This is an extremely difficult question, because God's ways are not our ways, neither are God's thoughts our thoughts.

We mustn't forget that. And that means that we can't be fully sure whom or what we're looking for; because as people who are separated from God by sin, we probably don't fully understand who Jesus Christ is, either. Moreover, it's simply amazing how much we <u>don't</u> let the <u>Bible teach</u> us who he is. Instead, we read the Bible with our minds made up in advance, and as a result we don't learn from it.

Perhaps we <u>assume</u>, for example, that God is great and powerful and that God works only in <u>spectacular</u> ways. But we also say that <u>Jesus</u> was God in the flesh. And when we look at Jesus, what do we see? a baby in a stable, a teacher, a friend of outcasts, a wrongly convicted prisoner who was executed. What <u>should</u> this teach us about God? Surely something about God identifying with the weak and working through weakness. We can learn that God's power is <u>strongest</u> <u>precisely</u> where the <u>weak</u> are doing something on their own behalf. Maybe <u>there</u> is where we should be looking for God. The strong don't need God's strength.

In Jesus we expect a law-abider, and we get, instead, someone who turns over the tables in the Temple, who heals on the day of rest, and whose disciples pick grain on the Sabbath. He is one who, himself, taught that God acts in ways that we don't expect, like giving a <u>day's</u> wages for an <u>hour's</u> work (Mt. 20:1-16) -- remember that parable? -- and like not being a respecter of persons, i.e., not comparing one person with another, but finding value in each individual.

Yes indeed, our God is going before us, making all things new (Rev. 21:5). And God is <u>in</u> the newness.

Is God in <u>everything</u> that's new? No. Of course not. Then how can we be <u>sure</u> <u>which</u> new thing is of God? The answer is, We can't. That knowledge is the work of the Holy Spirit -- which means that, as far as what we actually experience is concerned, we may be left simply with a conviction that something is right or that something is wrong. Oh, we may say we have the spirit, but the spirit that we have <u>may</u> be an <u>evil</u> spirit. The First Epistle of John recognizes this when it says that we must "test the spirits." (4:1) <u>How</u> do we test the spirits? Well, at least we can ask whether the new thing under consideration is in <u>accord</u> with the teachings of the <u>Bible</u> and with the <u>best</u> of the Christian tradition -- and that <u>doesn't</u> mean with two verses that support our own preference, but with the whole sweep of the Christian Faith, with the main thrust of the Christian message. Often the criteria may reduce themselves to the question, Is this new thing an expression of love?

In any case, the point <u>not</u> to be missed is that the question must be discussed. Since <u>we</u> cannot be <u>sure</u> whether God in the risen Christ is encountering us in a particular, new way, because <u>we</u> have only a <u>limited</u> perspective, and our minds are not wholly pure, we <u>need</u> the ideas and viewpoints of <u>others</u>, to provide us with a firmer basis for making a decision. And in the process of discussion, we had better be busy loving our enemy or those who disagree with us, because <u>they</u> may turn out to be more right than we first imagined.

Well, what does all that's been said boil down to? That sure is a presumptuous question! I can't answer it for you. But <u>God</u> may have been speaking to you this morning; and what is important to <u>you</u> is what <u>you</u> heard -- or perhaps even more, what you wish you hadn't heard.

But certainly somewhere in all of this is the notion that God is going ahead of us with power not simply to make a better world but to make all things new -- in ways that we really can't anticipate. So we <u>cannot</u> be <u>content</u> with everything just as it has been, and we will be <u>truly</u> Christ's disciples and earthly representatives <u>only</u> to the extent that we are receptive enough to new ideas, to different people, and to changed conditions to be willing always to look carefully for signs of <u>God's</u> will and God's presence in some very unlikely places. And this we will be <u>able</u> to do <u>only</u> by the power of the Holy Spirit, for which we fervently pray. Amen.

Easter

"Another Consideration of Easter"

(Isaiah 53)

It's time to tell the Easter story again, and the preacher's problem is how to make it the Word of God to us.

The Word of God is a living word, sharper than any two-edged sword. The Word of God is a living word when it speaks to us directly: when it hits us between the eyes, pricks our conscience, surprises us, or makes us see something that we hadn't seen before.

So should we say that Christ rose from the dead, and that means that our boy won, and since we are his followers it also means that only we are right and that therefore we are superior to everyone else? We sense something wrong with that form of triumphalism, although it's a very common stance that the Church has taken -- and not only in the past.

Perhaps we will gain new insight if we consider what we are saying when we say, "Christ is risen." One way of understanding that claim is to say that it means that Jesus' way is God's way. In other words, Jesus' way of living and showing love continues to be the best way that we could be. It is the way that children of God, such as Jesus and such as us who have been baptized, behave. It didn't die out when Jesus was crucified.

But even when we accept that insight, we tend to get involved in arguments over the literal details of the story -- was there really an angel at the tomb? Could the women have gone to the wrong tomb? -- as though the main decision that has to be made deals with those details. As a result, we get sidetracked from the Christian claim that Jesus' way of behaving is God's way. But which decision is more important?

I want to argue that it's clear that the Resurrection means that Jesus' way is God's way, because what else would properly have prompted most people to believe the few who said they had seen the Risen Lord?

The new believers could have believed for the wrong reasons, of course. They may simply have been gullible. They may have wanted to escape from an unhappy life. Belief in an afterlife that the Resurrection made possible would have opened the door to such an escape. They may have become believers simply because their friends did. But do we want to say that the Christian Faith is based on nothing more solid than that?

No. It is because Jesus had been doing God's will all during his lifetime -- it is because he had been living in such a way that he had been overcoming death at every turn: making outsiders feel welcome, making the riff-raff feel that they were somebody, healing the sick, standing up to oppressive forces in society, providing hope to those who were looking for a better world -- it is because his followers saw him doing those kinds of things that it was plausible to believe that he might indeed have been able to rise from the dead. We would not automatically say the same thing about our grandmothers, no matter how nice they are or were. But Jesus was different!

That makes Jesus' way of life very deserving of attention this Easter morning. The disciples thought so, too. When they asked what was significant about his life, they thought of the Old Testament's Suffering Servant motif. Jesus was obviously not the Messiah who was expected to free them from the Romans. Jesus was a different type of Messiah. He was not the Messiah because God was incarnate in him. They didn't think of that possibility until later. Jesus was the Messiah because he suffered.

I suspect that, when we think of Jesus suffering, we think of Jesus providing the perfect sacrifice to God on the Cross for the sins of the world. You've heard of that before. We have inherited the theology from the Middle Ages that Martin Luther took over. But that theology only became dominant at the beginning of the age of chivalry, when honor was very important. The purpose of Christ providing a perfect sacrifice on the Cross was to preserve God's honor, which had been besmirched by humanity sinning against God. People couldn't be permitted to get away with that, so Christ paid the penalty in our stead.

Christ's crucifixion also was related to the Jewish sacrificial system, where animal sacrifices had to be made, in order for people to get back on God's good side, after sins had been committed. Paul used the Crucifixion to claim that Jesus had put an end to that old way of appeasing God. But the early Church, easily for the first four centuries, didn't have that vision of the significance of the Cross at all.

Rather than taking over the views of the Middle Ages, we would do well to go back to the Bible, to look afresh at what was going on in Jesus' life that led his disciples to think he might have been the one that Isaiah had talked about. When we do that, what do we find? We find that Jesus identified with the poor and the outcast. He ate with them. He went out with them. He came from among them. And he lived with them.

This interest of Jesus is reinforced in a number of ways in the gospels and epistles. We see it in the Magnificat, in which God favors a lowly servant, scatters the proud, brings down the powerful, lifts up the humble, fills the hungry, and sends the rich away empty. We see it in Luke, chapter 4, where Jesus says he was anointed to bring good news to the poor, to proclaim release to the captives and recovery of sight to the blind, and to let the oppressed go free. We see it in I John 3:17, which asks, "How does God's love abide in anyone who has the world's goods and sees a brother or sister in need and yet refuses help?"

These concerns tend to get crowded out during Easter celebrations, but maybe God wants us to hear them especially again at this time, when many people are present in church. They are concerns that are not lost on the peasants of Latin America, or on the vast majority of the people in central and southern Africa.

Maybe God is telling us that the way to improve society is by improving the bottom rung. After all, that's where most assistance is needed (even though it may not be where most assistance is directed). If so, and if Jesus' way is God's way, then what does that tell us about where God is calling us to direct our concerns?

Twenty percent of the people in our city live below the poverty level. Are we with Jesus in siding with the poor and the outcast? Or would we rather pass by on the other side, transferring to another school district? That, of course, is the comfortable thing to do.

Or does Jesus give us a vision of another way to go? If Jesus' way is God's way, and if God's way is what is best for us -- and why shouldn't it be? Doesn't God know better than any of us what is best? -- are we willing to die to our old ways and rise again to the new life that Christ can give us this Easter morning, as we commit ourselves to developing in the image of Christ?

But we have so little guidance, you say. What other congregations are making a noticeable effort to side with Jesus on behalf of the poor and of people on the fringes of society? If there aren't many, that just shows the blindness that sin causes.

Admittedly, this is a very complex problem. But Jesus was a pretty smart person. He realized the complexities, too. But that didn't mean that he put the problem out of his mind. On the contrary, he did what he could. He ate with "them." He associated with them. He worked on their behalf. Should we be doing any less?

Can we evade the call to wrestle with the complexities of power lording it over the weak, and of racial bigotry? Can we ignore the fact that tuition at our community colleges is moving beyond the reach of our poorer families, so that their children cannot benefit from the education that is needed in the twenty-first century? And can we ignore the fact that that tuition is increasing because money from taxes is not available to serve as an alternative form of financing those colleges? Taxes simply aren't high enough. Nor are tax breaks and tax credits and tax cuts allowing the state to raise enough money to fund children and family services adequately. Funding has dropped 14% in three years.

Can we ignore those facts? Or are we followers of Jesus, willing to share even our power, and our contacts, and our knowledge, and our money, until we get some action and see some changes for the better?

We might prefer, this Easter, to rally around our man Jesus, who did one more trick than anyone else, and ignore the life that made Resurrection possible. But the Holy Spirit may not let us.

"Life in His Name"

(John 20:31)

"Christ is risen from the dead, by death destroying death and to us in our graves giving life!" That's a modified version of a statement that is heard in every Eastern Orthodox church every Easter. And it ties in very well to the last verse of today's Gospel lesson: "[T]hese are written that you may come to believe that Jesus is the Messiah, the Son of God, and that through this belief you may have <u>life</u>!"

Easter is a time when the question often gets raised, Is there life after death? It should also be a time when we raise the question, Is there life after birth? Or are we already living in a grave, without even realizing it? For millions of people, life isn't anything to get excited about. It is a painful experience of merely getting by, existing minimally from day to day and week to week, just keeping on keeping on. For others in the same economic circumstances, however, life is a joy that is radiant in spite of surrounding conditions. I dare say that those people are plugged into a dimension of reality that our Gospel lesson, momentarily abridged, simply calls "life."

John's Gospel says that Jesus came to bring life! In chapter 8 [v. 12] Jesus says, "I am the light of the world. Whoever follows me will never walk in darkness but will have the light of life." Now certainly he is talking about some form of life other than merely breathing in and out. We're already doing that! But we get more than just a hint of what he's talking about when he says, in John 10:10, "I have come that [people] might have life, and have it more abundantly." Jesus gives us life at its best! He said, "I am the way, the truth, and the life" (Jn. 14:6). Some theologians have suggested that that means that Jesus is the way to true life. But what is true life? Why--and here I shall finally complete the citation from the last verse of today's Gospel--true life is "life in his name."

Now that's not a very helpful answer, unless you know how the inhabitants of the Ancient Near East understood what a name was. It wasn't just a label for a person--or a pet, or a place. Rather, a name was often thought to identify the essence of the thing, the core values or characteristics of the thing named. Not only did a name identify those features; it also bestowed them. So parents believed that they were imprinting or impressing a particular virtue onto a child, by the name that they gave that child. We see remnants of this view being carried over, nowadays, when we give girls names such as Charity, or Joy, or Faith, or Justice, or even Hope.

So life in the name of Jesus is life in his essence. It is life associated with his core values. It's life lived from the power that made him the kind of person that he was. It's life at its best!

But calling it "life at its best" doesn't quite capture the point, if we are the ones who decide what life-at-its-best is. It's not the best life according to our standards. It's the best kind of life according to God's standards. It's not the best quality of life that we can conceive of. It's the quality of life that comes from God. So it's a quality of life that we cannot generate ourselves. If we experience it, it will be because God has been at work in us. Indeed, it may actually be the very presence of God.

It's what John's Gospel, in many places, calls "eternal life." That's another phrase that we need to understand better. The Greek word for "eternal" can mean "everlasting," that is, just continuing on and on and on. But the phrase can also mean "depth of life, profundity of existence, high quality of life." That means that the good news of the Gospel isn't limited to a time after we die. It means that we can be in touch with the divine life and with victorious living in this life. It means that, to use a phrase from St. Paul, we can know the power of Christ's resurrection in this life! Indeed, that's what the Risen Christ offers and what faith permits to come to us in the Holy Communion.

We can know the power and presence of God, along with the quality of Jesus' life, in this life. For some people, that's an experience that raises them permanently from one level of existence to another. They were functioning at this level and now they are at this level. For others it is an ecstatic, mountain-top experience which they, of course, cannot maintain throughout their life but which was so evidently out of their control that they are convinced that it offers proof of the presence of God active in the world today. For many it is simply the power to resist temptation and to keep from being dragged down by the forces of evil into a noxious lifestyle.

But the reality also seems to be that we all are, in some way, out of touch with God, the Source of Life. As a result, we all, in some way, are living in graves of our own making. It seems that the LBW confession is right: "We are in bondage to sin and cannot free ourselves." Sin is separation from the Source of Life.

Well, what can we do to improve our condition? I just said that we cannot free ourselves. And we cannot know when and where God's Holy Spirit, which blows like the wind and sometimes is still, will be at work. But our text points the way when it says, "through believing you may have life in his name." Through believing.

The most rudimentary form of belief gets us oriented properly. It consists of believing Christian doctrines, somewhat like believing that Ankara is the capital of Turkey, even though you've never been there. But the belief that brings a better life is belief based on a relationship with God that relies on God's power and that clings to Jesus' teachings no matter what the pressures are to veer in another direction. In such belief, the Holy Spirit is already at work in us, even if we don't feel it.

It is a belief that keeps us in touch with other believers. Accordingly, it brings us regularly to church, so that we are in a place where God can get at us, through the preached Word and the reading of the Scriptures, through the language of the worship service, through the spirit-invigorating and soul-lifting music, and through Holy Communion.

It is a belief that causes us to choose the life that Jesus offers, because "down deep" we believe that the Easter message is true. We believe that God is at work bringing life out of death, even the death mixed with our own life.

It is a belief that draws us to long periods of prayer, as we commune with God spiritually and open ourselves to God coming to us.

And it is a belief that results, ideally, in our "always excelling in the work of the Lord" [I Cor. 15:58]. Because God can come to us not only in prayer and meditation and in church but also while we're fully involved in the rough and tumble of confronting the evils of the world. What is this "work of the Lord" that our faith leads us to engage in? Why, it's bringing life out of conditions of death--in our interpersonal relationships, in everything that we do--even in how we vote. Bringing life out of conditions of death.

But there also is a belief that recognizes that death and resurrection are not limited to Jesus and to an afterlife but can apply to our own life, if we will die to our devotion to those things which separate us from God, the Source of Life, so that we can be open to the new life that Christ can bring.

Some people will not reach this stage until they have a tragedy in their life or until they force themselves to wrestle with what they really believe. But if the time comes when they have tried everything else and nothing has worked, then they finally may be willing to take the risk of the leap of faith, a leap that does not guarantee where they will land, but that offers the possibility that they will land in the Everlasting Arms. And then they will experience "life in his name."

Now, I could end here. But to do so would imply that none of you has ever experienced the power of God or a resurrected life in your own life. And I do not believe that that is true.

But if faith in Jesus, the Son of God, has been meaningful in your life, then the angel at the empty tomb has a directive for you. "Go and tell."

There is always a need to spread the word. Don't you know an un-churched person--at work, in your neighborhood, or among your rela-tives--whom you can ask whether they are involved with a church? Can't you assure that person, maybe only with one sentence, that faith in the God of Jesus has made a difference in your life? And can't you offer to take that person to your church, if ever they are interested? Do we have good news to offer, or don't we?

H. V. Kaltenbourn used to say, "Ah, there's good news tonight!" Well, there's good news this morning, too. Christ is risen from the dead! By dy-ing he brought God right into the jaws of death and destroyed its power. And to us who are less fully in touch with God than we could be, to us he can bring the very essence of his own life! If you are convinced that this is true, go and tell.

Pentecost

(John 16:4b-11; Acts 2:1-21)

"Who was that masked man?" Raise your hand if you recognize that question from the Lone Ranger program on radio or television?

The Lone Ranger was someone who fought for justice and was always on the side of the good guys in stories of the Old West. He always wore a mask, and he often would solve problems secretly and then leave a sliver bullet as a sign that he had been present. And as he rode out of town, calling out, "Hi-yo Silver, away!" you would often hear someone asking, "Who was that masked man, anyway?" It was only after he had done his good deeds that people started to think more carefully about who he was.

The same thing happened in the case of Jesus. It was only after his death that his followers had to confront the question of why he had been able to be so extraordinary. Why was he able to be so loving, so sensitive to people on the fringes of society, so willing to stand up against religious practices that emphasized outward performance but ignored motivation, so able to form groups of people who were concerned about each other, so much in touch with God and God's will? I didn't even mention healing, because there were other healers around, during his time, so _that_ didn't make him distinctive. He seemed to be the best kind of human being his disciples had ever met; and yet to think of him as merely human didn't quite catch the specialness about him. They eventually hit upon a metaphor, the metaphor "Son of God," to describe him. A metaphor takes two words that normally don't go together and puts them together, and as a result, we see things differently than we had seen them before.

"Son," a word for a human boy, and "God," the designation of divinity, do not normally go together. Everyone in Jesus' day knew that God didn't have a son; and if Jesus had called himself "the Son of God," he would have been stoned to death for blasphemy. (And, in case you didn't know it, the Bible never says that he said he was the Son of God.) Yet that phrase "Son of God" did seem, to the early Christians, to capture what they believed about Jesus.

Were they right? They were, if the Holy Spirit was testifying to Jesus, i.e., if the Spirit was guiding them in their thinking, as they pondered the question of who Jesus was and what his significance was. And our Gospel lesson today said that that's exactly what would happen, when the Spirit of truth was sent from the Father, when Jesus was no longer with us. So there's an important sense in which Jesus may well have been the Son of God, even if he himself never said he was.

Pentecost is about the coming of the Holy Spirit.

John's Gospel says that when the Spirit comes, it would "prove the world wrong about sin and righteousness and judgment." That's a strange sentence. What could it possibly mean?

It means, first, that the world was wrong in what it thought sin was. According to Jesus in John's Gospel, people are wrong "about sin, because they do not believe in me." Four other times in John's Gospel (3:19, 36; 8:21-24; 15:22-25), sin is depicted as unbelief. Now, you might say, "I thought sin was doing bad things." Well, it is. At least, doing bad things shows that sin is present. But why do you do those bad things? Jesus was always concerned about the motive of our thoughts and actions, the underlying reasons for our doing what we do. And here he is saying that we do bad things because we don't _really_ believe in him and therefore are not really committed to following him. Our problem often is that we are quite willing to call him "Son of God" and "Lord," but at a deeper level there is, within us, a disbelief that doesn't let us fully commit ourselves to him. It doesn't let us see the need to be led by <u>his</u> spirit. We would rather be led by ours; and, as a result, we end up not doing God's will. But, as Jesus says in Matthew's Gospel, 'Not everyone who calls me "Lord" will enter the kingdom of heaven, but only those who do the will of my Father' (7:21). So sin is unbelief, because if we don't take Jesus and his teachings seriously, we are more likely to do bad things.

Second, that strange sentence says the Spirit would prove the world wrong about righteousness--or justice, which is another way of translating that word--"because I am going to the Father." If Jesus was about to stand in the presence of God, that shows he's just and righteous and that his cause was vindicated, since nothing unjust can stand in God's presence. So if the Resurrection and Ascension show Jesus to be righteous, that means those who condemned him were wrong, and their standard of justice was wrong. And that's what verse 8 says that the Holy Spirit would do: prove that the world's standard of justice was wrong. It is sobering to notice that the most highly developed legal system of Jesus' day, i.e., the Roman legal system, and the most highly developed religion of his time were not able to deal with Jesus properly. Both of them had him executed, when he was innocent. That fact should keep us from being too confident that our own legal system and our own religious sensibilities can be relied upon to recognize the Spirit of God, when it is at work in the world. When God is at work, we may not see it. On the other hand, our laws have outlawed slavery and other forms of oppression since Jesus' time, so sometimes formal government does yield to the promptings of the Spirit.

Third, the coming of the Spirit would prove the world wrong about judgment, "because the ruler of this world has been condemned." The Spirit shows that the ruler of this world--today we might call it "the forces of evil"--have been judged and dethroned, because they were shown to be false in their condemnation of Jesus. They were wrong in their judgment. Stated another way, by misjudging Jesus, the world itself was judged. It was judged for not being open to the promptings of <u>God's</u> Spirit and for relying, instead, on its own preferences and prejudices. We always need to ask in what way we are facing the same dangers today. The Holy Spirit will help us, if we are willing to do God's will rather than ours; and today in particular we celebrate the coming of the Holy Spirit to the Church at Pentecost--and to our two members who are about to be confirmed.

Pentecost came 50 days after Passover, and, at the time Luke wrote the book of Acts, it celebrated the giving of the Ten Commandments on Mt. Sinai. There was a tradition that said that when God gave the Ten Commandments on Mt. Sinai, 70 tongues of fire hovered over the mountain, representing all of the nations of the world. So all nations were symbolically present when the Law was given. In other words, God's Law applies to everyone.

Luke puts tongues of fire into his account of the momentous event of Acts chap. 2, an event in which God now gives the Holy Spirit, in part to enable us to interpret the Law. And how important that gift is!

So many dear, religious people who want to do God's will think that what they need to do is to find a commandment in the Bible and then hold to it rigidly. But most Lutherans --and God-- know that life is more complex than that. A <u>commandment</u> cannot be aware of all of the factors in a situation that need to be considered, in order for God's will to be done in that situation. But <u>people</u> can be aware of those factors. And that's why God the Holy Spirit is present, to guide us as we weigh the significance of the various considerations. That's why, also, we need to pray for that guidance. And it is why we need to stay in close spiritual touch with God, so that we can dare to exercise the judgment we must, when we and others are faced with difficult moral decisions. An awful lot of misery has been caused by people who simply follow rules, without thinking about their consequences.

In our first lesson, the Spirit unexpectedly comes upon the apostles, and they speak about the mighty deeds of God, in languages that all can understand. On some Pentecost Sundays we also read about the confusion of languages and the scattering of people at the Tower of Babel. In stark contrast to that mythical event, the Spirit in Acts 2 speaks with a power that unites people.

But many scholars question whether that event took place exactly as the author of Acts depicted it. They point out that there isn't any evidence that the Holy Spirit ever again gave people the ability to speak foreign languages they didn't know to others in the same room. They also notice that the nations whose languages were spoken just happened to be all of the countries to which Christianity had spread at the time Acts was written. So perhaps what we have here is a symbolic representation and listing of all of the countries in which the Gospel had been preached, by missionaries inspired by the Holy Spirit. Notice: the work of the Holy Spirit isn't missing, in this interpretation, it just takes another form. (In that form, the Holy Spirit is with the missionaries, some of whom were probably also the apostles).

[Then there is something the average person would not notice about Peter's speech. Peter probably spoke Aramaic, like Jesus and the average Jewish fisherman. But Peter quotes the prophet Joel from the Greek [Septuagint] translation of the Hebrew Bible. That means that Luke, who did speak Greek, is likely to have inserted that quotation into Peter's speech. Why would he do that? Well, rather than treating the life of Jesus and the early Church as something uniquely new, some Gospel writers went overboard in looking for Old Testament passages that might possibly apply to New Testament events. Those passages usually did not apply; and here we have an excellent example. As the text reads, Peter is saying that the coming of the Holy Spirit was a sign of the last days, "in which the sun shall turn to darkness and the moon to blood." Well, the moon didn't turn to blood. It still hasn't, and it has been nearly 2000 years since Peter allegedly spoke those words. It seems to be time to conclude that Luke picked the wrong prophecy to apply to the Pentecost event].

The Festival of Pentecost presents us with a joyous source of hope and also a challenge. The source of hope is that the Spirit of God _is_ present and at any moment can invade our lives and transform us fully into the kind of person that God wants us to be. Perhaps you have experienced the power of God at work in your life in that way.

The challenge is to cause us to think about just what our relationship with God is. Do we come to church out of habit but then ignore God the rest of the week? Do we slowly drift away from God, by slowly drifting away from the Church? Or are we active in the church, while still holding onto some favorite sinful inclinations that we really don't want to let go of? That's all it takes to keep the Holy Spirit out. You see, God does not want to turn us into robots. The Spirit will not force us to commit ourselves fully to God. We have to will to do God's will. And if we are holding onto some sinful inclinations, we are obviously not willing to do God's will fully.

Actually, every time we pray the Lord's Prayer we are asking God to be powerfully present in our lives. When we say, "Thy Kingdom come," we are praying not only for God to change the world but for the Kingdom to come to us, for God to transform us. There is an ancient variation of the Lord's Prayer which, instead of saying "Thy Kingdom come," says, "Let Thy Holy Spirit come upon us and cleanse us." Isn't that what we want? If we pray the Lord's Prayer seriously, then we will want to be cleansed, we will want to be doing God's will, and we will be opening the door to God's empowering Spirit.

The Spirit can make us ecstatic when it comes. It can cause us to speak gibberish--what St. Paul calls "speaking in tongues"--as we praise the God whom we adore. But it can also come in ways that we can't detect, nudging us to do something good that we might not otherwise have been inclined to do, or giving us the deep peace of knowing that we are fully under God's care.

But as some of you know, you are not likely to get that way until you have risked entrusting your life completely to God and have committed your will to doing God's will--only. When you have, then you can follow Martin Luther, who confessed <u>his</u> faith in words that our confirmands and some of you may have learned, namely, "I believe that Jesus Christ, true God, begotten of the Father from eternity, and also true man, born of the virgin Mary, is my Lord, who has redeemed me, a lost and condemned creature, delivered me and freed me from all sins, from death, and from the power of the devil,...in order that I may be his...." This morning you have the opportunity, again, to be his.

Just as the Holy Spirit moved powerfully upon the apostles on that first

Christian Pentecost, the power of God can move mightily through this congregation this morning. And here's what I'm going to suggest that you do. When the offering is collected, be sure each of you holds that plate; and don't just put money into it, put yourself into it. And if someone else puts in the offering, you put in your hand. Let your offering symbolize your entire self, so that when the offering plates are brought up to the altar, you can symbolically rededicate yourself to the God who can lead you into all truth.

Trinity

"The Divine Trinity"

Trinity Sunday marks the theological pinnacle of the Church Year. Today, Christians draw together all of the insights into what God is like that we dealt with partially, during the other seasons of the year. In Advent, for example, we remembered God the Father, as Him from Whom the Savior was to come. At Christmas, Good Friday, Easter, and Ascension Day, we celebrated or commemorated moments in the life of God the Son. And last Sunday, at Pentecost, we celebrated the coming of God the Holy Spirit. Today we affirm that when we speak of God, we are referring to all of that.

God is the almighty Source, high and lifted up, the absolute in perfection and principle, not dependent upon human assistance or upon the created order at all.

But God is more than that. Christians believe that God is not simply abstract but that God became concrete, here on earth, in our history, as one of us, and therefore that God's reality (within human limits) and God's perfection <u>can</u> be realized here on earth. Not everybody who believes in God believes that. Jews and Muslims don't, for example. In their view, the purity of almighty God would be tarnished, if God were to become actually embodied here on earth. When God comes, they say, everyone dies. You cannot look upon God and live (Ex. 33:20). When God comes, the sinful order of things is so changed that it's completely different from the way it used to be. Are things so much better, they ask, since Jesus walked the earth? And if not, doesn't that fact make it clear that God's perfection simply cannot be realized here on earth?

This question pushes us even deeper into the nature of God and lays us right at the feet of the Holy Spirit. For Christianity teaches that it is precisely the "job" of God the Holy Spirit to make it possible for God's perfection to occur on earth. The Holy Spirit makes it possible for God's will to be done.

The significance of Christ is not simply that God once was embodied here, but that the principle has been established that God <u>can</u> take concrete, earthly form. And that's where we all fit into the picture. Because

Christianity is all about God taking shape, becoming real, being present--in us, by the power of the Holy Spirit. That's what Paul means when he talks about "the upward call of God in Christ Jesus" (Phil. 3:14), and about 'growing up into him who is our Lord and head' (Eph. 4:15), and about our 'having the mind of Christ.' What we mean when we speak of being more like Christ is: being more Godlike--being Godlike in the way in which human beings <u>can</u> be Godlike, and that is by being fully human. <u>Fully</u> human: perfectly genuine, sensitive to others, loving, trusting, open, faithful, caring--as only Jesus has ever been. Not our tarnished kind of human; Jesus' kind. That's what Paul has in mind when he speaks of 'receiving adoption as sons' (Gal. 4:5). Our goal is Jesus' kind of sonship, just as it is the divine goal that God be All in all. God wants to be in everyone, just as God once was in Jesus. As Jesus once embodied the best, so God's goal is for the whole world to embody the best.

That's not happening very quickly, is it? And it's easy to understand why some people believe that there must be a powerful evil force in the universe, equal in power to God, which keeps thwarting the divine impulse for good. It's easy, also, to understand why some biblical writers and some people today speak of a cataclysmic end to the world, when God will invade it and suddenly transform it is a flash. That seems to them to be the only way that evil can be overcome. Well, those people at least are correct in implying that God is not interested simply in tidying us up the way we are. For God to be at work in us, for the holy God to be present in sinners, means that the profoundest of changes takes place in us. How extensive that change is is another matter. Sometimes it affects our entire personality and our whole way of looking at things. At other times, it means that we just don't feel like teasing our sister or brother any more. At all times, however, it means that we become more fully human, which means that we make God more concrete, in the way in which Jesus made God concrete. And every time that happens, in every small way: when hatred melts, when the timid person becomes appropriately more aggressive, when we become willing to risk our own security or comfort for some worthy purpose--whenever something like that happens, it is appropriately called the result of the work of the Holy Spirit, because we cannot fully explain why it occurred just at that moment, and because it does present us as being different from the way we were--whether the change counts as a cataclysmic one or not, there's no denying that we have become different--and because in that difference we carry out God's will and so make God real, here on earth.

Why aren't more such changes taking place? If God the Holy Spirit enables us to be like Jesus, why is there still so much evil? The answer is, We don't know. At a time when modern human beings are able to control more and more of the world around them, this question reminds us that there still are dimensions of reality that we are not in control of. We are not in control of the ultimate mysteries of existence. And this is one of them. On this matter we simply are presented with a choice. We can believe that Goodness is ultimately powerful and is worth supporting--or not. There is no proof, either way. There is only faith, only commitment to whatever we choose to believe.

But if we are committed to the Good, or want to be, and if we believe that there is a Power reinforcing and even directing our good efforts, then we are reflecting belief in the Triune God: the Good empowered concretely: Father, Spirit, Son. And in that faith we will take action to work out our own salvation, and our society's salvation, and the world's salvation, because we believe that God can be at work in us, as God strives to transform the world and to become All in all--because we believe in that kind of God.

*****

Another significance of the Trinity--and one that most people overlook--is that it makes the point of how important Jesus is. If it weren't for Jesus, the Christian Church would not have had to develop the doctrine of the Holy Trinity. That doctrine can get so confusing that ministers and priests are sometimes driven to say, "Well, it's ultimately a mystery. We just have to believe it." Or, what's even worse--because God ultimately is a mystery--they will say, "It's part of God's revelation, and we just have to accept it." Well, if by that they mean that the teaching that God is one nature in three Persons was revealed to somebody one day, they are simply wrong. The doctrine was developed over a period of 300 years, before it was officially promulgated as a teaching of the Church at the First General Council, held in Nicaea in 325, when the Nicene Creed was hammered out. And just a peek at that history will show how important Jesus was.

First of all, we must realize that every doctrine about Jesus is an interpretation. If people kept diaries at the time that Jesus was crucified, no one would have written something like, "Today the Son of God was nailed to the Cross." Jesus did not go around saying, "I am the Son of God." That was an interpretation of who he was, which the community of believers made many years after his death.

You will be able to understand better what I'm talking about if you try to imagine yourself as one of Jesus' followers, about two weeks after his death. You had been captivated by Jesus every time that you were in his presence. You were touched by his gentleness and yet his strength of character; by his openness to everybody and his caring concern, especially for the poor, the outcasts, and the powerless, whom he spent so much time with; by his calm faith in his heavenly Father, who, he said, was not a distant potentate but was so close to each of us that we could call Him "Abba," the diminutive form of the Hebrew word for father, which could appropriately be translated "Daddy." Maybe it was that faith and that communion with God that enabled him to disobey the laws that were supposed to help us to be good but sometimes just seemed to stand in the way of what was right. And of course you were thrilled with his preaching of the coming Kingdom of God; and the more time you spent with him, the more you began to feel that something new and Godlike was already happening here, among his followers. But now he was dead, and with the passage of time, you and others were asking, "Who <u>was</u> he?" Because, of course, you couldn't forget him.

Even the Resurrection didn't answer that question. It just indicated how important he must have been during his lifetime. Remember, not many people are reported to have seen the Risen Lord. Most of the first Christians had to believe what someone else told them. And if Peter had told you that God had done something special for Judas Iscariot by raising him from the dead, you might have been a bit skeptical. But when someone told you that Jesus had been raised from the dead--yes, that just might be possible. He certainly was extraordinary!

But how did the early Christians explain that extraordinariness? One of their first suggestions was that he was someone whom God had adopted after his resurrection.

But that explanation didn't account for his extraordinary life, and behavior, and teachings. How could those early Christians explain the source of those superior qualities that they had encountered in Jesus? The qualities certainly were human qualities, but they always seemed to have a brilliance about them that wasn't found in other, tarnished human beings. Can you imagine the awe that must have come over the first person to think that the best way to describe Jesus was to call him the "Son of God"? And yet, some such metaphor had to be used. No ordinary human classification was adequate.

But calling him the "Son of God" didn't automatically make Jesus the eternal Second Person of the divine Trinity. When the first Gospel was written, namely, Mark's Gospel, probably 35 years after Jesus' death, it appears that people believed that Jesus became the Son of God at his baptism. A little later, however, he was thought of as becoming the Son of God when he was born, as the Christmas stories in Matthew and Luke suggest. Eventually, however, he was pushed all the way back to the beginning, right into God. So that when the Gospel of John was written, probably 60 to 70 years after Jesus' death, he was treated as the Word, who was with God "in the beginning."

Well, what were those first Christians doing, with their interpretations of Jesus? I think they were saying to themselves, "Now that Jesus is dead, we can't go back to the old life, because he has shown us a new way of life that makes us really alive! He has given us a taste of what life should be! Why, Jesus' way of life must be how God always intended life to be, even before Jesus was born! Jesus was the embodiment of something that always has been true." And with the help of the Greek metaphysical philosophy of their time, the best way that they could depict the notion that Jesus' way is what God intends for all of us was, eventually, to construct the doctrine of Father, Son, and Holy Spirit together as one God. But it was an uphill fight, and we can always wonder whether those who were declared to be heretics might not have been right. Because the doctrine of the Trinity was opposed by many devout and sincere people who believed that God is One, and transcendent, and holy, and that God could not remain so, if divinity were to include the physical and the earthly. During the Council of Nicaea, these opponents lobbied hard for their position. They even brought in dancing girls and developed chants, accompanied by tambourines. Their most prominent chant was *"ēn pote hote ouk ēn:"* "there was when he was not," i.e., there was a time when the Son of God didn't exist: Christ was merely the first-fruits of God's creation: the Son was a perfect creature, but he was not fully God.

In contrast, the Nicene Creed says that he was "begotten, not made, being of one substance with the Father," and that it was by him, the Son, that all things were made. What this orthodox and catholic teaching intends to preserve is the claim that God's involvement in our salvation is total and not second hand. God's very essence is not merely abstract but includes the concrete. God's will is that God take concrete form here on earth, and God arranges for that in the power of the Holy Spirit.

One way of thinking of the Trinity, therefore, is to conceive of God as being potential, actual, and the catalyst for making potentiality become actuality. God is Father, Son, and Holy Spirit: potential, actual, and catalyst. And that's why there are moments of perfect good in a sinful world.

But to restate our point: we wouldn't have this concept of God, if the first Christians had not been very impressed with Jesus. It would seem proper, therefore, for us not to get so caught up with interpretations about Jesus that we fail to study carefully and prayerfully what we know about his life and his teachings. Such study will also have to be done imaginatively, with the Bible in one hand and the newspaper in the other, as Karl Barth (a major Protestant theologian of the 20th century) said, because what Jesus said and did in the first century will have to be translated into terms that are appropriate for the 21st century. What he said about turning the other cheek will have to apply to all the different types of people who need a second chance. What he said about peace and about faith will have to apply to everything from raising children to gun control legislation to worldwide armament distribution. What he did about healing will have to be made relevant to the question of national health insurance. What he did about feeding the hungry will have to be brought to bear on everything from Meals-on-Wheels to tariff policies to national and international food production management.

If we take time to consider how his teachings apply to the 21st century, we shall give the Holy Spirit a chance to drive their truth home to us and to guide us in their proper application. As a result, we, too, may have the experience of being as impressed with Jesus as his original disciples were. In our actions that follow, then, there is a chance that we, too, shall be part of God's Self-realization, as the Holy Spirit enables us, God's adopted sons and daughters, to make real the Father's perfect will.

"The Triune God"

(Matthew 28:19)

It's all Jesus' fault. If he hadn't taught and behaved in such an outstanding way that, after he was gone and his followers asked, "Who was that masked man, anyway?" and their answer was, "Why, he was actually God in the flesh!" -- if that hadn't happened, the doctrine of the Trinity would not have been developed.

But it did happen, and it caused Christians to claim that God is not just an ultimate, abstract Principle or even a universal spirit, but that God is almighty enough also to be physical and material, as in Jesus of Nazareth.

This view makes the Christian God different from the God of every other religion. Neither Buddha nor Confucius claimed to be God. As far as I know, neither most Hindus nor most scholars of Hinduism claim that Krishna was actually a real person. He is just a mythological figure of Hindu scripture. And whereas Christians say, "the Word became flesh," the most that Muslims would say is, "the Word became Book," with Mohammed as the mouthpiece through whom the divine words of the Koran were uttered.

But with Jesus as God in the flesh, what kind of God do Christians believe in? Well, you know the answer, and you heard the formulation in today's Gospel, although it took the Church three centuries to decide just what those words mean and how they are related to each other. In order to say all that we believe about God, we have come up with the claim that there is one God, Who is Father, the generator of the material universe, Son, who reflects his Father's love and brings us wayward people back to God, and Holy Spirit, the spirit of the Father -- the same spirit reflected in Jesus -- still with us.

Probably the most popular way we have depicted our claim that we believe in only one God, even though three "Persons" are involved, is through the triangle -- and through three intersecting circles.

A triangle form can also be used in depicting the following statements:

The Father is God. The Son is God. The Holy Spirit is God. The Son is not the Father. The Father is not the Holy Spirit. The Holy Spirit is not the Son. There is only one God.

When we say that God consists of three Persons, we are not talking about three people. We are certainly not talking about one person with three heads. No, the Ancient Church got the idea of "persons" in God from Greek drama, in which one actor would portray several different characters by holding up a mask indicating which character was being portrayed. The mask was called a *persona*. So by going off stage and coming back with a different mask, one actor could easily play three different roles.

And initially, the idea of three Persons in God was our way of talking about how God appeared to <u>us</u>, as, for example, creating, redeeming, and sanctifying. It was one God appearing to us behind three masks or in three modes of being.

But eventually that view was rejected, in favor of one that said that the three Persons existed within the divine Reality directly; they were not just ways in which <u>we</u> perceive God. God "Himself" really is Triune. For the sake of convenience, we assign specific functions to each of the Persons, but the final doctrine that developed says that each Person is present in the other and hence in the work of the other. The three Persons interpenetrate each other; and no Person of the Trinity does anything apart from the others.

We call the Father the Creator, for example, but John, chapter 1 (v. 3), says, "All things came into being through [the Word, i.e., the Son], and without him not one thing came into being." And remember that, in the Genesis creation story, the Spirit of God brooded over the face of the waters (1:2). So there you have all three Persons involved with creation. And remember what I said about the Holy Spirit being the spirit of the Son who reflected the spirit of the Father. It isn't just the Holy Spirit's spirit.

So the Ultimate Force of the universe, the Reality that underlies everything, is triune. What is the significance of that, and how can we understand how that might be?

St. Augustine proposed an answer to the <u>second</u> question, by suggesting that we think about what it means to say, "I love myself." According to Jesus, it's O.K. to love ourselves, since we are to love our neighbors as ourselves. When I say "I love myself," there is a lover, namely, me; there is an object of my love, which is also me; and there is the loving, the energy and act of the lover on the beloved -- all three involved in one person.

Now let's return to God. The Church teaches that the Father did not create the son, as an artist or a builder creates things, that is, by using materials, such as paint or wood, which are not their actual selves. Rather, the Father begets the Son from His own substance or self, just as parents beget children from the substances of their own bodies. So the Son is God, because the Son is of one substance, or nature, or Being with the Father.

But if there was a time when only the Father existed, then the Son would not be eternal and therefore not be fully God. So the ancient Nicene Creed says that the Son of God was begotten of the Father "before all worlds," which means before time even began. That means that the begetting is timeless, or, thought of within time, it is continuous. And that means that whenever you have the Father, you have the Father generating the Son. Stated another way, God exists only and always as an Absolute that is reaching out (as in through begetting), an Absolute that is in relation.

In relation. Here is a key point. The purpose of the doctrine of the Trinity is to identify Ultimacy as relational, God as always in relationships.

What kind of relationship? Well, the Bible says that God is Love (I John 4:8). The Bible doesn't say, here, that God has love for others, although that is true, too. It says that God is Love. Love implies a relationship. There are at least two involved. God can have love for someone with whom God is relating. But for God to be love, the relationship has to be within God. And so it is. The relationship within God is not only that the Father begets the Son continuously but that the Father loves the Son, and the Son loves the Father; and the Spirit is the bond of love between them. This is not a dead relationship but a dynamic and ongoing relationship, second after second. And since it is the nature of love to reach out, it is not a love only within the Trinity. The Spirit is the divine love that reaches out to us, as well.

And that's the kind of God that we believe in. Not a reality that is waiting for us to meditate our way to it, but one that is always reaching out in love.

That God was evident in the Hebrew Bible, too, reaching out to choose the people of Israel, and to give them the Ten Commandments, and to prompt the prophets to call people back to faithful obedience. It is the latter role that Judaism emphasizes, and it is an emphasis that we must not ignore. We may prefer to focus our attention on how God loves us and forget about all the things that we can do to bring God's love to others. But we shouldn't forget that.

But if God, Who is Love, is always in dynamic and outgoing relationship, that means that the Christian God doesn't exist in the abstract. So you should not expect "God" to be a meaningful word for you, unless you are in a relationship with God.

The good news is that God is the kind of reality that enters into relationships. The doctrine also says that God, as the absolute Father, is His own firm anchor and is not tossed about by those relationships. To deal with God, to rely on God, is to rely on a firm foundation indeed!

Let me close this way: People sometimes say, "It doesn't matter what you believe, as long as you believe in God." On the contrary, Christianity urges us to see that it does matter what kind of God you believe in. The doctrine of the Trinity offers us God as the absolute power of love, not aloof but in relationship with us, not abstract but providing concrete examples in the life and teachings of Jesus, and actively present, to give us the power to reflect the divine love in the world around us.

July 4th/6 Pent (A)

"Political and Spiritual Freedom"

(Romans 7:15-25a)

Today we celebrate freedom. It is the 4th of July, and so we celebrate political freedom. It is the occasion of a baptism, and so we celebrate spiritual freedom.

When are you free? Your first thought might be, "When nothing has any control over me." But when there are no controls, you don't get freedom, you just get chaos. What if you could not rely on the law of gravity working reliably (to cite an extreme example)? What if there were no laws and no moral standards that everybody shared, so you could never be sure how people would act or what you would be permitted to do? Your freedom to act and to do things the way you want them to be done would be much more limited than if there were laws and standards that everyone acknowledged and agreed to follow. So you are free not when there are no controls but when you know and accept what the limits are and are able to work within them. (Laws and rules that are followed eliminate lots of uncertainties).

We could spend the rest of the morning talking about how to define "freedom"--and you may want to do that at lunch--but let me propose this definition: We are free when we are able to make choices that we find acceptable and are able to carry them out. I added that last phrase, because you could be in jail and choose to leave (which would be an acceptable choice to you), but if you could not carry out that decision, you would be reminded very quickly that you weren't free. There are some poor people who do not feel free, because they are constantly aware that they can't do what they would like, because they don't have enough money. Others are resigned to their financial limitations and, as a result, feel much more free, as they live within their restrictions. Whether or not one should accept one's financial situation is a whole other topic.

Increasingly, during the course of early American history, the colonists were feeling that, under the rule of King George III, they were not able to make choices that they found acceptable. They wanted a much greater "say" in determining what the rules would be that governed their society. So on July 4, 1776, they declared their independence. Today is Independence Day, and we still celebrate it, because freedom flourishes when we follow rules that we have a voice in establishing. (Please check on whether your children or grandchildren know the significance of this day. Some teachers have told me that they've found students who think the reason for the day is to go to a parade, have a picnic, or watch fireworks).

So we are politically free. But "I do not understand my own actions," said St. Paul. "For I do not do what I want, but I do the very thing I hate. [...] I know that good does not live in me--that is, in my sinful nature. For even though the desire to do good is in me, [TEV] I cannot carry it out. [NIV] For I do not do the good I want, but the evil I do not want is what I do." I remember the King James translation: "The good that I would I do not: but the evil which I would not, that I do." Later Paul says (in the New English Bible translation), "Thus, left to myself, while subject to God's law as a rational being, I am yet, in my unspiritual nature, a slave to the law of sin. [TEV:] Who will rescue me from this body that is taking me to death? [NEB:] God alone, through Jesus Christ our Lord!"

While we rightly celebrate out political freedom, humanity has a need for a much deeper freedom, and we can celebrate that freedom, as well. Paul found that he was not free, because he could not always carry out the good choices that he intended. Others are not even free to make good choices. Our problem is that we are separated from God. We are separated from God's Spirit and God's power and God's goodness--which means, as Paul found, that there are dark forces at work in us which keep us from always doing God's will. In other words, "we are in bondage to sin," and, apart from faith in Christ, "we cannot free ourselves." Our normal inclination, guided by our sinful or unspiritual nature, is to make life meaningful and enjoyable for ourselves, without regard to God's will. In that way we are in rebellion against God. We are trying to save our lives in the way that we think best. But Jesus said, "Those who would save their lives will lose them. Only those who lose their lives for my sake will find them."

So what is called for is a conversion, converting our old, sinful lives into new ones--ones that we have surrendered to him and that we have committed to doing his will. We have to be willing to give up the old wineskins of our sinful nature, so that we can receive and retain the new wine--wine is the symbol of life--so that we can receive the new quality of life that comes when we have yielded our will to God. For then the Spirit of life in Christ Jesus sets us free from the law of sin and death. (Rom. 8:2) When we are genuinely open to Christ's Spirit, we are freed from the compulsion to sin and from the living death that results. As Paul says in II Corinthians 3:17, "where the Spirit of the Lord is, there is freedom," because, as we experience the new life that Christ gives: the cleansed and re-invigorated life that comes from God, we have no desire to seek a more fulfilling kind of life by acting against God's will.

This conversion is symbolized in baptism. Paul asks, "Do you not know that all of us who have been baptized into Christ Jesus were baptized into his death?" He continues, "We were buried therefore with him by baptism into death, so that as Christ was raised from the dead by the glory of the Father, we too might walk in newness of life." (Rom. 6:3-4)

Here is the pattern of dying and rising again that is at the core of the New Testament. It didn't just happen on Easter. The same power at work then will be at work, we fervently pray, in Evan, the baby who is to be baptized today, when, as a young teenager, he will confirm that he believes what his parents and sponsors will confess for him this morning and he will have a chance, freely and personally, to commit his life to Christ. It is a pattern that he and we can follow every time we symbolically put ourselves, along with our offering, into the offering plate, and every time we come to the altar rail. It is a pattern--this dying to self and rising again in surrender to Christ--that can occur at any time and in any place when we are struck by the need to stop merely "playing church," to stop resisting God, and to acknowledge that St. Augustine was right when he said, "You have made us for Yourself, O Lord, and our spirits are restless until they rest in You."

There are people here, this morning, who know the freedom of being in the right place in their relationship with God. There are others who know that they need to make a change. But we all can believe the promise of God that, since we were buried by our baptism into Christ's death, God can raise us to life at its best, through the Holy Spirit that stands at the door of our heart, knocking, and waiting for us open the door--maybe again, maybe for the first time. We also can believe in the freedom that follows, even if we do not always consciously experience it, and that is worth a picnic, and fireworks, and two parades: one when we go up for communion and one when we leave the sanctuary for the wider world on this 4th of July.

"Faith for the Best Kind of Life"

I invite you to use your imagination to return with me to the 1500s, the end of the Middle Ages, when life was hard for most people, a veritable "vale of tears," and the only hope for something better was a hope in an afterlife in heaven. But that same hope brought with it the fear and dread of another form of afterlife, namely, purgatory and hell, filled, according to the popular imagination, with flames, and pain, and continuous thirst, and devouring demons. Even on earth, devils were said to prowl around trying to lead souls astray. Martin Luther even claimed to have thrown an inkwell at one. What a different view of life from what we have today!

Whatever hopes you have for a better future, for many people here it's likely that most of them deal with a time period much nearer at hand than a time after you die. And whatever genuine dread and anxiety you may occasionally experience, I suspect that *none* of that dread has to do with the possibility of being snatched by the Devil and of being thrown into hell. Yes, our views today are quite different from those of Luther's time, and a good part of the reason for that difference is due to Luther himself.

Nowadays, to strive for what is good means to strive for a better world, for more sensitive and even-handed justice, for greater opportunities for the powerless, for a greater sense of the worth of individual human beings, for respect for the environment, for the well-being of our families, and for improved interpersonal and international relationships. In Luther's day, to strive for what is good meant to pray and to fast and to give alms and to attend church daily and to say the Rosary and to do other pious things in order to get into heaven. Monks had more time to do those things, so when Luther was almost struck by lightning, instead of continuing as a law student he decided to enter a monastery.

There he soon became the most zealous monk in the abbey, trying to do everything he could possibly do to make himself acceptable to God. But he was never sure about whether he had done enough. God is holy and righteous and demands perfection. The sinner could not be admitted into heaven. So Luther went to confession daily, confessing every sin that he could think of, even every thought that might be displeasing to God.

But maybe he had overlooked something. He eventually started to hate God for making such demands, and that made him even more miserable, because he knew he was supposed to love God. But he hated the righteousness of God, which required such perfection of imperfect people.

Meanwhile, he had been studying Hebrew and studying the Bible. And one day as he began to examine Paul's Epistle to the Romans, his eyes fell upon the 17th verse of the 1st chapter, and it was as if heaven had opened up to him, which is a way of saying he got a new insight into how to think about God. What Romans 1:17 says is, "The person who by faith is righteous shall live." People become righteous or, to use another translation, they become justified, i.e., they become acceptable to God, not by what they do, but by faith -- faith that God accepts them. That gave Luther a completely new lease on life

What gave Luther that new outlook on life was an insight actually into the very Being of God. Let me explain how that was possible. As a result of studying Hebrew, Luther knew that Hebrew nouns are based on verbs. And he applied the insight gained from that knowledge to this epistle, even though the Epistle to the Romans was written in Greek. Stay tuned. He came to believe that God's righteousness was not a static standard that we can't attain -- not a noun -- but a dynamic power -- an action verb -- a power that makes *us* righteous. God is the force for good in the world, not only setting the standard of goodness in any given situation but also making it possible for the goodness to take place: empowering us to be good, if we trust in *God's* way. And for Christians, God's way is not something vague that we have to guess about. God's way is Jesus' way.

In one respect, "justification by faith" isn't terribly meaningful to us nowadays. We aren't preoccupied with the question of how we can find a gracious God, i.e., of how we can become acceptable in God's sight, of how we can get God to like us. We have learned what Luther learned about God's unrelenting love for us and for all of humanity. Besides, sometimes we're not even sure whether "God" is a meaningful word any more. We often seem to be able to get along quite well without God.

But when life isn't going well, or when we can pull ourselves away from our *own* problems long enough to look at society in all of its forms of disharmony and at the world at large -- when we become baffled by the problems of the world and don't know in what direction the solution lies -- then we may be ready to rediscover that Jesus' way is God's way. Then we may see again -- or even for the first time -- that what makes for goodness in the world, what will make the world into the *best* that it can be, is love in action: concern for the powerless and for people on the fringes of society and at the bottom of the world's economy, efforts that foster peace -- in a word: what Jesus taught.

But knowing what needs to be done in general terms is not the last step. The difficult next step is to find ways to implement love in specific situations. Intelligent people of good will can do that.

But even intelligent people will hesitate to do what they intellectually know is right, if it means that they will have to be hurt a little bit in order for many others to benefit: They may have to give up some power, in order for many others to gain some power. It is in circumstances like that that one's faith is tested. Because it is then that you are forced to ask whether you really believe in Christ and in the type of goodness that he taught.

Or do you just believe in Christ but do what's best only for yourself, anyway? If so, you don't really believe in Christ. Belief in Christ doesn't mean believing primarily in doctrines about him. Belief in Christ means believing that his way is the right way. It means endorsing what he taught and what he stood for. Jesus said exactly that when he said, "Not everyone who calls me 'Lord' will enter into the kingdom of heaven, but the person who does the will of my Father."

And if you do believe in the goodness that Jesus taught, are you willing to take the risk of implementing that goodness because it's right, even if you don't appear to benefit directly? *Without* that risk-taking faith, the good will not be done; God's will will not be done; and your behavior will not be acceptable to God.

So we, too, find it to be true, as Luther did, that it requires *faith* to be righteous, i.e., it requires *faith* to take the risk of doing God's will, and that only people with faith will truly live, i.e., truly be in harmony with the abundant life that God is, rather than merely existing in what may be called "a state of living death," separated from the life of God.

Do you see the new twist that I've given to the traditional doctrine? Luther said that in order to be righteous or acceptable to God, you have to believe, believe that Christ died for your sins, which is a way of saying believe that God considers you worthwhile in spite of yourself.

And I think that's correct. The modern twist applies the word "righteous" not to your inherent worth but to your behavior. It says that there are times when, in order to do the right thing, you have to give up or, at least, risk losing some of the sources of your security. In order to do the right thing, you have to risk losing your security. That is when faith really comes into play, because then you have to decide whether you really trust God and God's truth and God's power, or whether you will continue to cling to your own sources of security, such as capital gains. It is then that faith is really needed, in order to do the righteous, or just, or right thing.

The risk of faith that brings life and righteousness can apply to your personal life, if you ought to be doing something that you're afraid to do, even though you know it would be good for you. If it also seems to be in accordance with God's will, then the full power of God will endorse you, if you will take a chance and act.

The same thing applies on a broader scale, too. People who believe in the dignity of the individual, and in providing opportunities for the powerless, and in rights of self-determination may have to take risks to implement those ideals. Boards of Education may have to take the risk of giving teachers the right to bargain, rather than presuming that only the Board has the wisdom to know what is best for them. White people on committees in racially mixed neighborhoods may have to relinquish some of their seats, so that racial minorities can be represented on the committees. Suburbanites and farmers may have to vote for the state to spend more money to improve inner cities. The problems there may not be solved otherwise. Americans may have to be willing to pay more for bananas, so that Guatemalans can earn a living wage. If God wants us to be concerned for the poor, as Jesus' own ministry certainly indicates, then it's doubtful whether God cares whether the poor are Mexican or American or Canadian. It would seem to follow that what should be done should be to take steps that are most likely to help those who are least well off and therefore who need the help the most. And if the natural resources of our planet are to be saved for many future generations to come, enormous risks will have to be taken to change the way our international economy functions, risks and changes which few people have even imagined or considered at this point but which may well have to be taken, in order to insure a healthy environment and sustainable economic well-being for most of the people of the world.

Just as Luther's insight freed people for such practical consequences as finding dignity in very many forms of work (and not only in the priesthood), so his emphasis on faith continues to have application today, freeing us from preoccupation with ourselves, and challenging us to trust the God Who loves us and therefore to do God's will "no matter what," since it is in doing God's will, i.e., in doing the best "no matter what," that we and the world find *life*.

"When You Really Believe in God"

(Matthew 16:25)

Last year in the Reformation Day sermon we considered the theme that Lutherans believe summarizes the very essence of Christianity. That theme is that we are justified by grace through faith. Since such a claim might evoke nothing more than a mighty yawn, nowadays, we considered how that theme could be understood in <u>this</u> century. We saw that it deals with how we are saved.

Incidentally, what does it mean to be saved? What are we saved from? Martin Luther's answer was that we are saved from sin, death, and the Devil, all of which amount to the same thing. That is, all of them stand for being separated from God. We are saved from being separated from God. Or, to be saved is to be united, in some way, with God or to be in harmony with God. In 21st century terms, to be saved from sin, death, and the power of the Devil means to be saved from participating in evil and from doing things that endorse the forces of death and that lead ourselves and other people away from the best kind of life that we and they could have.

In order to be saved from those things, we saw last year that we may need to have the kind of faith that is willing to take risks in order for us to do God's will. For we are saved when we have the faith that dares to do what is right.

Luther placed an awful lot of emphasis on faith; because in his view, faith doesn't just deal with what you believe about God. Faith affects your relationship with people, too. And it affects it in a very powerful way.

Listen to what Luther said about faith: "O, when it comes to faith, what a living, creative, active, powerful thing it is! It cannot do other than good at all times. It never waits to ask whether there is some good work to do. Rather, before the question is raised, it has done the deed and keeps on doing it."

Christians at their best do good not because they should, not because God wants them to, not just because it's better for society, not because they think God's law demands it, but because their relationship with God causes them to <u>want</u> to do good and gives them the <u>power</u> to do good. Faith is active. And an active faith in God results in a spontaneous activity on behalf of the good that doesn't wait to be told what must be done but that instinctively reaches out to where the need is and takes action that is appropriate. It reaches out, because it is motivated by faith in the God Who is love. That divine love has reached out to the believer, filling the believer with so much love that the believer overflows with a love that reaches out to others.

Let's take a look at the type of faith that generates that type of behavior. First of all, that type of faith is not primarily beliefs. It's not simply accepting the correct doctrines. That doesn't mean that doctrines aren't useful. They have developed over centuries and often are a composite of insights concerning what God is like and also concerning what God is not like. That is, doctrines can sometimes be useful in keeping us from attributing to God things that Christians down through the ages have not found to be true about God and God's will. But while doctrines can keep our thinking straight, believing doctrines doesn't mean we know God any more than we know the President of the United States, if all that we know are some facts about him or other people's reactions to him.

Faith at its most profound is not simply beliefs. Faith can also describe a relationship, much like a relationship between two people. There is a gospel song that's <u>not</u> part of the Lutheran tradition that sings about encountering God in a garden, where God walks with you and talks with you and tells you that you are God's own. The song proceeds to speak of the joy that is shared in that encounter with God. Making allowances for the anthropomorphism involved, that is the kind of relationship that you, too, can have with God. God's presence and the reality of God's power can be felt and experienced.

A central feature of that relationship, on the believer's part, is trust in God. Even among human beings, when we say "I believe in you," we can also mean "I trust you." A faith that trusts God is a faith that liberates us from preoccupation with ourselves. It trusts in God's love and in God's care and in God's power, and in so doing it frees us to be concerned for others. Such trusting reliance on God also frees-up our energies, so that we can move ahead naturally to do the good that we see needs to be done.

But why don't Christians always behave that way? Why does Luther's statement about the spontaneity of good deeds generated by faith seem like such an exaggeration? Well, you may have your own answers to that question. The question certainly is more complex than the way I am going to deal with it this morning. But let me suggest one answer by returning to that trustful faith that we've been considering. How do we get a faith like that?

In answer, let's direct our attention back to our baptism. Since Lutherans believe in infant baptism, the Church calls us to consider what <u>God</u> was doing for <u>us</u>, even before we could lift a finger to help ourselves. God was accepting us, which means also that God was saving us. God was bringing us into a community of believers, i.e., into the Church, through the efforts of other people on our behalf.

But I think the main point in recalling our baptism is to confront us with God's gracious action on our behalf, precisely at times of our greatest helplessness. If this is how God acts, if God acts on our behalf especially when we are helpless, then this is a God Whom faith can fully rely on.

It is a sound Christian principle: to focus on God's action on our behalf. And salvation, however it is understood and whatever we are saved from and whatever we are saved for -- salvation comes and will come from God alone.

But perhaps what we need, in order to experience Luther's dynamic faith, is to experience or to acknowledge a state of helplessness analogous to our condition at the time of our baptism. As long as we think we can help ourselves or do good by our own strength or according to our own lights, we are not likely to feel any need to rely on God or to trust God. There are many ways in which we <u>can</u> help ourselves, and we shouldn't pretend that we are helpless when we are not. But on the matter of being intuitively certain of what is right and of voluntarily walking the extra mile to do it, we don't seem always to be able to help ourselves.

I suggest that we are helpless here because we have not fully acknowledged our spiritual helplessness without God. We are holding back from God, at points where we ought to be entrusting ourselves to God. What we need is to surrender ourselves completely to God. That action would reflect a faith that takes trusting God seriously, wouldn't it? Interestingly, total surrender to God is the foundation of Mohammedanism. The correct name for that religion, Islam, means "surrender."

Jesus said, "Those who would save their life will lose it; but those who lose their life for my sake will find it." Jesus wasn't talking about losing your life by dying in battle or by dying from old age. He was talking about committing yourself to him and his cause, with nothing held back. In a word, he was talking about "surrender." That, paradoxically, is how you find life! Not the kind of life that you give to yourself. Not the kind of minimal joy that you eek out in your daily existence. But the abundant life that comes from God, to the person whose total self is yielded to God.

Jesus puts it another way in John's Gospel. "Unless a grain of wheat falls into the ground and dies, it remains alone; but if it dies, it bears much fruit" (John 12:24). The grain has to stop being a grain, before it can become something different and better. Your old sinful self has to relinquish itself to God, in order for it to be open to the transforming power of God. You will not be able to rise above your present, imperfect, humdrum existence unless you stop holding onto that type of existence, unless you stop being so devoted to it, unless, figuratively speaking, you die to it, so that a new kind of life may arise in you, by the power of God. Here once more is a central theme of the New Testament, the theme of dying and rising again, depicted paradigmatically in Jesus' death and resurrection.

The apostle Paul, in describing his experience of the same thing, said, "I have been crucified with Christ; it is no longer I who live, but Christ who lives in me" (Galatians 2:20). "Christ ... lives in me." No wonder he could add, "But whatever gain I had, I counted as loss because of the surpassing worth of knowing Christ Jesus my Lord. For his sake I have suffered the loss of all things, and count them as refuse, in order that I may gain Christ and be found in him ... that I may know him and the power of his resurrection" (Philippians 3:7-10).

The Christian claim is that it's OK to stop clutching tightly even to your life, trying to give it meaning and purpose on your own. It's OK to surrender yourself completely to God, because, as a matter of fact, it is only then that you will find life at its best. It's only after death that resurrection comes. It's only after turning yourself over to God that you really permit God to work within you, using your own untapped energies to bear much fruit.

That's the intellectual justification for this message. Assuming that we have free will, God cannot transform our lives, making us the kind of people we were meant to be, unless we permit it, i.e., unless we submit our will to God's will.

And it is precisely that submission that is the source of Luther's faith. Not the kind of faith that barely hangs on, but the kind of faith that is willing to risk letting go, surrendering totally, committing yourself completely. That is the kind of faith that finds life that overflows in abundance.

Ref

"Christians Can Create Their Own Ten Commandments"

(Jeremiah 31:31-34)

What if I were to tell you that you could make up whatever moral rules you wanted? Some of you would have a field day! Think of the different rules that you could devise. "Take whatever you want" might be one. Or "drink a keg of beer every Friday night." Or "thou shalt not be chaste." The possibilities are endless!

Well, it may surprise you to learn that Martin Luther said that Christians can make up their own Ten Commandments. To understand what he had in mind, let's take a look at what he thought the purposes of God's moral laws were, in general. Actually, there is a debate among theologians as to whether there are two or three broad uses for the Law. (When I say "the Law," I mean the Ten Commandments and all of the other moral rules that you can find in the Bible).

The first use of the Law was stated by St. Paul when he said, "The law is our taskmaster to lead us to Christ." God's laws tell us how we should behave and what our motivations should be; but if we're honest, we have to admit that we don't always follow those laws 100%. Now, if the laws come from God, then breaking them says something not only about how we treat each other but also about how we treat God, about what our relationship to God is. As the psalmist said, when speaking to God, "Against Thee, Thee only have I sinned and done this evil in Thy sight" (Psalm 51:4). That's an important point. Immoral behavior is not a matter of breaking impersonal laws. It is a form of thumbing our nose at God: It is a violation of what is ultimately best--for both ourselves and our society.

And if you should happen to notice that the Ten Commandments deal mostly with our relationship with other people and not with our relationship with God, perhaps that's a clue as to just how sacred individual people are. Luther emphasized that fact when he said, "We meet Christ in our neighbor." So when we mistreat our neighbor, we are mistreating Christ.

As sinners, therefore, we are in need of healing the breach in our relationship with God. We need God's forgiveness. And so the Law, which we have broken, leads us to Christ, whose life and teachings demonstrate God's love for us, in spite of ourselves and the punishment that we deserve.

The Law also leads us to the <u>Spirit</u> of the <u>Risen</u> Christ for the power and will to live in accordance with it. As Paul himself bemoaned, "The good that I want to do I don't do. The evil that I don't want to do: that's what I do. Who will free me from this body of death [i.e., from these inclinations that kill the abundant life that I <u>could</u> have if I were in harmony with God]?" His answer: "Thanks be to God, Who gives us the victory through our Lord Jesus Christ." Faith in Christ and acceptance of <u>his</u> way give us the power and will to obey God's laws, which means, simply, to behave in a way that is ultimately best.

But Paul and Luther weren't thinking only about our <u>own</u> difficulty with being moral when they said that the Law leads us to Christ. They were thinking of the entire history of the human-divine relationship, starting with the basic <u>rupture</u> in that relationship, as depicted in the story of the Garden of Eden. Thanks to human disobedience, the peace and harmony of the Garden had been broken; and although God made it clear, at Mt. Sinai and other places, how people could make themselves acceptable to God, the experience of the <u>prophets</u> was that people simply <u>would</u> not or <u>could</u> not follow God's laws. They needed a savior with greater power than their own.

That's where Jesus comes into the picture. When his followers thought about his crucifixion, they asked, "Could it be that on that Cross a perfect human being was making the perfect sacrifice, once and for all, for the sins of the world, in a way that replaced the <u>yearly</u> sacrifice of unblemished lambs in the Temple in Jerusalem?" Yes, that's what they thought had happened, and the conclusion that they drew was that if that sacrifice <u>healed</u> the broken relationship between God and humanity, then anyone who acknowledged that that reconciliation had taken place was also reconciled to God (was included among those whom God found acceptable). That's a somewhat involved way of saying God loves us in spite of ourselves; but it <u>is</u> a way of showing how the Law--and our inability to fulfill it perfectly--can be used to make us aware of God's love and of our inability to earn it.

There is a second use of the Law, according to Luther. God's moral laws were intended to apply not just to believers but to societies in general. God's Law is intended to provide guidance to legislatures and town councils, when they deliberate to decide what laws and ordinances to pass.

God wills that people live in communities that are not chaotic but where order is preserved, where we are protected from murderers, and where thieves are punished. So Christian faith applies not only to how we treat other individuals but also to how we vote and, understood properly, to how our government should behave.

But then there's the question of the third use of the Law. Most denominations say there <u>is</u> a third use for God's Law, and that use is to provide rules for leading a Christian life. Much of what Luther said opposes that third use, and that piece of information usually surprises most Lutherans. But Luther argued that Christ's sacrifice freed us from the curse of the Law. The Law is a curse for people who think that they can get on God's good side by following it. It is a curse first because it leads them to think that their <u>salvation</u> is essentially under <u>their</u> <u>control</u>, and second because, in the long run, it will lead only to defeat, as we find that we <u>don't</u> follow the law perfectly. The Christian, said Luther, is not under the Law but under grace. To be under grace is to be ruled by God and not by rules. To be under grace is to be related to God and not to rules. Christians at their best have surrendered their lives to God, in such a thorough way that the Holy Spirit rules within them. God has <u>transformed</u> their <u>sinful</u> inclinations into Christ-like inclinations. They are on God's wavelength: they have the mind of Christ: they intuitively know what is right. They don't have a need to follow rules. Indeed, "for <u>freedom</u> Christ has set us free," as the Apostle Paul wrote (Galatians 5:1).

Here Luther demonstrates some very sophisticated ethical thinking. For he realizes that no rule can be <u>relied</u> upon to cover any <u>particular</u> ethical situation adequately. The details of a situation may just be too complex. As a result, rigidly following a rule might require us to ignore factors that simply cannot be ignored if God's will is to be done, i.e., if we are to provide the most moral and ethical behavior possible in the particular circumstance.

It is in connection with <u>such</u> situations that Luther says that Christians can write their own Ten Commandments. They can do so if they are so in tune with God and have become so morally sensitive that the moral rules that <u>they</u> would say they should follow would probably <u>be</u> the <u>best</u> ones under the circumstances.

The general principle that Luther is following here does seem to reflect an <u>essential</u> element of the Christian Faith, which is that we are to orient our lives to God and not to rules. That is, we are to live our lives, day by day, receptive to the promptings of God's Holy Spirit to make us sensitive to what the morally best behavior would be in each of the decisions that we make and the actions that we take. That is what it means to walk with God. Such faith in God creates flexible people, because they are willing to be led by God, Who knows what is best at any given moment--better than they do. So to say, "If you want to live a Christian life, follow these rules," is tantamount to denying the power of the Holy Spirit to guide our actions from minute to minute. It is a way of denying the freedom of God and of rejecting the freedom for which Christ has set us free. It is as though God were to say, "You're free!" and then a church were to say, "Now here are some lovely chains to control your behavior."

BUT Luther is also famous for another insight that would seem to suggest that we should not throw out the Ten Commandments too quickly. Luther <u>also</u> taught that Christians are *simul justus et peccator*, simultaneously righteous and sinful, both saint and sinner. We are saints because God lovingly chooses to view us that way. And because God does love us, we feel secure enough to respond by behaving lovingly, from time to time. But Luther knew, as all perceptive Christian theologians have known, that we are part of a sinful world and do not always live like saints. Indeed, there may be <u>nothing</u> that we do that is morally <u>perfect</u>. Our motives may <u>never</u> be 100% pure. The love that <u>we</u> express, in whatever form, is never as selfless, never as complete as God's love. We almost always have to make compromises. "You can never satisfy everyone," as we say, and so some people get hurt to some degree, and justice is not fully done.

We don't always trust God; we don't always live faithfully. We are not <u>always</u> at our best, and so we can't always <u>trust our moral instincts</u>. Especially when we have to make compromises, our instincts are likely to be biased in <u>our</u> favor, and as a result, we may not do what's best for the entire situation.

Clearly <u>then</u>, the Ten Commandments can serve as useful reminders. We are called to live in a close personal relationship with God, but that doesn't mean we have to throw away God's moral roadmap. Indeed, in a complex world, <u>our</u> moral instincts may not always provide sufficient guidance for solving a complex moral problem. When we don't know <u>what</u> to do, God's laws can at least point the way. They can do that because they have weathered the test of time. Under most circumstances, they indicate the right thing to do. In fact, if <u>you</u> were to create your own set of Ten Commandments that you would want everyone to follow, you probably would <u>not</u> do what I suggested you might do at the beginning of this sermon. You would not, for example, create a command that says,

"Take whatever you want," because <u>you</u> know that if everyone were to follow that commandment, nothing of yours would be safe. <u>Your</u> rule would be encouraging a chaotic society, and you wouldn't want to live in a society like that. I wouldn't be surprised if the Ten Commandments that <u>you</u> would develop would look very similar to the traditional ones.

But if they were developed in the abstract, in your room, for general application to whatever situation might come along, they would be no more certain to guarantee a correct moral decision (to say nothing about correct moral behavior) than the traditional Ten Commandments. Because they, too, would have the limitations that all general rules have: They wouldn't be able to take into consideration the specific circumstances of a particular situation. That step must be taken by people. Accordingly, it must be taken by you and me, when we're faced with a moral choice.

In a particular situation, we cannot be <u>sure</u> <u>what</u> God's will is by looking at a rule. That's because God is not a tablet of stone. When Christians try to understand what is ultimate, they depict God as alive and personal, fully aware of all of the details of <u>each</u> specific situation and capable of willing the best for each situation.

That's why all churches, whether or not they believe in the third use of the Law, are not content simply with teaching rules. (Remember, the third use of the Law was to guide us in how to lead a Christian life.) The churches' primary aim is to put us in touch with the God revealed in Jesus Christ, so that we might have the <u>mind</u> of Christ and be as sensitive in the way <u>we</u> treat people as Jesus was. Sometimes the churches succeed in putting us in touch with God. And when we think about <u>why</u> they succeed, we say with awe and reverence that the Holy Spirit has been at work, the spirit that blows where it <u>wills</u>, so that we cannot predict when it will come or how long it will stay. But when it comes, we become like the person who had encountered Jesus and later said, "I was blind, but <u>now</u> I <u>see</u>!" When the Holy Spirit is at work within us, we who must take so many factors into consideration <u>can</u> have the mind of Christ, i.e., we can think the way Christ thought, and in the specific moral situation that confronts us, we <u>can</u> see what the will of God is (when the Holy Spirit is at work in us), and we <u>can</u> have the inclination and the power to do it.

"Down with 'Thou Shalt Not'!"

(Exodus 20:2-17)

How many times have you heard the words, "No!" "Don't do that!" You've probably been hearing those words for longer than you can remember. I say "for longer than you can remember," because our memory is dependent upon our knowledge of language. Apparently our memory is based on words and concepts, so we remember almost nothing about what happened before we could talk.

Yet long before we learned to use sentences, we were exploring the fascinating world around us. We were putting things into our mouth, and we were crawling into places that we shouldn't have tried to get to, and we were touching things, and, over and over again, we were being told not to. Usually those admonitions were for our own good. When you haven't experienced much of this complex world, it can be helpful -- indeed, it can be absolutely essential to your own well-being -- for someone to point out what the limits are.

The same thing was true in the infancy of Western civilization. There were all sorts of things that people could do, but for the well-being of society as a whole, there were certain things that had to be forbidden. These were reflected in the Ten Commandments. And just as it still makes sense for us not to touch a hot stove, so the prohibitions in the Ten Commandments still meaningfully steer us away from actions and thoughts that are not healthy for society as a whole.

But children grow up. And when they do, the role of the parent changes also. With grown children, the parent is concerned not only that they realize what the limits are but that they channel their energies in useful ways and that they develop the talents that they have, both for their own good and, again, for the good of the wider society of which they are a part.

Between the time when Moses gave the Ten Commandments and the time when Martin Luther wrote about them in his *Small Catechism*, Western civilization had had an opportunity to do some growing. It is a sad commentary on human society that, during all that time, we had not outgrown our need for the prohibitions in the Ten Commandments. That fact makes clear the pervasive reality of sin, both in ourselves and in our social, political, and economic institutions.

But between the times of Moses and Luther, Jesus had lived among us; and in word and deed he taught the ultimate reality of love. Love is not a stance of avoidance; love reaches out. Because God is love, Jesus encouraged us not simply to avoid doing bad things but to direct our efforts at doing good things. "Do unto others as you would have them do unto you." "I give you a new commandment, that you love one another, even as I have loved you," he said. So if you think the will of God is all about what you shouldn't do, think again.

Luther did. As a Christian, he took the negative Ten Commandments -- not all of the Ten Commandments are negative, but he took the negative ones and directed our attention to their positive implications. He asked, How can these Commandments stimulate us to reflect to others the love of God in our lives? If love underlies everything, so that behaving lovingly is the way that we function best and the way that people interact most humanely, what else is implied in the Ten Commandments besides mere prohibitions?

Listen to what he taught about the command "Thou shalt not kill." He said, we are "not to hurt our neighbor in any way but help him in all his physical needs." Notice that Luther doesn't get involved with distinguishing between different degrees of murder, as is necessary in a court of law, if justice is to be done. He goes to the heart of the negative statement and says we should not hurt anyone in any way! Think of how broad that statement is! Even hurting people in little ways is a form of killing them. But then Luther moves right into the positive implications of the commandment by calling us to help our neighbors in all their physical needs.

Killing puts an end to our physical life. The opposite is to promote people's physical well-being. How? Well, what would you suggest? By seeing that everyone has adequate food, and water, and housing, and health care? By eliminating environmental pollution and by providing for everyone's physical safety, including adequate maintenance of bridges? The more you think about promoting life, rather than ending it, the more you become aware of how vast are the implications of this one little commandment.

Let's look at what Luther taught about "Thou shalt not steal." Luther said that the commandment means that "we do not take our neighbor's money or property, or get them in any dishonest way, but help him to improve and protect his property and means of making a living." When viewed with the eyes of love, "Don't steal" means "help your neighbor improve his property." And if your neighbor is not just the person next door but the person in need (as Jesus taught in the Parable of the Good Samaritan) -- or the country in need (so that we are now talking about international economic arrangements on behalf of undeveloped countries, possibly at the price of our own "high on the hog" lifestyles) -- you begin to get a sense of the range of God's love that awaits your action and mine, in order for that love to be expressed.

Luther goes on. "You shall not bear false witness" means we should explain our neighbor's action in the kindest way possible. "You shall not covet" means we should always help our neighbors keep what is theirs.

So if you think you have kept the Fifth Commandment because you haven't killed anyone, you are letting yourself off too easily. At least, if you have caught the Christian vision of what love requires, you eventually will have to confess, in the words of the Episcopalian prayer, "we have left undone those things which we ought to have done." If you acknowledge the insight behind Luther's understanding of the Ten Commandments, you will never be smug about how good you are. And you won't think of the Ten Commandments as just a bunch of prohibitions.

We all leave undone things which we would do if we were more loving. You can probably think of how that applies to you.

Does Luther tell us how we can be better at being more loving? In looking for an answer, it's important to know that everything that Luther says about each of the Ten Commandments he relates to our love and trust and respect for God. That's the clue. If we behave lovingly, if we take the risk of doing what is right, even though we might not personally benefit, it's because we love God and trust that God's will or God's ways are what is really best.

But what if we don't much love God? Not that we hate God but just that we don't have strong feelings one way or the other. Well, first of all, you don't have to limit love to an emotion. You might think of it as an orientation or a commitment to what is best. If you are not oriented or directed toward what is best (i.e., toward God), you may be foolish but you are not alone. You are in the category labeled "sinner." And Jesus' call to all of us, since we are all in that category in some way, is "Repent!"

But the primary reason why Christians can love God is because God loved us first. That is why God reached out to Abraham, and it is the point of the teachings and actions of Jesus. The Gospel message is: God loves you. Ya see, the theory is: when you are loved, then you can love in return.

Now it's true that some people can be loved and yet not love in return. That's another version of the category labeled "sinner." (The reasons why a person might fall into that category for that reason are too complex for us to consider right now.)

Others may simply not have experienced God's love. They may be turning their backs on God, with the result that they are not sensitive to God's presence. Does that describe you? Or they may be holding back from committing themselves to God. Does that describe you? Or they may simply be in situations where God's love is not evident or essential. Those who are living in comfortable circumstances are likely to fall into that category.

But to those who receive God, i.e., to those who trust in God's love and who are seeking God's will and trying to do it, to them is given the power to become God's own children. And just as children inevitably are reflections of their parents, so the sons and daughters of God are enabled to express the love of God.

To sum up, the love of God controls us, as it controlled Luther, if we treat the Ten Commandments not just as a list of things we shouldn't do, but also as a goad to prompt us to be helpful to people and to form a vision of what is required to move toward a better society, where relationships are such that there is no need to kill, or steal, or be unfaithful, or lie, or to envy. Such a society is achieved not simply by refraining from doing bad things but, in innumerable and creative ways, by taking positive steps to improve present conditions.

"Christians Are Free Servants"

(Jeremiah 31:33; John 8:36; Galatians 2:20)

Martin Luther said, "A Christian is a perfectly free lord of all, subject to none. A Christian is a perfectly dutiful servant of all, subject to all." This seems to be a paradox. How can you be both free and a servant, subject to no one and subject to everyone?

Well, let's look at the first statement and ask ourselves what it is probably <u>not</u> saying. It can often be useful, when you're trying to solve a problem, to ask what it is <u>not</u>.

In the first statement, Luther says, "A Christian is perfectly free and subject to no one." Does that mean that Christians don't have to obey the laws? Obviously not. Luther also said that God intends everyone to obey the laws of society, under normal circumstances, as a means of maintaining harmony in our dealings with one another.

In a totalitarian state, are Christians free to say whatever they want to say about the government, without being subject to mistreatment? Of course not. Fortunately in the United States, we can express our opinions, even, presumably, if they are antithetical to our country.

Do all Christians have economic freedom, because they're all rich? No. In fact, some of the deepest faith can be found among people who are very poor. That doesn't mean Christians with money shouldn't be concerned about those who are poor. The Acts of the Apostles, in the Bible, reports that the very early Christians used to share their wealth with one another, so that none of them had financial problems.

But it seems clear that when Luther talks about the freedom that Christians have, he is not talking about legal, or political, or economic freedom. He is probably talking about spiritual freedom, which today often is closely connected to psychological freedom, or just to the way we think about things and the way we behave, or to our relationship with God.

What keeps us from being free, in this sense? Sometimes it's fear. Sometimes that means lack of trust. Sometimes it's lack of self-confidence, uncertainty that you can do what needs to be done. It's as though you don't have the assurance and the power needed for the task at hand. Perhaps that's because we're not fully in touch with the "Lord God of power and might," as Lutherans and others sing in what in Latin is called the *Sanctus*. At the core of spiritual freedom is our relationship with God.

God calls for full commitment, but we hold back. Rather than doing things God's way, we want to do them our way -- as though God's way were designed to make us miserable. Yet is that likely? Isn't God identified with what is best? But when we want to do things our way, rather than God's way, the story of Adam and Eve is played out once again. That's what makes it true. Adam and Eve were not real people; but the myth about them is true, because it describes the truth about everyone. Everyone, in some way, rebels against God and so is cast out of Paradise, away from the best kind of life that harmony with God would bring.

Stated another way, when we hold back from full commitment, we cut ourselves off from being fully plugged into the Power Source. The whole point of the Gospel is that God has broken down the barriers that separate us from God. And yet we hold back. We believe in God -- sort of. We trust God -- sort of. We do God's will -- some percentage of the time. And so our fears remain, and we don't feel free.

We haven't quite grasped the insight that is at the center of the Muslim religion, which is that faith in God means *al Islam*, the surrender -- of self to God.

And yet Jesus said the same thing when he said, "Unless a seed falls into the ground and dies, it remains alone. But if it dies, then it bears much fruit." When Jesus speaks of the seed dying, he is calling us, in metaphorical language, to do what Islam calls "surrendering."

And isn't it true, what Jesus said? A seed is just a single seed, even though it has potential for much more, as long as it holds onto itself and keeps being a seed. But when it lets go of itself, when it turns itself over to the soil and the water and the warmth of the sun, then it becomes much more: a tree, or a bush, or an ear of corn on a cornstalk. That all happens only after the seed dies to itself, so to speak.

When Jesus talks about bearing much fruit, he is talking about what we do on earth. But before we can bear that good fruit, we first must die to our preoccupation with ourself; we must give up our self-centeredness; we must turn over our life to God.

"Unless a seed falls into the ground and dies, it remains alone. But when it dies" -- when it stops being its old (shall we say its "sinful"?) self -- "then it bears much fruit." As long as we are trying to save our life and give it meaning and purpose apart from God's will, we will lose our life. Oh, we won't die; we just won't have the abundant life that Christ said he came to bring. (In John 10:10 Jesus said, "I have come that you might have life, and have it more abundantly!" And he wasn't talking about another world. He was talking about our life in <u>this</u> world).

Jesus said at another time, "Those who would save their life shall lose it." But then he continued, "But those who lose their life for my sake shall find it." "For my sake" means for what Jesus believed in and what he stands for. And since Christians believe that what Jesus believed and did reveals what God is like, we have come full circle in our thinking: When we lose our life for Christ we surrender our life to God, and, as a result, we get it back in the best way that it could be.

In fact, then we can say with the Apostle Paul, "It is not I who lives, but Christ who lives in me." That's what makes you free. And "if the Son makes you free, you will be free indeed!" Faith in the God revealed in Jesus Christ releases the power and energies deep within us, because it gives us the will to direct them in the way they <u>should</u> be directed. And when we are fully on God's side, our fears can vanish, because we can know that the ultimate force of the universe is endorsing us. Then we can say, with Luther, that we are perfectly free lords of all, subject to no one.

But then an interesting thing happens. Are we free in order to be selfish? How could that be? We died to ourself: we gave up preoccupation with our own wants and our own concerns and our own self-fulfillment when we turned our life over to God. That frees us to be sensitive to the needs of others, and to be willing and able to help them out. So Christians at their best can be said to be servants of all and subject to all -- not under compulsion, not because they <u>have</u> to be, but because the Power of Love to which or to Whom they surrendered themselves flows back into them and empowers them to reach out naturally and givingly to others.

That type of service can apply on many levels, too. It can affect your decision about your future vocation: how you will spend your time and how you will contribute to society. It can affect how you carry out your present job. It applies not only to life at home or in town, but also to your willingness to vote to increase taxes, if the money will be used to help people whom you don't even know.

Well, how is it with you? Are you free to be a Christ to your neighbor? (That's another way in which Luther talked about this matter. We are to be Christs to our neighbors. We are called to embody Christ's love and to make it available to our neighbor.) Are you free to be for others? Or do you still need to know the transforming love of God? Are you still holding back?

God has cleared the way. <u>God's</u> love is unconditional. God awaits your response.

"'And the Shepherds Returned:' Scientific Fact and Christian Vision"

(Luke 2:20)

How many of us remember, as kids -- or even as adults -- doing something that would have been OK if we were careful or if we had behaved responsibly, but, instead, we over did it in some way -- and then it happened: The ink spilled or the milk, or the glass broke, or someone got hurt. We didn't mean to do it. We didn't intend it to happen. But it did.

Human civilization seems to be behaving the same way toward the earth and our environment.

What was wrong with manufacturing what people want? Nothing, as long as there weren't a lot of people and our natural resources seemed endless. But we are coming to see that there is a limit to the amount of iron and copper and coal and oil in the ground. The time will come when we will have used it all up.

Oh, that won't come during our lifetime, although it may start to. Some estimates say that the United States will run out of oil in 50 years. But even if it doesn't come even during our children's lifetime, what is our moral responsibility to future generations? Don't we have a responsibility to preserve a high quality of life for as long as we can, for as many people as we can? If you were to be living in the year 2206, wouldn't you want the people back in 2006 to have thought so -- to have left some natural resources for you?

And when we are using much of those resources not to make what we need or even to make things that would be nice to have, but to make things that we don't really care much about but which we buy anyway (since they're on sale in the store or catalogue), fully expecting to throw them away in a short time -- thereby contributing to our growing waste disposal problem -- then we are behaving like irresponsible children, and we need to think seriously about the consequences of our actions.

Letting factories pollute our rivers was a cheap way of letting them dispose of their wastes. After all, wouldn't the rivers wash the refuse away? But then we found that there weren't any fish in those rivers any more.

We in the Midwest improved the poor quality of air around our factories by building taller smokestacks to send the smoke far into the sky. But we didn't realize -- or we didn't admit that we knew better -- that the sulfur that factories were spewing into the sky would fall out of the sky 1 mile or 2,000 miles away, where it would kill fish and plant life in the lakes in the Adirondack Mountains in New York State, because it was making the water too acidic. For the same reason, it has also started to turn trees into posts without leaves, just as its cousins have done in Slovakia and in other parts of Eastern Europe.

We enjoy our cars and our air conditioning and the products of our factories, but we are beginning to see that their exhausts are so polluting our atmosphere that we are not letting the earth cool off, with projected negative consequences called "the greenhouse effect."

In other cases, chemicals from convenient aerosol sprays and refrigerants are finding their way into the upper atmosphere and destroying the ozone layer, which protects us from the harmful ultraviolet rays of the sun.

Massive forests have helped to save us in the past, as their trees have consumed carbon dioxide and manufactured oxygen. But these forests in our own country and tropical rainforests in Brazil, Indonesia, and elsewhere are being cut down nonstop.

The endangered condition of the spotted owl has made us aware that if we continue logging operations in the Pacific Northwest at the present rate, in only twenty years we will have cut down all of the oldest softwood trees in the world. Why are we continuing these logging operations? To save 30,000 jobs and many small mill towns in Washington and Oregon. That would seem to be a worthy objective, until you realize that in twenty years, those same jobs and towns will be in jeopardy anyway, but by then there will be no more ancient trees, they will all have been chopped down. Will the world be better as a result? Are we being responsible stewards of the earth if we do not look ahead to see what is coming?

As you will recall from the map of South America, the big bulge in the northeast is mostly Brazil, and most of Brazil is the Amazon rainforest. Already today, on a map of South America you can draw lines around large patches of the rainforest that are totally barren, patches encompassing millions of square miles, completely devoid of trees. That's a lot of land that is no longer absorbing carbon dioxide and making oxygen.

The Amazon forest is being destroyed for at least four reasons. One is that the Japanese like the mahogany that is grown there. A second is that unemployed people from the crowded cities are clearing the jungle with the slash and burn technique, in order to eek out a living as farmers. But the poor soil of the former jungle allows them to farm the same land for only one or two years, and then they have to move on, slashing and burning some more. A third reason is Americans like hamburgers. And just as South Americans are being paid more to grow coca for cocaine than they're paid for any other crop, because Yankee yuppies and prisoners of the ghettos want it, so the forest is being cleared to provide land to graze cattle, so that fast food restaurants can give us more cholesterol than we need. A fourth reason is that the trees are being used -- as long as they last -- as cheap fuel for iron-smelting plants.

When we point out the devastating consequences of what the Brazilians are doing, they ask us what <u>we</u> are doing to improve the environment. Are we doing anything more than talking and studying? And when they find that our President lets the automotive industry save a little money by not requiring really effective emission control standards (by saying that the standard will be met if the <u>average</u> car in a fleet meets the standard, rather than requiring <u>all</u> cars to meet the standard), the Brazilians find it difficult to understand why they, a Third World country, should have to sacrifice, when people in the prosperous and comfortable United States can't seem to take the environmental crisis seriously.

And what about the need to feed, house, educate, and find work for the world's increasing population? This is a problem in large measure of macroeconomics, and if you don't know anything about it, how will you be able to make a rational decision concerning whom to vote for in future elections?

The long-term future is even more bleak. Have you ever thought about it? I mean the really long-term future. Even if we manage to avoid destroying the world by a nuclear holocaust, scientists tell us that eventually the sun's gravity will pull the earth into the sun and the earth will burn up. Or else the sun will run out of hydrogen and helium fuel and will swell into a giant red ball that will devour the earth in that way. Eventually, the sun's energy will totally burn out, as other stars have done, and the sun will become a black hole in the sky.

Before then, as our overpopulation chokes us off of the earth's surface, some of us may be able to live on gigantic space stations orbiting around the earth, if we still have the raw materials with which to build the space stations.

Somewhat later, as the earth's climate gets too hot because it is being pulled into the sun, the climate on Mars presumably will change, and we may be able to colonize Mars. But as I said, in the long run, there is a good chance that the human race will be obliterated.

Well, we have looked into the Abyss. In view of what we have seen, is life "all sound and fury, signifying nothing," as William Faulkner has proposed? How should Christians react to this view of the future?

The reaction of some people will be to adopt the thinking of some New Age cults, especially those groups that say we are all one with the universe, anyway; each individual is God; and if things go wrong, it is because we have wrong thoughts. They do not take seriously the forces that science talks about. Modern Christians would say they are kidding themselves.

Some Christians will become very religious, as they understand what it means to be religious. They will basically withdraw from the problems of the world into prayer groups, worshipping the Lord and trying to save their own soul for an afterlife.

Martin Luther poked fun at both of these responses. He did so most cleverly in a Christmas sermon, when, after reading about the shepherds visiting the baby Jesus, he changed the words of the Bible and, instead of saying that the shepherds returned to tend their flocks, he said, "and the shepherds returned, shaving their heads and entering monasteries." The two responses I have just described are modern versions of entering monasteries, and that, of course, is precisely what the shepherds did not do.

In Luther's faith, God is still at work in the world, and through Jesus Christ we are given a vision of the world at its best, symbolized by the Kingdom of God, when God reigns or rules. Just as Jesus' own faith and behavior brought a taste of the Kingdom, i.e., made the world better, we, too, as his disciples, are called to be active in the world, as conduits of God's power, making the world in our time a better place. The shepherds returned, you will remember, to their daily tasks in the secular world.

With regard to the long-term future, science may have miscalculated, although that is not likely. Something extraordinary may take place. But even if not, our job is to keep faith with the Bible's vision of a world of peace and harmony (Isaiah 2:4; 11:6-7; 32:15-18; Ezekiel 34:25-29; Amos 5:11, 15, 24; Micah 4:4; Matthew 5:38-44; 25:37-40; Luke 4:18; 10:27; II Corinthians 5:18-19; Galatians 5:1; Revelation 21:1, 3-4) -- peace and harmony brought about because there are no large gaps between the rich and the poor, where the resources of the world, our house, are shared and used wisely, as exemplified by the way the early church members shared all of their possessions (as the book of Acts [2:44-45] reports), and where nature itself shares and is permitted to share in the glory of God.

What kind of people will we be when we are living on the space station? Will we have a keener sense, then, that we're all in this together -- even though we see that that's already true for us on spaceship earth?

By the time the human enterprise ends, will we have caught the biblical vision? Will we have created societies where misery is minimal, so people don't feel the need to take addictive drugs to escape it? Will there be opportunities for education and personal growth and meaningful employment that are not restricted by racial or ethnic considerations? Will we who are at the top have learned how to share with those on the bottom, without being compelled to? Will we have found ways of measuring the economy that reflect the impact of environmental pollution and the social disruptions caused by whole towns losing their economic base? Will we be sensitive to skewed distribution of income, which our present way of measuring the Gross National Product does not register? (We might be pleased that the GNP of a Third World country has been constantly rising, but that statistic does not tell us that all of the increase is going to the five wealthiest families, as is often the case.)

Christian faith, based on the Bible, offers us a vision to build our life around. It gives us a reason for living now, as God's people, even if the long-range prognosis for our planet is bleak. Because we have seen that we can clean up polluted rivers, and we can provide for the homeless, and we can give children a good education, and we can overcome oppression and sex-discrimination.

This is a vision that requires that we learn a lot and that we cultivate a great breadth of awareness of the world around us, because the forces that oppose the vision are at work in a great variety of ways. It may well require that we show leadership in sacrifice, as we move society away from the high-on-the hog living that is causing our technological culture to destroy its environment. We may have to learn how to do without air conditioning. We certainly will have to be willing to pay more taxes, because money will be required to pay for rectifying the problems that have been created. But Christian love generates a giving stance, not a selfish one. And as disciples of Christ, we cannot expect to be greater than our master, whose own death showed that sacrifice is often necessary, if something worthwhile is to be accomplished.

But because the Bible's vision of a world of peace and harmony, in its environmental, political, economic, and social dimensions -- in addition to the military one -- because the Bible's vision is <u>God's</u> vision, we may be sure that the power of God, the guiding spirit of God, the persistence of God will be with us, as we live to do God's will in the wider world, while also tending our particular flocks.

OTHER IMPORTANT TOPICS

17 Pent (B)

"Starting Again"

(Genesis 2:24; Mark 10:2-16; Hebrews 1:1-4; 2:5-12)

Our scripture readings today begin with the first basis for Christian marriage: "A man leaves his father and his mother and clings to his wife, and they become one flesh."

Jesus refers to that verse when asked about divorce. He's against it. He points out that when two become one flesh, they are no longer two, but a unity. That needs to be all the more true when children come along.

The writer of the Epistle to the Hebrews says that Jesus "is the reflection of God's glory and the exact imprint of God's very being." That means that Jesus' behavior shows exactly the way God wants us to behave, and his teachings are the same as God's teachings. God is perfect, so Jesus' teachings are perfect.

But we live in an imperfect world. In an ideal world, we would do exactly what God wants us to do. But in a world full of sin, and self-centeredness, and bad examples, and mistakes that cannot be undone, we are nudged more and more into being unlike Jesus. And the nudging is so gentle and yet so persistent that we don't realize that anything is going wrong with the life we are building for ourselves, until we stop to take a look at our patterns of behavior and the situation we have gotten ourselves into.

Sure, ideally no one should get divorced. But what do you say to a wife who is being mercilessly beaten by her husband time and again? My guess is that most of us can think of examples of circumstances under which we could justify a divorce. If we could foresee those situations occurring in the future, it would probably be better not to get married at all. Some couples in pre-marital counseling discover that there are difficulties in their relationship that they had better try to work out before they actually get married. And they work hard with a professional counsellor. And often they overcome those difficulties; but sometimes they decide that they're really not good for each other, and they go their separate ways.

But what happens when children are already present? Children need strong support from both parents. Are the parents reluctant to get married because they expect too much of their own relationship in an imperfect world? Or would marriage just be making a mistake even worse? These are not easy situations to sort out.

The good news is that into this darkness and confusion and uncertainty and helplessness and sometimes hopelessness, God "has spoken to us by a Son," through whom even the world was created and who is the standard and goal toward which the whole evolutionary process of the human race is moving. He has "made purification for sins;" and those who turn to him and are sorry for the mistakes and sins of their past can have those sins totally washed away, and they can begin again, like a new baby, only now with God's support and, if they will pray frequently for it, also with God's guidance.

We don't need to keep repeating the mistakes of the past. Especially if we are young, we don't need to be trapped in our present situation. Most of us can use our mind and our strength to do things differently, to improve our situation, and we can get others to teach us how, if that's what we need. When Jesus said that the kingdom of God belongs to such as little children, I believe he was pointing to the absolute trust that little children have. The kingdom of God is the reign of God or the rule of God in our lives, and Jesus is hinting that if we are willing to trust God to guide us, our future can more and more be brought into accordance with God's will.

People who were attracted to Jesus and his teachings kept finding reasons to hang around him and to hang around each other, and eventually the Church was born. The Church is a group of people who are called to reject the sin of the world and to live their life in accordance with God's will, supported by the power of the resurrected Christ. The Church is also a hospital for sinners, because its members do not always succeed. But by joining in worship on Sunday, they are forgiven, and strengthened, and enabled to have a better week ahead than they otherwise might have.

And they provide a community of support for each other and especially for children who may not be getting the spiritual and religious guidance that they might otherwise get at home. It takes a village to raise a child, and the church community is an important part of that village. Into that community, Caleb is coming this morning. He is literally starting his life again--this time, as a child of God.

But he doesn't know it, and he is not committed to it. There are teenagers here, on the other hand, who had the same thing happen to them, twelve or so years ago--in most cases. But they are now being given the chance to confirm that the faith expressed on their behalf at their baptism is the faith that they themselves accept. They, too, are starting again, this time to develop an awareness of being part of God's people that goes all the way back to Abraham, and to learn in concrete terms what God's will for them is and what the beliefs are of the larger, Christian family that they are part of.

They--and all of the rest of us--can awake every morning and remember their baptism, the same baptism that Caleb is about to experience. That's what Martin Luther said we should do. One of last year's confirmands asked me whether I remember my baptism every morning, and I said that I didn't. But I might, if I had done something wrong that was gnawing at me, or if I was weighed down because I made a mistake that I wished I could undo. I've had that experience since coming here. I would remember my baptism, because baptism was the first time that we started again. It was the first time that God accepted us and loved us in spite of ourselves, even before we even asked for that love. It was the time that God promised to be with us for the rest of our life. So remembering our baptism means reminding ourselves that we can repent of the past and begin afresh, every morning, with renewed determination to do better in the future.

If God promised to be with us during our life, some might ask why their life isn't turning out to be better than it is. Well, God isn't with us like a puppeteer, pulling the strings to make everything come out right. God is with us, luring us in the direction that we should go. But with our free will, we often choose other paths. And they have consequences, don't they?

Yet every morning, business people--in fact, everyone who earns a paycheck--who have been sliding into ethically questionable practices can stop themselves and decide to start again in a moral direction. Lazy and irresponsible people can determine to change. Married couples who are seeing the flame of their relationship die down can start again--not with someone else, but with conscious attempts to rekindle the interest that brought them together originally and to celebrate the attractive qualities that they have discovered in each other as their relationship has deepened. The teenager who has, in some way, let God and the Church down, can, by the grace of God, start again. And retired people now have time for new forms of service to the community and the church, or for finally fulfilling that vow to read the Bible cover to cover. It is never too late to start again--and not only in connection with reading the Bible.

And the person to start again <u>with</u> is Jesus. The writer of our epistle lesson said, "Long ago God spoke to our ancestors in many and various ways by the prophets, but in these last days he has spoken to <u>us</u> by a Son." This was the writer's way of expressing what the coming of Jesus Christ meant to him. It was a new, unexpected, intimate, and personal revelation.

A prophet says, "Thus says the Lord." But time and again, Jesus quoted the wisdom of the law and the prophets--"You have heard it has been said"--and then had the audacity to add, "But <u>I</u> say to you." There is something so compelling, to authoritative, about what he has to say about the God we claim to believe in that we can <u>understand</u> why the people of his day said, "Never did anyone speak like this man." Somehow when he speaks, it can be as if God were speaking to us directly, personally, and even disturbingly, with transforming power and with standards and clues for experiencing life at its best that many people, even 2000 years later, find worth following.

When I speak about starting again with Jesus, I do mean that it is <u>Jesus</u> we have to begin again with--and not some theory about him. He makes his own impression, if we are willing to <u>open</u> the closed doors of our mind and the locked compartments in our heart. And he makes it possible for <u>all</u> to start again.

4 Pent (A)

"Inclusiveness"

(Exodus 19:5b)

There is a message in this morning's scripture readings which doesn't exactly jump out at us. But it <u>may</u> be precisely the word that God wants to speak to us today.

In our lesson from the Hebrew Bible -- what we call "the Old Testament" -- God says, "the whole earth is mine." And today we would agree that God's love extends to the whole earth and to all of the peoples of the world.

Yet it is very normal for us to stick to our own kind, and to want to deal only with people who are like us. We feel comfortable being around people who see things the same way that we do; and it seems only natural not to want to bother with people who we don't understand.

That's the way the first Christians felt, too. They, of course, were Jews. And although they believed that Christ had risen from the dead, the only people they felt inclined to share that marvelous news with was other Jews. In fact, it took a special revelation from God -- as described in the Acts of the Apostles -- for them to realize that people who they considered to be unclean were accepted in <u>God's</u> sight and were worthy of as much love as they were. A direct revelation was needed to get them to stretch their interests and concerns, and only then did they conceive of their mission as extending to the whole world. Only then did it become concretely clear how wide the love of God really is and how inclusive human fellowship is intended to be.

<u>Luke</u>'s Gospel reflects the early Church's new awareness of inclusive love -- in many places. For example, at the end of this service we shall sing the *Nunc Dimmitis*, which comes from Luke's Gospel. There, the aged holy man Simeon sees the baby Jesus, who has been brought to the Temple in Jerusalem, and speaks of him as "a light for revelation to the Gentiles." Later, the gospels speak of John the Baptizer as preparing the way of the Lord, but only Luke quotes a passage from Isaiah that implies that Jesus is the savior of "all flesh" -- that is, of everyone. Luke also depicts Jesus

as sending some advance men into the despised region of Samaria, to prepare for his appearance there (9:52).

OK, we know all this. Today we generally agree that God's love is not limited to one tribe, or to one nation -- not even our own -- or to one race of people and that the Church's mission and the love of Christians is to extend to the whole world.

So that can't be the Word of God to us. Because the Word of God isn't what we already know. The living Word of God, sharper than any two-edged sword, is what cuts through our present understandings and confronts us with the Truth, the Truth which we, as sinners, are incapable by our own efforts of making ourselves see. At this most basic level, we, too, are more helpless and more in need of a shepherd than we would like to admit. And the Word of God is just such a shepherd. The Word of God is God's personal address to us. The Word of God is the kingdom of heaven at hand. It is God having an impact on us, an impact that changes us and the way we think and the way we behave. So the question becomes, What considerations related to our theme this morning would provide the Word of God to us?

Well, what about "them"? Would you really want to have "them" in our church? What if a whole bunch of "them" moved into your neighborhood? Now, if the word "them" conjures up a specific group of people in your mind, then those are the people that still have to be included in your circle of love. Those are the people who pray that God's grace would be mightily at work within you, so that you would be able to find room in your heart for them.

You see, Jesus prayed that all people would be made one, just as he and his heavenly Father were one. And Paul in his letter to the Ephesians speaks of Jesus breaking down the barriers that separate us. Notice: breaking down the barriers, with the implication that anything that sets up barriers between people is working contrary to God's purposes. We need to be very sensitive to this truth, as we consider the role that religion should play in our society, in our schools, in the worldwide fellowship of believers, and even in our Lutheran family. The Christian vision is for all people to be one. That vision is realized as we are open to God's Holy Spirit, which enables us to reach out, to include, and to be willing to be included. There is much more yet to be done, isn't there?

A city planner in a neighboring state had such a vision, and he tried to implement it in the area of housing. He and his planning board were in charge of developing a large new addition to the city, and they proposed to mix the income-levels of the housing, so that high, middle, and low-income houses would be scattered throughout the development, rather than having all of the houses of the same size grouped together. The planning board felt that people at different income-levels need each other, to set examples and to learn from each other. But the residents of the city would have none of it, and the plan was totally rejected. When given a chance to implement our Christian faith -- when provided with the opportunity to make the vision of unity concrete -- we prefer to remain separate. Boy do we have a long way to go!

We fail to see that when we call people to have faith in God and when God calls us to draw closer to Himself, God is actually calling us to draw closer to each other. Let me illustrate how that is so. Pretend I have a blackboard here. I'll put a letter "G" in the middle of the blackboard. That represents God. Then I'll scatter dots all over the blackboard. Each dot represents a person. Now I'll ask each dot to move closer to God. And do you see what happens? As the dots close in on God, they move closer to one another, until they ultimately are all united, all being equally included within the radiance of God's presence. They are all united both to God <u>and</u> to each other.

Well, that's nice in theory; but we're not very good at putting it into practice, are we? We would rather complain about how, when you clean up the slums and build new housing there, the poor people who move into that housing turn it into another slum within six months. We would rather complain, instead of realizing that the way you take care of property often depends, first of all, on whether you own the property, and secondly, on how you've learned, from your neighbors and your parents, how to take care of it. If everyone in your neighborhood throws garbage out the window, or leaves it in uncovered garbage cans or oil drums, where would you get the idea to behave any differently? If, on the other hand, poor people were scattered throughout a neighborhood where people did take care of their property, they would have a different model to learn from. Different standards would be expected of them; and their behavior might change. Of course, it might not. If we were living in that neighborhood, we'd have to have faith that their behavior could change, and we'd have to be willing to speak with them if it didn't. We'd have to risk the possibility that our neighborhood might deteriorate. We'd have to believe in the value of accepting and encouraging those people, just as we believe that God accepts and encourages us. Faith is always risky. Faith requires trust in the yet unseen. But this faith can make a concrete difference in the real world.

It _is_ something other than merely believing doctrines. It's the kind of faith that accomplishes physical things. It's the kind of faith that moves mountains.

But poor people wouldn't be the only ones who would benefit from this housing arrangement. Many of us could learn from many of them. Because, often, they are more genuine than we are. They are more giving. They are more willing to share. And that willingness strikes home when you realize how little they have! Jesus knew. "Blessed are you poor," he said.

Someone was talking about a low-income family and the landlord of the house that that family was living in. This person knew both families and he said, "You know, I actually liked the poor people better that I did the rich people." I could imagine myself saying something like that. But do you see the sinful presupposition involved in such a comment? Why should I be surprised to discover that poor people can be nice? Why do I presume that having money determines what a person's value is?

Why would a person with money not feel content to live next to a person from a lower income-level? Would there be no common humanity that could be shared? Would the rich person feel that he still had not succeeded in establishing his superiority, because he had not fully separated himself from people with lesser wealth? And if we can sympathize with that feeling, what does that say about _our_ ultimate values and the source of what makes _us_ feel significant? In the Christian view, we don't have to bother with making ourselves superior, because we already are daughters and sons of God. Let me say that again. We already are sons and daughters of _God_! We are accepted by the highest standard of the universe! That should be enough. Is it? And how else will unity come, if all of us are busy proving that we're superior to other people?

No wonder we have a confession of sin at the beginning of our service every Sunday! No wonder the Church talks about the need for the Holy Spirit to be at work within us! Because as much as we know these things to be true, we don't seem _able_ to implement them. We need to be transformed, and there seems to be no transforming power within us. "But thou, O Lord, have mercy upon us."

Let me move to one final consideration, based on the wording I once saw on the cover of a church bulletin. That wording said that Christ's compassion isn't limited to people in dire need of food. "Affluent people... also need our Lord's sensitivity and concern," the statement said. The question is, Do we understand fully what that statement implies, or do we understand just half of it? The statement suggests that affluent people need to <u>receive</u> our Lord's sensitivity and concern. And that is true. But does it stop there? Isn't it true that people also need to <u>give</u> our Lord's sensitivity and concern? Isn't it true that they need to <u>have</u> and to <u>express his</u> kind of sensitivity and his kind of concern, and to take them with them into their economic behavior and their political decisions and their daily lives and their attitudes toward the non-affluent? Too often our Christianity stops with our receiving God's good gifts and being thankful. We may need to receive in order to give. But God also calls us to be conduits of His love: to be channels through which His love and power can be made known and can be experienced in the world. Martin Luther understood that fully. He talked about it in terms of having faith. He said, "What an active, mighty, vibrant thing faith is! It doesn't need to be told what good thing needs to be done, but before the request is even made it is out there doing it and it keeps on doing it!" Wow! But see, Luther was on some of the same wave-length as Jesus, who went out of his way to be with people on the fringes of society, to associate with outcasts and with those who were different from him and who were despised and rejected. They are the ones who need to be included. And we are his disciples. Amen.

24 Pent (C)

"Why Did the Disciples Follow Jesus?"

(Exodus 34:6b-7a)

I promised to preach on the question, "Why be a Christian?" and to-day I propose that we "start at the very beginning, a very good place to start," to quote from *The Sound of Music*.

The very beginning is with the disciples. Why did his disciples follow Jesus? After all, if they hadn't been followers of his, we would never have heard of him.

And the next question is, "Is what attracted them to Jesus what also would attract us?" If not, are we really following the founder of our religion, or are we devoted to concepts that didn't really come from the source of our faith?

Well, what do you say? Why do you follow Jesus?

You might answer, "Because he was the Messiah or the Son of God." We certainly do think of him that way nowadays, but he never said that he was either of those.

"He was a healer," you say. True, but historians tell us there were other healers in his day, just as there are faith-healers today.

"Well, he rose from the dead. Isn't that enough reason for following him?" Yes, but, for the most part, very few people said they actually saw him after his resurrection. Now, Peter said he saw him. But why believe Peter? Why was it plausible that Jesus might have risen from the dead? Could it be because he was overcoming death, in numerous ways, throughout his lifetime?

Today's reading from the Hebrew Bible describes one "abounding in steadfast love and faithfulness, keeping steadfast love for the thousandth generation, forgiving iniquity and transgression and sin." Maybe that's why the disciples followed him.

Let me give you <u>my</u> answer to the question. Like David Letterman, I, too, have a list of ten -- ten reasons why the disciples followed Jesus. That's a pretty long list to remember, so I've created a one-page handout, which you may pick up as you leave the church this morning.

Reason number (1) Jesus called people to new life, with God -- in this world. He burst onto the public scene saying, "Repent, for the kingdom of God is at hand!" (Mark 1:15) 'Turn from your evil ways and from the pattern of life that's destroying you. Don't continue life-as-usual. There's a better way. Become, instead, what God intended you to be or what you can be at your best.' The disciples followed Jesus because they were attracted to the possibility of having new life, with God -- in this world.

Second, Jesus didn't just preach change. He brought change. He cast out demons, that is, he healed people. And however we may understand those healings today, in his day they were seen as a sign that the power of Satan was being broken and that God's New Age, the Kingdom or rule of God, was coming in Jesus' own actions and teachings.

Third, Jesus went to where love was needed most: to outcasts, people on the fringes of society, to religiously disapproved people, who were called "sinners," because they were not trying to follow all 613 laws of the Jewish religion, and to scoundrels, such as tax collectors, giving them all a sense of self-worth, and building among them communities of love.

I wonder. Would we be anxious to have in church the kind of people whom Jesus associated with? Do we seek them out, as he did? Of course we don't (for the most part). It does raise the question of just what kind of followers of his we are. Doesn't it?

But by associating with outcasts, sinners, and scoundrels (people whom others turned their back on), Jesus was expressing what God is like, how God acts, and what God is concerned with. At least, that was the conclusion of his followers. And that was their third reason for following him.

Fourth, Jesus taught in parables that subvert conventional wisdom. His parables reversed our normal expectations. And that caught their attention, if nothing else.

Take the parable of the Good Samaritan, for example. A key feature of that parable is who the hero is. The hero is a Samaritan. The Samaritans were despised by the Jews, because they didn't worship in the Temple in Jerusalem and because they were half-breeds. That is, they weren't ethnically pure Jews, because they had intermarried with Gentiles in the area. Jews would have nothing to do with them. Yet in the parable, this "bad guy" is the one who is really good.

In the parable of the Prodigal Son, the younger son gets his inheritance and squanders it in riotous living. But instead of the father punishing him when he returns, he accepts him and celebrates his return.

The passion that finally drove Jesus' disciples was relief at being liberated from their complicity in systems that were destroying them. Through Jesus, they had found the power to act against the normal expectations of their society.

Jesus' unconventional wisdom also led to a new view of God: not a God Who was high and lifted up and far away, but One Who was close to them. Which brings me to Reason 5.

Jesus taught that God is gracious. He taught that the most basic reality is grace. What is grace? A religious answer is, "Grace is God's undeserved favor." A slightly more secular answer, but nevertheless a true definition, is, "Grace is the occurrence of the unexpectedly good." For example, consider being in school and discovering that one Friday you were to have a test in three different classes. That's a lot to study for, and when it came time for the third test, you knew that you weren't fully prepared. You hadn't studied for that test as much as you would have liked to. But then at the beginning of the class, the teacher announced that the test had been postponed for a week. That's grace. You didn't deserve it. You didn't expect it. But suddenly you had a chance to do much better when the test was finally given.

Jesus viewed life as a gift. He taught that we live in a world where good things do occur, even when there's no reason for them.

And he taught that rules and regulations do not have the last word (as a reflection of his new view of God). That's important, when rules are stifling you, rather than providing for your freedom. Rules can be useful. In conditions of chaos, you can't be free, because you don't know what's going to happen next. If there are no agreed-upon rules that everyone is following, you can't be sure how anyone will behave; and so you're not free to plan meaningfully for the future or to act with any feeling that your objectives will be achieved. In conditions of chaos, rules can be liberating. It's when there are too many of them, or when they must be followed even when they don't fully fit a particular situation, that they can be stultifying.

But since rules don't have the last word, Jesus' God is not simply fair. God gives even when we don't deserve it. Thank God, God isn't fair, or else we'd get what we deserve!

We find the clearest example of this claim in the Parable of the Laborers in the Vineyard (Matthew 20:1-15). Do you remember that parable? The owner of a vineyard hires some workers at the beginning of a day and says he'd pay them a day's wage. Then, at different times during the day, he hires additional workers. And at the end of the day, he pays everybody a day's wage. Well, it won't surprise you that the people who were hired first object, saying that they should get paid more because they worked longer. But the owner of the vineyard, representing God, says to one of them, "Friend, I am doing you no wrong. Did you not agree to work for me for the usual daily wage? Take what belongs to you and go. I choose to give to this last group the same as I give to you. Am I not allowed to do what I choose with what belongs to me?"

Or Luke 12:32: Jesus says, "Fear not, little flock, it is your Father's good pleasure to give you the Kingdom."

So, with all due respect to Martin Luther King, Jr., we're free already! You are under God's gracious care, and that faith can free you from being preoccupied with saving your own neck.

It can even induce you to take risks that will bring you even more freedom. Let me tell you a true story. When I was working in New York, one Monday in the early 1960s my boss came to work very disheartened. He lived "across the river" in New Jersey, and he was a member of his town's Urban League. During the previous weekend he had been canvassing in what might have been called "the Negro neighborhood," going door to door asking residents to sign a petition that would have helped to make life better for them. (I don't remember what the specific proposal was.) But time after time, the person who came to the door did not want to sign the petition, saying, "Uh, no, we'd rather not get involved. We don't want to cause trouble." They were afraid to confront whatever needed to be confronted, presumably in the White Establishment. They didn't feel free (or safe) to do so. And because they didn't feel free already, they didn't take action so that they could be even more free at last. Sisters and brothers, by God's grace you are free already!

Reason 6 Jesus taught that God's grace is available to all, not just to Jews. And that meant that Jesus was open to -- and accepting of -- all types of people. He broke all barriers (crossed all lines) between sexes, races, classes, and nationalities. Not only are other nationalities included in God's grace, but also those who are hated, those who are rejected, those who are sorrowful, the poor, and the hungry ... are blessed by God. (Luke 6:20-23)

And God's grace (and love and respect) are available even to women! That was a radical notion in Jesus' time! In his day, a rabbi was not supposed to speak with a woman in public. If a woman had a question about religion, she was to ask her father, or husband, or brother -- at home. But you remember the Mary and Martha story . Martha is busy in the kitchen and wants Mary to help her. But what is Mary doing? Jesus is talking with her -- in public. I say "in public," because where could they have been? They were not in the kitchen. That was part of Martha's complaint. They would not have been in the bedroom. So either they were in the front room, which you could look into from the street, or they were on the roof, which could be seen from other buildings. Both were public places. Jesus was the first women's libber.

Seven The disciples were attracted to Jesus' <u>ethics</u>, because God's <u>grace</u> is the basis for Jesus' ethics. Jesus understood ethics as our response -- in gratitude -- to how God treats us. How does God treat us? God loves and accepts us even though we are unacceptable. So you should be merciful, as your heavenly Father is merciful. (Luke 6:36)

And Jesus understood ethical judgment, whereby rules are created for how we deal with each other, to be the result of new moral empowerment by God. "Make the tree good," he said, "and the fruit will be good. You can't expect a bad tree to produce good fruit." We're talking here about a person's changed inner motivation -- all the work of the transforming power of God.

Eight The disciples liked the fact that Jesus wants a genuine response. When asked to give a sign, so that people would know that they should follow him, he said [in Mark's Gospel, the earliest one] that no sign would be given to show that his teachings were divinely sanctioned. There would be no special miracle. Jesus wants a genuine, affirmative response to what he taught and how he behaved, not to something else. He doesn't want to coerce us. He wants a pure heart.

Nine Jesus was willing to oppose evil systems and hypocrisy and to stand up for his beliefs, even to die for them. His faith gave him the freedom to do so. With that faith, he was the most free person who ever lived. Is that attractive, or what?

Finally, Jesus and his disciples looked forward to the coming New Age. Note: not to going to heaven but to the coming of the Kingdom of Heaven to earth. He began his ministry by saying, "The Kingdom of Heaven is at hand." There was an expectancy that at any moment God could do something great. What a formula of faith for overcoming despair! If you don't think God is dead, then God can still do something great in your life, at any minute! Are you watching for it? Or have you lost the truth of Jesus' teaching?

The disciples also were getting a taste of the New Age already, in the presence of him whose love made laws more humane, and made broken people more whole and healthy, and brought God more close to us, and even accorded dignity to scoundrels. In fancy, figurative language, they were experiencing the Kingdom of God proleptically, in the presence of him whose love cast out the works of darkness and brought light to his small band of followers, that is, brought new power and a new vision of how the world might be.

Is that worth following? You bet it is!

Why did the disciples follow Jesus?

1. Called people to a new life, with God -- in this world.

   Don't continue life as usual. There's a better way.

   Become what God intended you to be or what you can be at your best.

2. Didn't just preach change but brought it.

3. Went to where love was needed most.

4. Taught in parables that subvert conventional wisdom.

5. Taught the ultimate reality of grace.

   God is not simply fair: God gives even when we don't deserve it.

   "Fear not little flock, for it is your Father's good pleasure to give you the kingdom."

6. God's grace is available to *all*, not just to Jews.

7. God's grace is the basis for Jesus' ethics. Jesus understood ethics as:

   Our response -- in gratitude -- to how God treats us

   The result of new moral empowerment by God ("Make the tree good and the fruit will be good.")

8. Wants a genuine response to what he taught and how he behaved.

9. Willing to oppose evil systems and hypocrisy and to stand up for his beliefs -- even to die for them.

10. Looked forward to the coming New Age.

   The disciples possibly also were getting a taste of the New Age already, in the presence of him whose love made laws more humane, and made broken people more whole and healthy, and brought God more close to us, and even accorded dignity to scoundrels.

   They were experiencing the Kingdom of God proleptically, in the presence of him whose love cast out the works of darkness and brought light to his small band of followers, i.e., brought new power and a new vision of how the world might be.

16 Pent (B)

"Tolerance Toward Outsiders and Insiders"

(Numbers 11:24-30; Mark 9:38-41)

In our Gospel reading today, we have a lesson in tolerance--tolerance toward all groups that are not identical with an organized church and its traditional teachings. Jesus said, in Mark 9:40, "Whoever is not <u>against</u> us is <u>for</u> us." This is consistent with the usual disposition of Jesus to break down social barriers and be inclusive. Just because the others are not part of our group doesn't mean they're not doing good. If they're not standing in our way, they're not hurting our cause. Indeed, it can be said that they are even fostering our cause, because they are making it possible for us, as disciples of Christ, to do what we are called to do.

At a luncheon, recently, I was eating with two faculty couples, all four members of whom have lived extensively overseas, and they were struck by how intolerant religions can be. Much of the suffering in the history of the world has been caused by religious conflicts, from Muslim conquests at the beginning of their history, to the Crusades, to the Thirty Years' War, to conflicts in India, to the conflict in Northern Ireland, to Bosnia, to the creation of refugees in Sudan, to much of the motivation of al-Qaida, today. Now I wouldn't want to call the exploits of Genghis Kahn or any of the wars the United States has participated in "religious wars." But there is no denying the reality of religious intolerance. And since all religions endorse respect for fellow human beings, there would seem to be no excuse for it.

But it does show how important religion and religious groupings can be to people. If only they would take the "love" part of their religion with full seriousness! And it does show the danger of certainty, in a field that is not fully within human comprehension. (Which does not mean you should not be fully committed to your faith--indeed, you only get full benefit with full commitment--but you do need to be sure to include the part about loving others.) Religious intolerance also shows how pervasive evil is (and I presume its pervasiveness extends even to nice people like us).

This Gospel passage applies most directly to relations between churches, because the person Jesus' disciple wanted to stop was casting out demons <u>in Christ's name</u>. So a person working in the name of Jesus is for us, if he or she is not against us. The ecumenical movement, during the past century, has been fostering mergers, and altar and pulpit fellowship, and "full communion," based in part on this assurance of Jesus that others who are working in his name are for us, if they are not directly against us.

Churches are also cooperating with secular groups, on the basis of v. 40: "Whoever is not against us is for us." Why not, as long as we share the same goal? Well, some might caution, their motives may be different, or they might stab us in the back. Now, we don't have to be naive about cooperation with non-Christian groups. We should be wise as serpents while being harmless as doves. But one significant question may be, How important is the end result for which both of us are working? Verse 40 would seem at least to urge us to give the other group the benefit of the doubt. The others may genuinely be "for us" and our cause, even though their methods or their base of support may be different.

But if you know your Bible well, you will also remember Jesus saying, "Whoever is not with me is against me, and whoever does not gather with me scatters" (Mt. 12:30). That's the direct opposite of "Whoever is not against us is for us."

It is possible to reconcile the two statements, however, by noticing that when Jesus said, "Whoever is not with me is against me," he was talking about people who were <u>not</u> doing God's will, people who were challenging his ability to cast out demons, whereas earlier he was talking about people who <u>had</u> been doing God's will. When doing God's will, even as an outsider you are given the benefit of the doubt and are considered to be <u>for</u> Christ. When not doing God's will, you are against him.

Also, in this second statement he is talking about people who might have said that they were guided by God's Spirit, since he speaks out against blaspheming against the Holy Spirit. In other words, he is talking about those who were part of God's People and yet who were working against him. So this second statement ("Whoever is not with me is against me") applies even more specifically to people who are <u>in</u> the Church--not to outsiders--and yet are not doing God's will. They are not gathering with him, and since they are not with him they are against him. Put another way, he does not want the Church to be a divided kingdom.

But as I wondered how many of you really needed a sermon on tolerance, I noticed again the First Reading which was paired with today's Gospel, and I thought of the need for another kind of tolerance which just might apply to us.

In the First Reading, God's Spirit is given to 70 elders. Now you've heard me say more than once that 70 is the number that was understood to be the number of nations in the world. So the sending of the Spirit to the 70 could be a symbol for the Spirit coming to all people.

When the Spirit rested on the 70, they became prophets. Prophets are not fortune-tellers, not people who predict the future. A prophet is one who is sensitive to God's will and speaks out on God's behalf about present conditions.

In the story in the Book of Numbers, Eldad and Medad were not selected to go to the tent of meeting, but God worked through them, as well. Even though they remained in the camp, the Spirit rested on them, and they, too, prophesied. And just as one of Jesus' disciples tried to stop those who were healing in Jesus' name, so Joshua tried to stop Eldad and Medad. But Moses said, "I wish the Lord would give His Spirit to all His people, so everyone could be a prophet" (CEV).

The point of the story is that anyone can contribute. We can't predict where the Spirit will be at work. So those in charge mustn't stifle voices from the fringes. Those from whom you would least expect it may bring God's unexpected truth. This applies even--and perhaps especially--to activities where children and teenagers are involved. As our bulletin's "Thought for the Week" said, a month ago, "The small voice in the corner may herald the truth. Make certain it can be heard."

So the question for us is, Are Eldad and Medad in our congregation? Do they hear God's promptings in some unique way? And are others in the congregation open to what they are saying?

8 Pent (A)

"Evangelize!"

(Isaiah 55:11; Matthew 13:1-9, 18-23; Romans 8:5-9)

I've come to preach the Word of God. Of course, whether it is the Word of God will be up to God.

It's interesting: We use that phrase "the Word of God" in three different ways. Often we call the Bible "the Word of God." It doesn't call itself that; and if you think about it, if what we mean by "the Word of God" is God speaking to us in the present, then a book compiled almost 2000 years ago doesn't fully quality -- certainly not if God is alive and well and capable of addressing us directly, today.

One of the greatest theologians of this past century, a Reformed theologian named Karl Barth, said, "The Bible is the Word of God when it becomes the Word of God for you," i.e., when God uses the words of the Bible as catalysts or vehicles for speaking to you directly. When, as you're reading the Bible, something hits you between the eyes, shakes you up, pulls the rug out from under you, makes you realize something you hadn't realized before, nudges you in a new direction, or in some other way has an impact on you, that could well be God speaking to you through the words of the Bible. We shouldn't trivialize the notion of God speaking. If we do encounter God, we're not likely to forget it right away.

That's partly why Jesus, also, is referred to as "the Word of God," Jesus seen as the concrete expression of God, through his teachings and his actions. People didn't forget Jesus. On the other hand, there are many, even here in [town], who do not know him.

The sermon, too, is sometimes called "the Word of God." The preacher is certainly more alive and present than a series of printed words or a figure from the past. But like the Bible, the sermon -- or some parts of the sermon -- will actually be the Word of God only if God uses it to speak to you directly, to give you a new slant on things, to overwhelm you with the divine presence, or possibly even to irritate you.

Let's see whether God speaks to you, through the sermon, this morning. The sermon will refer to all three of today's scripture readings.

In the Epistle, I want you to notice verse 9. Listen to it carefully. "Anyone who does not have the Spirit of Christ does not belong to him." Say that out loud with me. [Speak] This time, everybody say it again. [Speak] O.K. "Anyone who does not have the Spirit of Christ does not belong to him." In verse 15, Paul says, "you did not receive a spirit of slavery to fall back into fear." So, verse 31, "If God is for us, who can be against us?" [TEV] I'll return to these verses later.

We move, now, to today's Gospel lesson. It is the familiar parable of the sower of the seed. The second half of the Gospel-reading says the sower is sowing the Word. That can be a way of talking about evangelizing. "All power is given to me in heaven and on earth," said Jesus to his followers. "Go ye, therefore, and make disciples of all nations." Are you doing that? If you are, there's always more to be done. Isn't there? I'd like to see more [denomination] in central [state]. Wouldn't you? I'd like to see more active members of this congregation. Wouldn't you?

If you belong to Christ, surely you know an unchurched person--at work, in your neighborhood, or among your relatives--whom you can ask whether they are involved with a church. If you have the Spirit of Christ, surely you can assure such people, maybe with only one sentence, that faith in the God of Jesus has made a difference in your life. And certainly many of you could offer even to take that person to church, if ever they are interested. If they say they are too busy on weekends, you can respond that that's precisely why they need to go to church: to break out of the busyness treadmill and take time to think about the more fundamental matters of life.

You might say, "Well, first our congregation needs to get a minister." But that's not true, for at least two reasons. First, you can tell outsiders that the great thing about your church is that you have a number of different preachers, so they can get exposed to a variety of perspectives.

And second, this is your church. You are the people of God in this place. You are the people whom Christ calls to sow the seed and to make disciples. You can organize to consider new ways to attract people to church, just as you can organize to see that the bricks get tuck-pointed, without the minister, and to run a bake sale, without the minister. Besides, as good Presbyterians, you know that the minister is only the "teaching elder." All of the other tasks of the congregation are in your hands.

Jesus once said, "A sower went out to sow." But he didn't continue the parable by saying, "The sower very carefully prepared the soil, removing all of the rocks and weeds. And then he plowed the soil in straight rows, 12 inches apart. Then he placed the seed very carefully in the rows and covered the seed with a half inch of soil." No, he said, "A sower went out to sow and just started throwing the seed everywhere. He threw it on the highway. He threw it in the bushes. He threw it on the ground. He threw it on the rocks. And, of course, most of it was wasted. The weeds came up and choked off some. The sun came up and burnt off some. Birds ate a bunch of it." Most of it was wasted. You get that kind of result when you sow seed that way. But amazingly, about 10% of it actually took root and came up; and it was miraculous and the farmer called it a great success.

Here's a strategy for evangelism. Try a lot of different ideas, and some of them may work. "Oh, but we've never done that before." All the more reason for doing it! Maybe if we had done it, we wouldn't be in the shape we're in now.

Would I be wrong in guessing that if all of your children and in-laws and grandchildren were in church next Sunday, our attendance would be double what it is today?

And then if you had a coffee hour right after church in the vestibule, all of those younger people could meet one another and discover that they're interesting enough to want to come back and get to know better. And when one person brings a visitor, others wouldn't just say, "Nice to meet you" and let them leave. Several of you would talk with that person over coffee, to make him or her see what nice people you are and to feel that this is a place where they are welcome.

And if there isn't an electric outlet in the vestibule that would allow you to set a coffee urn on a table, along with some cookies and some fresh grapes or apple-slices (for people who are smart enough to stay away from cholesterol-producing foods), a pitcher of lemonade will probably do just as well.

And if you set it all up outside the church in nice weather, so much the better. Outsiders would see all of those people around the church, and if you did it consistently enough, they might be prompted to come over to see what's going on.

Here's another thought. How about once a quarter bringing contemporary Christian music into the church? Are there five of you who would be interested -- who can sing, or play the guitar, or play the electric keyboard? That's all it would take to lead the musical part of the worship that Sunday. You might be surprised how readily the Holy Spirit can make an appearance through upbeat music. The [judicatory] office can direct you to appropriate pieces.

"Oh," some of you may be thinking, "that fellow doesn't know us, or what we've already tried, or what our situation is." And if you're thinking that, you would be right. So let me stop making random suggestions and hit the ball back into your court.

How does the Spirit of Christ in you prompt you to respond to Christ's call to make disciples? I'm told that in Carlinville, 50% of the people do not belong to a church. Is the situation very different in this town? What does the Spirit of God want you to do?

I once heard a minister talking about this parable who said that the test is not in the seed but in the soil. The seed is all good. What kind of soil are you? Are you the path, or the rocky ground, or the thorns? Or do you have good soil? The good soil is our potential for responding to God. God can turn one seed into 100. God can do amazing things in us and through us, if we choose to provide the proper soil and join God in the effort. God has not given us a spirit of fear. God is rooting for us. Indeed, God gives us a spirit that takes the risk of doing something different, because it trusts that God can bring something good out of the effort. We may have to do a lot of praying, before we take the risk. OK, that's what we may have to do, in order to be on God's side. The nonbeliever remains in the flesh, turned away from God and trusting, for security, in the way things have always been done, and in the things they have control over, because the nonbeliever finds it hard to believe that there really is a God who is active in the world today.

Many biblical scholars believe that the parable Jesus actually told stopped at verse 9. I won't take time to go into the reasons why, but if that is the case, then Jesus may have told his parable in response to a question about why he kept on preaching, when he didn't always attract many followers. And Jesus answered, 'Well, I'm just like a farmer sowing seed. Lots of it doesn't come up, but some of it does exceptionally well; so I don't give up.' We who have the Spirit of Christ will follow his example, not giving up but continually trying something new, so as to give God a chance to make it work.

Finally, we have the rare opportunity to test whether the Bible is true; because in Isaiah 55, God says, "my word ... shall not return to me empty, but it shall accomplish that which I purpose, and succeed in the thing for which I sent it." God's Word calls us to make disciples and to sow the Word. Sooner or later, we shall see whether God has accomplished that objective through us.

18 Pent (A)

"God Isn't Fair"

(Matthew 20:1-15)

Both the Bible and a sermon can be referred to as "the Word of God," and both can irritate you or make you wish you hadn't read it or heard it.

We might be irritated by a sermon because we are all sinners, and that means that, in some important ways, we are out of touch with God. Being out of touch with God, we may view things quite differently from the way God considers them. And we may be very comfortable with our views, even though, from God's perspective, they're wrong. So when God nudges us toward a new way of thinking, we may become irritated at the possibility of having to change. I don't like having to change, either.

With regard to the Bible, today's Gospel lesson sure seems to qualify as a catalyst which God might use to speak to us directly, whether or not we want that to happen. What a shocker today's Gospel is! And what a superb example of why people remembered Jesus' parables! They remembered them because very often Jesus' parables undercut conventional wisdom, breaking into and challenging our way of thinking with God's way.

In the parable for today, the person who owns the vineyard hires workers at different times during the day, doesn't specify how much he'll pay them (except for the first group), and then pays them all the same! Raise your hand if you think that's fair. Nobody thinks it's fair. Our society and our economic system don't work that way. Now, the fact that there's a difference between our system and God's way suggests that there may be a flaw in our system. And that's why this parable still enables God to speak to us today.

The owner of the vineyard, who surely represents God, asks, "Am I not allowed to do what I choose with what belongs to me?" But what he does doesn't strike us as being fair.

Here's the first lesson: God is not fair. Thank God, God isn't fair! If God were fair, we would get what we deserve! And unless you've been perfect all of your life, you should be happy that God applies a different standard.

But notice that the vineyard owner doesn't give the people he hired first any <u>less</u> than what he promised. He is just more generous with the other workers than we would have expected. Of course! He's God, and Ultimate Reality is abundantly gracious. That's what it means to say, "God is love." Love isn't parceled out based on whether you've earned it. Love is giving, even when we <u>don't</u> deserve it. That's the kind of God we have!

That's why Christianity teaches that we are saved by grace. "By grace are you saved, through faith ... not by works, lest anyone should boast" (Ephesians 2:8-9). Even during our lifetime, the Spirit of God rescues us not when we can do things to save ourselves, but when our back is up against the wall and there seems to be no way out. Then we are saved by grace, by God acting in ways we would not have anticipated, or we are not saved at all.

<u>There</u>'s another lesson found in this parable: God acts in ways we don't expect. That possibility can be very comforting. If we believe it, it means that even when there seems to be no reasonable solution, God's ways are not our ways, and God is that kind of reality that does the loving thing at the most unexpected times. Surely the Hand of God is present when an unexpected peace "breaks out" in the Middle East, for example. And it means, in our own lives, that if we have faith in this kind of God, we should never fall into despair. We should never give up. God can always do the unexpectedly good.

So our parable tells us what kind of God Christians believe in. But consider something else. When Christians describe what God is like, very often we are describing what we consider to be the ideal standards or the highest form of behavior for human beings, as well. We don't say God is loving and forgiving and generous and the prince of peace, for example, but that doesn't have anything to do with the way <u>we</u> should behave. On the contrary, those are the very ideals that we, at our best, will be able to embody and carry out. So when we idolize Jesus' sacrifice on the Cross, as another example, we are really saying that we agree that sometimes sacrifice is necessary, in order for something worthwhile to be accomplished.

So Jesus is being consistent with his teaching about the abundantly generous God in this parable when he applies that trait, in the Sermon on the Mount, to our <u>own</u> behavior, by saying "if any one forces you to go one mile, go with him two miles; and if anyone wants to sue you and take your coat, give your cloak as well" (Matthew 5:41, 40). The principle is clear: Because we can trust in a generous God, we don't have to cling tightly to our own possessions or our own self-preservation. We can be generous, because we know that they are not what save us.

God's love has been poured out, unstintingly, to us. If we believe that -- if we believe it so fully that we have experienced the warmth and even the transforming power of that love -- then we know that God's love frees us to pass that love on, to be loving and giving and generous to others.

In Luke chapter 12, Jesus brings together dramatically the theme of God's generous love and the response that we can be empowered to make, when he says to his disciples, "Fear not little flock, it is your Father's good pleasure to give you the kingdom." That's in verse 32. Then, in the very next verse, he says, "Sell what you have, and give to the poor" [+ Mark 10:21]. First, God gives; now you do likewise. Should we sell everything? Well, here we've stumbled into another big issue, the question of appropriate use of our possessions. I'm not going to try to deal with that, this morning. But notice this insight: the purpose of God's love is to have an impact on society. God doesn't love us just so that we can feel good but so that we can be freed to take action to improve the world around us.

Speaking of improving society, the unexpected generosity of our parable may say something about affirmative action programs for racial minorities. There are people who consider those efforts, too, to be unfair. After all, they didn't own slaves. They would rather continue to enjoy the benefits of being part of the majority, where they can rely on employers and other people in decision-making positions to be biased in favor of their race. And they would rather not acknowledge the obstacles continually being thrown up to members of minority groups, even when those minority-group members are economically successful. Several years ago, for example, *USA Today* reported that, in big cities, 20% of the taxis hailed by Blacks did not stop for them, as compared with 3% of those hailed by Whites.

The generous God of love, who acts in unexpected ways, has a longer-term perspective than we do. Aware of the misery of slavery-days and of the continuous deprivation that has been the lot of most of the ancestors of slaves, God may be asking, "Do you begrudge my generosity?" or, in the words of the King James Version, "Is your eye evil because I am good?" As part of the big picture, this may be the point at which sacrifice is occasionally required on our part, so that God's will may be done on earth.

Well, how do we get the inclination and determination to sacrifice? What enables us to live up to our highest ideals? Where do we get the power to be loving, generous people, in response to a loving, generous God?

The answer is by letting ourselves be conformed to the image of Christ, i.e., to become more like Christ. And why would we want to do that? We would want to be more like Christ, because Christ restores to us the image of God in which we were created. In other words, Christ helps us to be more like Adam before he sinned.

And how do we let ourselves be formed in Christ's image? The answer is by surrendering ourselves to God: by ceasing to hold onto those imperfections that keep us from being the best kind of people that we can be: by letting go of our preoccupation with ourselves -- and that's especially hard to do when you're in pain -- by not being all tied up in ourselves: by dying to ourselves, as St. Paul put it, so that the Holy Spirit can come into us and melt our hearts and regenerate us and give us a new quality of existence altogether.

Some of you may know what that experience is. If so, you will also know whether, today, a recommitment to Christ is in order.

To others I can only say that no one can predict when and how the Holy Spirit of God will work. But there is no question that God can work on you and make you a better person -- indeed, make you the best kind of person that you could possibly be!

It also seems, unfortunately, that, through an act of will, a person can keep the Holy Spirit out. We can choose not to have anything to do with God. We can choose to resist God's Spirit and not to let God have any effect on us. Is that what you want to do?

Let us pray. Take our lives and let them be consecrated, Lord, to Thee. Help us to be children of the light and not of darkness. Enable us to do Your will in the same power of love with which You have loved us, through Jesus Christ our Lord. Amen.

Christ the King (A)

"God and the Value of People"

(Genesis 1:27; Matthew 25:40; Romans 6:1-4, 12-13)

It surprises many Americans to learn that most people in Europe don't believe in God. While this country was struggling for its independence during the Age of Enlightenment, Western Europeans were learning that the technical functioning of the world could be understood quite well without reference to God -- a lesson that all Americans in the twenty-first century should have learned, although there still are prayers for rain in times of drought.

But even in this most church-going of all industrialized nations, as much as 30% of the population says that it has no church preference or affiliation. 30%! That's an astonishingly high number, compared with 40 years ago. Forty years ago, in the early 1960s, the number was only 3%. In the town that I moved from, 50% of the people were not members of a church. Granted, you can believe in some kind of God without going to church. But in view of the European experience, and in view of the fact that the number of nonbelievers in academic circles also is quite high, it becomes interesting -- and it might even be quite important -- to ask whether or not it matters whether a person believes in God.

In an article in *The Atlantic Monthly* over a decade ago, Glenn Tinder, a political scientist at the University of Massachusetts, said it matters. He said that if people stop believing in God, there will be no theoretical basis for affirming the universal dignity and basic equality of all human beings. Not everyone will deserve respect, because there will be no reason to claim that each individual is intrinsically valuable.

Now you might be asking, "What is the connection between believing in God and believing in the dignity of the individual?" Let me give three answers.

(1) First, we are created in God's image. Well, what does that mean? If God is actually or potentially everywhere, then it cannot mean that we look like God. In order to have an appearance, there have to be limitations which show where your features end and something else begins. But if

God is infinite and therefore limitless, there are no defining limits that let God have an appearance. That's partly why we say that God is spirit.

There have been a number of interpretations of what "image of God" means, but one is that we human beings have the capacity for transcendence. Just as God is not the same thing as the everyday world that we encounter, so we, too, can rise above our daily existence and can commune with God. All people can decide upon values and have the ability to be aware of a higher reality than our mundane world. That makes human beings -- each one of us -- unique among the plants and animals, a uniqueness that would not exist if there were only the mundane world and no transcendent God to enable us to commune with "Him." Is it plausible that puny us should have the power of transcendence but that there be no transcendent Higher Reality?

(2) Then there is the doctrine of justification by grace. Christians believe that God loves us and accepts us in spite of our personal deficiencies and failures. That means that our personal worth comes not from what we succeed in accomplishing but from the undeserved grace of God, from God's high regard for us anyway. In other words, our value has transcendental backing. It does not have to be self-evident. But will people be willing to attribute that kind of intrinsic value to others, if they don't believe in God, Who gives them that value?

What these doctrines mean is that people are not just objects, to be used for whatever purpose we want to use them and then to be discarded. As Emmanuel Kant said, people are ends in themselves and not simply means to achieving someone else's ends or objectives.

(3) But you may want to protest: <u>Must</u> people believe in the Fatherhood of God in order to believe in the brotherhood of man (as the old phrasing used to run)? Can't we just see that people are all quite similar and realize that they would want to be treated the way we want to be treated?

Well, let's look at some evidence. The Greeks in the Periclean Age, in the most brilliant period of Western civilization but before the coming of Christianity, did not believe that everyone had a basic worth that couldn't be annulled.

Plato understood love as something you direct toward something or somebody that is worthwhile or beautiful or handsome or of high quality, not something you direct toward inferior or base products or people. Everyone did not have equal value, in his view. And he was the founder of Western philosophy! It was a new idea for Christians to claim that God loved even the unlovely.

When the great philosopher Friedrich Nietzsche declared that God was dead, because he saw that Europeans in the 1800s sure were acting as though God didn't matter anymore, he also denied the validity of democracy and of the claim that everyone was equal. He said that people had obligations only to their equals and not to subordinates. Aristotle had said the same thing. One is to have respect only for people who are strong and creative and who are leading purposeful lives. A person should get respect only in proportion to the quality of that person's performance. If you can see how that thinking can make some sense, you can see the direction that our thinking might take, if we stop believing that God "thinks" otherwise.

Marx and Lenin and Stalin, all denying divine reality, all said that the single individual did not matter. What was important was the outcome attained for the group.

Well, when the equal worth of each individual person is denied, the universal value and dignity of human beings also, rather quickly, becomes denied. In its place comes something more limited, like nationalism, ethnic pride, or religious extremism. From those perspectives, not everyone is a child of God, only everyone in our group. What happened in the former Yugoslavia or in the thinking of al-Qaida terrorists reflects what happens when people stop believing that the intrinsic worth of each individual is guaranteed by a transcendent God, a God not limited to a particular tribe, nation, or religious sect that might worship some distorted version of God.

And when equality and universal human dignity are denied, can the abolition of liberty and freedom be far behind? If everybody is not equal and is not intrinsically worthwhile, then perhaps those who are inferior are not worthy of having complete freedom. The abolition of freedom is not far behind for literally hundreds of thousands of underage girls (12, 13, and 14 -- even as young as 8) who are being sold into prostitution by their families in Thailand, India, Nepal, the Philippines, and elsewhere.

These are the consequences of not believing in God. They show that it is not at all clear that we can always rely on people to ascribe dignity and intrinsic worth to all human beings. Instead, people are degraded, because, left to our own devices, we make decisions in accordance with no higher standards than expediency and self-interest. So if human relationships are not to deteriorate any further, belief in God would seem to be important.

But you might be thinking, "Well, we believe in God. Why are you saying all this to us?" Right, we should know better! Yet doesn't a lot of sin consist simply in our not acknowledging the intrinsic worth of another person?

How should we treat other people? Answer: As though each were as important as Christ -- because each is. "Just as you did it to one of the least of these my brothers and sisters, you did it to me" (Matthew 25:40) -- as today's Gospel reading says.

Martin Luther said, "We meet Christ in our neighbor." This means both that our neighbor can bring the demands and the consolation of Christ to us, in the needs and the assistance of that neighbor, and that the neighbor is to be treated as though she or he were Christ. This is another way in which Christians assert the ultimate worth of people.

One noticeable way in which that worth is <u>not</u> being acknowledged nowadays is in the degeneration of sexual ethics, prompted by various forms of the entertainment industry. Appropriate sex occurs as part of a close, developed <u>relationship</u>. But when people are portrayed and treated simply as bodies, it's much easier to think of them as things to be used than as persons to be related to -- persons with feelings and values and a mind of their own.

Jesus tells us not to look lustfully at the opposite sex (Matthew 5:28) -- or, by extension, at whatever sex attracts you. Why not? Because if you're thinking of that person as a "hunk" or a "piece," you're probably not thinking of that person as a child of God, as a genuine human being. The very words themselves show that the intrinsic dignity of the full person is completely missing.

Let me digress for a minute. One holiday weekend, Barb and I visited a church where the sermon asked where the seat of love is. Is love based in the emotions or in the will? Most of us probably think of love as an emotion. But in Christian theology, love is based in the will. We are called to love God and our neighbor not with a passion that might be directed to a "real living doll" but with our will. We are called to will to love others, givingly and sacrificially, even if they are unlovely and even if they don't deserve it -- as God loves us.

So in response to our Lord's command, we can, by an exercise of our will, decide <u>not</u> to give vent to inclinations to look lustfully at another person but rather to treat her or him as a complete human being, made in the image of God.

But sexual ethics may not be a stumbling block for you. Your problem -- since we all are sinners, I assume you have <u>some</u> problem -- your problem may be that you are always critical of other people or in some other way are not recognizing their intrinsic dignity. Fortunately, we believe in God, so we know better and can do something about it. We can decide, by the power of the Holy Spirit and with the help of serious prayer, to change our behavior. And "if we confess our sins, God, Who is faithful and just, will forgive our sins and cleanse us from all unrighteousness." Amen.

"The Cost of Discipleship"

(Mark 8:27-38)

There are signs that God really wants us to hear today's Scripture reading. This is the Sunday when we planned to kick off a year in which we emphasize "Call to Discipleship." Our women have returned from their retreat, during which they had a Bible study on discipleship. Our Tuesday lunchtime Bible Study series is dealing with discipleship. And today's Gospel presents the most profound way in which one becomes a disciple.

Since we are having a contemporary service, where we deviate from traditional patterns, I thought I'd change the objective of the sermon, too. Instead of emphasizing just one point, I thought I'd turn it into a teaching sermon.

I'm doing that partly because, two times in our Gospel the strange title "Son of Man" is used. That phrase has a long history in the Bible, and it has had different meanings at different times. It was first used in Ezekiel 37:3, when Ezekiel is shown a valley of dry bones and God asks, "Son of man, can these bones live?" In that setting, the phrase means "mere human being," as in "puny mortal, what do you think?" It means the same thing in Job 25:6.

Then in Daniel, chapter 7, after describing a vision of a series of world empires that follow one another in the form of horrible beasts, the Kingdom of God is presented, in verse 13, as coming "like a son of man," that is, humanely. The phrase here is a simile. It is saying that the Kingdom of God will come gently, just like the Lord's Servant in Isaiah 42:3, who will come, not like mighty generals of the past, who rush into a city on a chariot that runs over anything in its way and at a speed that would blow out any candles burning along its path, but so gently that "a bruised reed he will not break, and a dimly burning wick he will not quench."

Next, the simile was transformed into a title of a community or a person through whom God's Kingdom was to be established on earth. In the book of Enoch, in intertestamental writings, the Son of Man would end the present age and bring in the Age of Come.

So in Mark 8:38, we find Jesus saying, "Those who are ashamed of me and of my words..., of them the Son of Man will also be ashamed when he comes in the glory of his Father with the holy angels." Notice that here Jesus applies the title to someone other than himself. Right? I mean, if he were talking about himself, he would normally be expected to say, "Those who are ashamed of me, of them I will also be ashamed, when I come in the glory of my Father." It sounds as though he's applying the title of Son of Man to someone else also in Matthew 10:23 ("When they persecute you in one town, flee to the next; for truly I tell you, you will not have gone through all the towns of Israel before the Son of Man comes") and in Mark 13:26, where Jesus says that in the last days "they will see the Son of Man coming in clouds with great power and glory."

Later, the "Son of Man" title was applied by the gospel writers to Jesus, explaining his authority to forgive sins and to heal.

With this background, now let's take a look at our Gospel reading. It begins, in verses 27-30, with a great confession of faith, which surely is the first step to discipleship. Peter says, "You are the Messiah" or the Christ. But then Jesus sternly orders them not to tell anyone. Isn't that strange? Except that many biblical scholars think that Jesus didn't actually say that. He didn't say, "Don't tell anyone that I'm the Messiah." It makes sense that he should not say that, if he really thought of himself as the prophet of the New Age when the Son of Man would come, as the passages I just quoted from Matthew and Mark indicate. If that's who he thought he was, then the title of "Messiah" is a later interpretation of who he was. But when people then would ask, "If he was the Messiah, why didn't he say so?" Mark provided an answer by adding the verse that says, "he sternly ordered them not to tell anyone about him."

Our Gospel then moves to verse 31, where it is claimed that Jesus taught them that the Son of Man must suffer. That's odd, because the Jews did not think of the Son of Man as one who would suffer. He, as Jesus said, was supposed to come on the clouds in great glory. And if Jesus was applying the title of Son of Man to himself and saying that he would undergo great suffering, then his prayer in Gethsemane, asking to avoid suffering, was a charade, since he would have known all along that he would have to suffer. Or was this verse, also, written by Mark -- notice: there are no quotations from Jesus here -- in an effort to explain Jesus' awful death? If so, then Mark is simply reflecting what the very early Church finally concluded, namely, that Jesus was the Son of Man, but that the Son of Man expected to suffer and, indeed, had a mission to die, to die for the sins of the whole world.

Our Scripture passage then moves to the call to discipleship. Dietrich Bonhoeffer, that German pastor who was executed by the Nazis for his part in an attempt to assassinate Adolf Hitler, wrote a book entitled *Nachfolge*, Following After. Significantly, it was translated into English as *The Cost of Discipleship*. In it, Bonhoeffer says, "When Christ calls a person, he bids that person come and die."

Verse 34 reads, "He called the crowd <u>with his disciples</u>." The verse specifies the disciples, because they had never made the commitment that Jesus is now speaking of. And what is that commitment? Listen. "If any want to become my followers, let them <u>deny themselves</u>." Not give up meat on Friday or deny yourself a luxury during Lent, but deny yourself. There is a cost to discipleship at its fullest, but it pays off. Even Bonhoeffer, in prison and as he went to the gallows, thought so. The cost is giving up our devotion to our own best interests and following Jesus' way, which really is the best way anyway. There needs to be an essential cessation of treating yourself as #1. I have done that, but there seems to be a need to reaffirm it again and again. I suspect we all do it imperfectly.

"And take up their cross and follow me." Not wear a cross on a lapel pin or a necklace, but be willing to die for your faith. (Now you see how much easier it is to invite someone to church, and even to extend your invitation a second time.)

"For those who want to save their life will lose it." Here we're talking about trying to give your life meaning and purpose apart from Christ; living life to the fullest, <u>outside</u> the will of God; or conserving energy; or protecting yourself from the demands of others, or from the risks of having to deal with others, or simply from harm. Such people will lose the life that Christ has to offer -- here, in this life.

"And those who lose their life for <u>my</u> sake and for the sake of the gospel...:" those who are excited about spreading the good news -- the good news of God's love and God's reliable presence, the good news that the Kingdom of God is always at hand: that the unexpectedly good always can occur, the good news that we <u>can</u> die to inhibitions about inviting someone to church or inviting them to meet other people who are followers of Jesus -- those people will save their life.

Instead of the word "save," <u>Matthew</u> 16:25 (and one other place) has "find:" find life. Not just preserve what they have, but find life at its best. Jesus said, "I have come that they might have life and have it more abundantly." Jesus said he was the way to true life: a life of selfless love, a life in touch with the Source of boundless energy, a life free from sin.

In an imperfect world, no one has that life completely. But Christ gives us the formula for finding it, namely, by shifting our focus from self to Christ, by giving up our preoccupation with ourself and withholding desperately onto what we have, by figuratively dying to our sinful way of life and rising with and by the transforming Spirit of God to a better quality of existence.

If you have never tried this kind of surrender to Christ before, there is no time like the present. It will empower you to be a disciple. Besides, what will it profit to gain the whole world and forfeit the chance for <u>this</u> kind of life?

10 Pent (C)

"Transformative Prayer"

(Luke 11:1-13; Colossians 2:6-15)

In previous sermons, I have pointed to the need for sacrifice, so that opportunities can be made available to minority groups that have not had them in the past. Christians are sometimes quite happy that Jesus sacrificed <u>himself</u> for our sins, but we don't always notice the broader insight that sometimes sacrifices are necessary on our part in order for something worthwhile to be accomplished.

That is especially true nowadays. The many problems with the environment and with the horrendous national debt and with the budget deficit are unlikely to be solved, without significant sacrifice.

The appointed lesson from the Hebrew Bible, which was not read today, was about Naaman, the Syrian leper, who went on a long trip to Elisha, the prophet, in search of a cure for his leprosy. He was hoping that Elisha would perform a miracle, but instead, Elisha just told him to wash seven times in the muddy Jordan River. Naaman wanted a more spectacular event. But someone pointed out that he would do anything to get cured -- wouldn't he? -- so why not do what he was told? God does not provide miracles when we can do things ourselves.

I thought about applying that lesson to the need for recycling, as a small and not glamorous but necessary step in preserving our environment. But that hardly would be an example of sacrifice. Sacrifice would have to do more with not using air-conditioning or not travelling by air, so as not to spew jet exhaust into the atmosphere. I don't know whether it will ever come to that, but if it does -- and for all of the forms of sacrifice that <u>are</u> required -- there are resources in Christian faith that should enable Christians to take a leadership role. Consider it: Christians as leaders in sacrifice.

Those resources don't consist simply in the symbol of sacrifice and in the call to follow our Lord in doing God's will. They come from a relationship with God that so changes us that we naturally want to do God's will and we have the power to do it.

All of Christian ethics is based on this assumed relationship. Christian ethics describe how the people of God behave when they have surrendered their lives to the God revealed in Christ and have become his daughters and sons (John 1:12-13). Notice I said Christian ethics <u>describe</u> how Christians behave; they don't merely assert how Christians <u>should</u> behave, because the children of God have been born of God and so, at their best, <u>naturally</u> do God's will. The ethics that Jesus taught did not simply guide us to live prudently in this life. They set the highest of standards; and left to our own resources we will not be able to follow them. We need God's power to do that.

How do we get that power? Scripture says, "Ask, and it will be given you" (Luke 11:9). Oh yeah?! Do you always get everything you ask for? How shall we deal with a statement like that? Rather than trying to show that the Bible is a factually accurate report of how the world operates -- or even of how God operates -- in all respects, it would be better to regard the Bible as a book of faith, written by and for believers. A professor of mine once said, "We have been taught that the Bible is a treasury of truths which we must believe. Perhaps it would be better to think of the Bible as a pack of lies which we <u>may</u> believe." With regard to the sentence we are considering ("Ask, and it will be given you"), we could doubt that God can be relied upon in that way, and, as a result of doubting, possibly sink into despair; or we could choose to believe that the statement might be true, thereby keeping hope alive.

But notice that even Jesus does not stop with this sentence, leaving us lazy or acting like greedy, spoiled children. His very next word calls us to be fully engaged in exerting our own effort. The very next word is "Seek!"

And what is promised if we do so? "If you then, who are evil, know how to give good gifts to your children, how much more will the heavenly Father give the Holy Spirit to those who ask him?" How many of you thought, "Is that all?" No riches, no success, not all of those things that so many TV evangelists offer. Just the Holy Spirit. <u>Just</u> the Holy Spirit! But the Holy Spirit is God! Jesus is claiming that prayer can make us filled with all the fullness of God! And we are right back to what is needed, in order to be able to do God's will.

The Greek and Russian Orthodox call it "divinization." They say the whole point of Christianity is to present the claim that God became human so that human beings could become divine. Not that we lose our human limitations and are able to know what is happening in some other city at this minute, for example, but, essentially, that we overcome sin and are able to live life confidently, faithfully, at its morally best, as Jesus did. That's what our epistle lesson called "coming to fullness of life in Christ" (Colossians 2:10).

How do we come to fullness of life? By rejecting the less-than-full way-of-life that we give ourselves. By ceasing to cling to what attracts us but what we know is evil. Here's the hard part, but there's no way to get around it. A life separated from God, not devoted to doing God's will, is what Jesus called "old wineskins." And you will remember he said you cannot put new wine into old wineskins. Wine is the symbol for blood, which is the symbol for life. New life in Christ won't stay in old wine-skins. It leaks out, because we are not devoted to doing things God's way (which is, of course, the best way).

Our epistle lesson calls the old wineskins "the body of flesh." That was Paul's way of talking about being turned away from God, oriented toward and devoted to those things that don't fully satisfy but which we treat as gods, in our devotion to them and in our seeking after them, because we think they will make life meaningful and pleasureful in the long run. They won't. That orientation must be cut off from us, as skin is cut off in cir-cumcision. The old wineskins are the life led by Adam after the Fall. It must be destroyed. Only then can new life appear.

"All this is from God." But you can keep it from happening. Or you can let God work.

In a few minutes we will sing a hymn that was probably sung the first time some of you committed your life to Christ. You will know how firm that commitment has been to the present day and whether a renewed commitment is in order. Others may have been confirmed as a result of believing some stuff and going along with what was expected. If your faith today were no stronger than that, you might not be sitting in a pew this morning. You, too, will know how firm your commitment to Christ and his way is and whether the word "divinized" would describe the state of your being.

Take the opportunity you have now to open the door to God wider, as we stand to sing the sermon hymn.

10 Pent (C)

"Possessions, Power, Relationships, and the Kingdom of God"

(Luke 12:32-34; James 2:1-7, 14-17)

Some people regard the sermon as the Word of God. By calling it that, they don't mean that everything that the minister says is automatically correct. What they do mean is that the primary purpose of a sermon is not to get people to nod in agreement with the logic of the conclusion of a carefully constructed presentation. (Of course, they don't want people to nod off to sleep, either.) Rather, the purpose of a sermon is to enable God to speak to you directly. A sermon is the Word of God -- or better, it be-comes the word of God's address to you -- when something hits you in a way that never occurred to you before, when a new idea or a new insight grabs hold of you, when you are challenged, or freed, or made angry by something good, or when you are overcome by a conviction. In brief, when the sermon has an impact on you, that could be the Ultimate bring-ing itself to your attention. And that will happen to different people through different parts of the sermon, as the words of the sermon touch upon each individual's unique combination of background, interests, problems, and needs. So the preacher cannot know when he utters the Word of God, if he or she does. But the listener can know, if the listener is open to God's own promptings.

God? What's God? If you take a philosophy or religion course in any academically respectable college today, you will quickly learn why all of the old proofs of God's existence no longer hold up. In addition, there are all sorts of good reasons why the word "God," today, should be totally meaningless. There is no way of demonstrating conclusively the reality of God. Yet Christians believe in God. Where Christians get their notion of God from is Jesus. Because Christian faith says that if there be a God, and if that God were to take human form, God would look like Jesus. Or, stated with a bit more sophistication, Christians believe that what is most true and ultimately real about reality can be seen in the behavior and teachings of Jesus Christ. Not that we know all about God and agree that Jesus is a good example of God, but that only because of what we find in the life and work of Jesus are we led to the conviction that there is God at all, i.e., that there is a profundity of resource and meaning in the universe that we are not normally in touch with in our workaday world.

Jesus is called the Son of God, that is, the incarnation of love and perfection, because Jesus is what it means to be fully human. All of the rest of us are less than fully human. All of the rest of us don't love with the full range of sensitivities and with the depth of commitment that it is possible for human beings to have. If you want to know what it would be like to be a fully authentic person, look at Jesus.

When Christian theologians looked at Jesus, they developed a radically new understanding of God, embodied in the doctrine of the Trinity. We will not examine that doctrine this morning, except to notice that it presents God as a relationship, symbolized as Father, Son, and Spirit. The Father loves the Son and gives Himself eternally to the Son, and the Son eternally loves the Father and gives himself to the Father. God is a relationship. The underlying pattern of reality is relational. And what sort of relation is it? The Father and Son love each other. The way in which things are truly meet and right is when the relationship of love prevails.

The Bible says that we are created in God's image. What that means will depend upon how we understand God. And that understanding has changed over the centuries. Originally, the writer of Genesis probably was thinking of God as almighty power. Since God was the powerful Creator of the universe, humanity reflected God's image in that Adam was told to name the animals, that is, to exercise power over the created order: to subdue the earth.

In the Middle Ages, theologians were impressed with the intelligence of human beings in comparison with animals, and the "image of God" came to mean people's capacity to be rational, just as God was rational.

Recently, some theologians have looked at God through the doctrine of the Trinity and have said that to be in the image of God means to be in relationship with others. That means you are not in the image of God as an isolated individual. And that certainly makes sense from all that we know about human sociology and psychology. People are social creatures. We need others from the moment that we are born; we are molded, shaped, and influenced by other people constantly; and we would not be the way we are apart from our social environment. And that is part of what it means to be an authentic human being. Our true self is not just our individual self but encompasses a larger concept of self that reflects our relational nature. In the image of the God Who is a relationship, our true self includes, ultimately, all of humanity.

Now, does Jesus, the revealer of true humanity, the source of our notion of what the word "God" might mean, confirm this notion of our essential relatedness, or not? Surely he confirms it. His emphasis was not on withdrawing from the world to find his true self in meditation but on active engagement with the world, in healing, in teaching, in reaching out to people, and even in arguing with the religious leaders of his day.

But Jesus, the concrete embodiment of true humanity, reveals an emphasis that our abstract concept of relationship does not catch. When you study Jesus carefully, you can't help but be struck by the kind of people he went out of his way to be with. They were the people on the fringes of society, whom proper religious people would have nothing to do with. They were the poor people, the halt and maimed and blind, and worse, the Quisling tax collectors, traitorous Jews who agreed to extort taxes for the Roman government from their fellow Jews, and Zealots, bigoted political fanatics, and Samaritans, racially mixed and religiously impure. These people Jesus affirmed, not in their evil actions but in their essential humanity. These people were part of his relational self. He could have been in their shoes. Indeed, he cared enough about them to feel that they were part of himself.

So it should not be surprising that in this morning's lesson he goes so far as to say, "Sell your possessions and give" to the poor [see also Luke 18:22], "for where your treasure is, there will your heart be also." He saw quite clearly that people with possessions tend to think that their possessions justify their being separated from other people. Through our possessions we try to be self-sufficient, so that we don't have to depend on other people. That means we don't have to relate to them or care about them, either. "For where your treasure is, there will your heart be." We do get caught up with our treasures.

The truth of this statement was driven home to me shortly after I bought my first stock. When you can invest in stock, you have a surplus of money. Your daily needs are being taken care of. If the Government should want to tax the profits you make when you sell your stock, so that it can get money to assist those who can't afford to buy stock, that strikes me as being completely in accord with Jesus' own concerns. Yet when a bill was introduced in Congress to reduce the amount of tax on stock profits, I found myself hoping that the bill would pass. I would get to keep more money that way. My stock really had become my treasure, and it was separating me from those who needed the money more than I did.

Jesus had a way of cutting into the heart of the matter. That's partly why he came to be called the Son of the Ultimate. The heart of the matter is the unity of humanity and the commitment to loving -- and therefore giving -- relationships that that unity calls for. Things that get in the way of those relationships should be wrenched out of the way. So sell your possessions, he says, if they create barriers between you and those in need.

St. Paul interpreted this command in a way that is slightly easier to live with -- but only slightly. He said, "Have these things as though you had them not." (I Corinthians 7:30c) Hang loose with your possessions. Be attached to them so little that if you had to give them up, you could do so without any problem at all. Because you could still have faith in God, and the God of love would continue to give.

How have Christians, in fact, dealt with their possessions in relation to the poor? For the most part, they have done so through individual giving to alleviate individual needs. The Christmas basket is perhaps the best symbol of this form of charity. From our abundance we give foodstuffs to the poor at holiday time, so their plight won't be quite so grim. After the holidays, of course, their basic situation will not have changed at all.

Back in 1910, however, Walter Rauschenbusch found that this type of individual giving was totally inadequate for the new, industrial age. He was a minister working in Hell's Kitchen, a very appropriate name for a section of Manhattan that was the garment district of the time, filled with immigrants who were crowded six to a room in six-story walk-up apartment buildings, with one toilet per floor and communal kitchens. Most of them were hired at very low wages for only a day at a time, so they could never be sure of having a steady income. And many of them worked in "sweat shops," which received that name because the people were perspiring while they worked, even though all they were doing was sewing, because they were sewing in upstairs rooms that didn't have any windows and therefore no ventilation. Rauschenbusch had come to Hell's Kitchen to win souls for Christ, one by one; but he found that alcohol and prostitution and thievery were winning souls for the Devil (so to speak) by the thousands. Clearly, what was needed was not one benevolent person doing a few good deeds, but a complete change in the structure of a society that permitted that type of overcrowding in living accommodations and those types of working conditions. Those changes were brought about by legislation. It became evident that, in the 20th century, the way to give alms to help the poor was through working for changes in public laws and in the unwritten agreements of our society.

A half-century later, through the civil rights movement, we became aware -- some of us did -- of an even more basic element in the relations between people, namely, the use of power. It wasn't that one race was clearly inferior to another. When the race that controlled the means to power, i.e., the avenues to education and significant jobs and leadership positions, made changes that enabled minorities to participate in the power structure, the minorities developed and blossomed just as whites had done. They didn't need whites to assist them; they just needed whites to relinquish some of the power that they held. Here is God's challenge to us. Once again the injunction to "give alms" takes a new form.

Among adults, genuine relationship can take place only between equals. Genuine love can be exchanged only by equals. If the way in which we help other people succeeds in keeping them weaker than we are, then we aren't really taking them seriously, we aren't relating to them as equals, we aren't loving them as ourselves, and we don't fully see the unity of ourselves with their selves.

There needs to be more equal distribution of power, because only then will equally valid interests and needs be given equal treatment. As well-educated and intelligent as any group might be, its own self-interest will always cloud its judgment of what is good for somebody else. This became clear to me in my own experience in labor relations, prior to entering the academic world. As enlightened as our management position might have been, there were times when the smooth functioning of our personnel procedures were more important to us than what we considered to be the minor inconveniences that they might cause to employees. Well, there was no reason why employees should have seen it that way. And had the balance of power between labor and management been different, the employees probably would have been treated differently -- by that same enlightened management.

If relationships are to be genuine, if humanity is ever to be one, if the poor are to overcome their poverty, if peoples and nations are to develop and prosper freely and peacefully apart from revolution, it may be that the Word of God to people and nations with power is, "Give up some of your power." This is a difficult task, hardly any easier than selling our possessions. Yet Jesus pointed to what was essential for accomplishing it, at the beginning of our second lesson this morning. He said, "Fear not, little flock, for it is your Father's good pleasure to give you the kingdom." God will give what really matters. Paradoxically, believing that is the key to making a better world. Because if you believe that God gives the kingdom, which is what really matters, then you are freed from trying to hold onto what you think really matters (because what you would be holding onto couldn't be the kingdom given by God) and you are freed for doing whatever is necessary to make a more perfect world. Human action will bring in the kingdom, but only after God's strange, unpredictable presence gives us the faith that frees us to do so. And that is precisely the relationship that Jesus presents in Luke, chapter 12. In verse 32 he says, "God gives you the kingdom." Therefore, verse 33, "Sell your possessions and give alms," because the kingdom in which God is present is not found in possessions or in power. Those who can trust God know that.

But if the kingdom is to come at all, if the best in human relationships is ever to be realized, if love is ever going to reign, it will do so only through people who believe that: who believe that God is not found in our possessions of power. For, again, only those people will be willing to relinquish power in the interest of genuine relationships with the powerless. Only those people will be able to love all people fully and appropriately and genuinely, because their treasures will not be elsewhere.

Let us pray. Almighty God we have erred and strayed from Your ways like lost sheep. We have followed too much the devices and desires of our own hearts. We need to be transformed, O God, by the power of Your Holy Spirit, so that we may love all whom You love and be enabled to do what You would have us do, in the spirit and power of Jesus Christ, our Lord. Amen.

Trin (B)

"Being Born Again"

(John 3:1-15)

There is only one place in the Bible that talks about being born again, and it is in today's Gospel reading. Yet many Christians consider that statement to be the most important one in the Bible. Why is that?

Our theology says that people have fallen away from God and therefore are separated from life at its best. So a change is needed, to put us back in touch with God.

If you are unwilling to change, this sermon may provide you with some information, but you will keep it from giving God a chance to have an impact on you. Because there is such a thing as free will, and God will not force "Himself" on you. You've got to be willing to change.

Is there a need for change? Jesus thought so. His public ministry began with his saying, "Repent, for the Kingdom of God is at hand!" That means you are walking in the wrong direction and must turn 180 degrees and head in the opposite direction. This call to start over is presented in John's Gospel as the need to be born again, which also can be translated "born anew" or "born from above."

Most Christians understand today's Gospel lesson to be talking about Baptism. Verse 5: Unless you are born of water and the Spirit, you cannot enter the Kingdom of God. The water is the water of baptism, and the Spirit accompanies the words of the pastor, as the baptized is cleansed of original sin and begins again by being grafted into the body of Christ, the Church.

Others see these words as applying, also, to a genuine new beginning-- something you can actually experience.

There is a long history of people who claim to have been touched by God in some way.

St. Thomas Aquinas, that great medieval theologian of the Catholic Church, apparently had such an experience. After writing thousands of pages that shaped Catholic doctrine down to the present day, Aquinas had a vision or an experience of God that provided him with an awareness that he had never had before and with knowledge that he could not put into words. All he could do was say, "All that I have written is straw; I shall write no more." His personal encounter with God made all the difference.

Does God exist? Aquinas found that there was no verification of that claim without participation--participation in a relationship with God that brought an experience of the undeniable reality of God.

It is a relationship that Lutheran pietists, a few generations after Luther, were having.

It is something that prompted the Methodist movement in England in the 1700s, after John Wesley found his heart "strangely warmed," while listening to the preface to Luther's *Commentary on Romans*.

Then there was the Great Awakening in this country, which William James wrote about in *The Varieties of Religious Experience*. He gave many examples of what he called "Twice Born" people. What appears to be characteristic of the conversion experiences that he described was the presence of ecstasy and buoyancy in the people who had those experiences. And the world appeared to change, too. There was a sense of newness about it.

I can cite other examples that are much more recent. There was the college junior who, at the end of an evangelistic service, was overwhelmed by a surging of energy that he did not believe he was generating and to which he yielded his life.

There was a seminary student in Massachusetts who had a similar experience, but only hours after he left a revival meeting.

Another seminary student was feeling very depressed and was walking up a hill from one part of the campus to another when she was filled with a warmth that assured her that God had not deserted her.

Sometimes God is revealed through light. I know a man who used to go to church because he liked to sing in the choir. He endorsed Christian morality, but he didn't pay much attention to the doctrinal stuff, until one Sunday, when he was sitting in the choir stall, as people came up for communion. Everything became quiet and three columns of light appeared before him.

A final example, reported by a middle-aged Lutheran seminarian in the San Jose newspaper: This woman was sitting back on her heals, doing breathing meditation, when she began rocking from side to side, and she knew she wasn't creating the movement. At first she was afraid, but then she thought, "This is what it feels like to be filled with the Spirit." The rocking stopped, but before she could get over the shock of what had happened, it started again. She started praying, "Jesus, take control. I don't know what this is, but you do. Take control." And then, "I felt his presence. How can I explain it? I just knew that the source of life and love was with me."

One other thing to add. I have been surprised at the number of religion professors that I have spoken with who have had <u>some</u> such kind of experience of the reality of God. But not without a struggle. The experience didn't happen to people who took their religion casually.

A final important thing to add is a quotation from Larry Rasmussen, chief ethicist at Union Theological Seminary in New York. He says that some theologies expect to find "God in power, majesty, and light, in triumph, ecstasy..., and pure unadulterated experience. God is found, however, says Luther, in weakness and wretchedness, in darkness, failure, sorrow, and despair. God is not found <u>only</u> there, to be sure, but God <u>is</u> there in a special, crystallized, and saving way. God is present in a certain kind of suffering love and as a certain kind of power on the home turf of ... brokenness."

If you haven't had anything like the experiences that I've described, maybe you don't need them. If you have been a faithful follower of Christ all your life, you probably don't. On the other hand, "the wind blows where it chooses," and you could have some such experience before you leave church this morning, while you're singing the next hymn, when you come up for communion, or even sometime afterwards.

<u>You</u> will know how much you have been resisting Christ and how much you are in tune with God. If you know you have been slacking off-- if you know you have never been fully committed, this may literally be the chance of a lifetime for you. One verse of an altar-call hymn says that even though I am tossed about by "many a conflict, many a doubt; fightings and fears within, without," nevertheless I will come and recommit my life to Christ. Because "just as I am, your love unknown has broken every barrier down. Now to be Thine, yea Thine alone, oh Lamb of God, I come."

The refrain of another such hymn is "I surrender all." That's what it takes. There is no in-between condition that brings the same result. Either God is the Lord of your life and the Source of life-at-its-best for you, or you are. You can, of course, continue to get by with coming to church only occasionally, but you will be missing out on the quality of life that Christ can give to those who truly believe in him, and therefore trust him, and therefore are committed to him. Do you really want to miss out? Or is now the time to make a full commitment and surrender?

5 Easter (B)

"Where Should We Bear Fruit?"

(John 15:8)

I.

Our tradition considers the sermon to be the word of God. Does that mean that everything that the preacher says is the Word of God? No, the preacher is as fallible as anybody else. Nevertheless, the sermon <u>can</u> be the Word of God, when <u>God</u> makes it so. The sermon is the Word of God when God speaks to us through it. And when God addresses you, watch out! God's Word is sharper than any two-edged sword, you remember. God's Word cuts through the sin and blindness and lethargy that separate us from God and from each other and puts us in touch with a holy spirit, which gets us moving in new directions -- in accordance with God's will and purpose.

Ultimately, therefore, the <u>preacher</u> cannot make the sermon into the Word of God. That's in God's hands. But what a preacher <u>can</u> do is to direct our attention to matters that we may not have been considering lately, so that the Holy Spirit can be given the opportunity to nudge us into God's Truth.

When God comes to us, God always comes with both blessing and judgment. As sinners, radically separated from reality-as-it-should-be, we cannot expect God simply to pat us on the head, or even simply to strengthen us in the good that we think we're doing. As sinners, we keep misunderstanding what the <u>true</u> good is. So if, in a sermon, you hear something that you don't want to hear; if you find yourself thinking of lots of reasons why the preacher must be wrong; or if someone idea or phrase keeps bothering you and will not let you go, you can at least suspect that those words of the preacher are the Word of God to you.

II.

Our text this morning is the last verse of today's Gospel: "By this God is glorified, that you bear much fruit, and so prove to be my disciples."

Well, what about that fruit? What sort of fruit does God want us to bear? We know the answer to that question. We're supposed to be loving, supportive, kind, meek, bear one another's burdens (which means help the other person out), turn the other cheek, and wash behind the ears. Anyone who normally goes to church on Sunday knows those answers. Some people may need to be told them, but not us. And if we ask why we do not always bear that kind of fruit, we know the answer to that question, too: It's because we don't abide in the vine of Christ fully enough. Since we know all of those answers, they cannot be the Word of God to us, because the Word of God comes from <u>outside</u> our everyday understandings and hits us between the eyes.

What <u>could</u> be <u>God's</u> Word to <u>us</u>? Perhaps it has to do not so much with the <u>kind</u> of fruit that God wants us to produce, as with the <u>place</u> where it should be produced.

If we look at the Gospels carefully, we cannot help but notice where Jesus did his bearing of fruit. It was not among the rulers of his land, nor even among the church-goers of his day. No, Jesus spent an inordinate amount of his time with poor people, with -- in sociological language -- the lower class, with the outcasts of society, with the powerless, with people at the fringes. He was so much a part of their group that he even ate with them. He didn't just pass through, giving advice, but he had lunch and dinner with alcoholics, and ne're-do-wells, and the traitorous Jewish tax collectors who had turned against their own people to extort revenue from them for the Roman occupying forces, and with "sinners," those working-class people who just didn't try to keep all the rules that would make them respectable middle-class citizens like us. We read that the multitudes heard him gladly. But who were those multitudes? They were not the respectable shop-keepers, or office workers, or lawyers, or businesspeople. Those people had jobs to do. They weren't available to hear Jesus. Who was available? Well, people out of work, waiting to be someone's hired hand, farmers in between planting and harvesting season, lepers, the halt, maimed, and blind, servants doing the errands, perhaps some shoppers, but mainly -- in a word -- the masses. And the masses are at the bottom of the economic heap. Jesus moved and acted mostly among the poor and the outcasts of society. Those people by the wayside that he healed wouldn't have been there if they could have afforded proper medical attention.

Jesus' disciples walked with him. Jesus' disciples went where he went. And how is it with his 21st century disciples? Are we walking where he walked? Are we even glancing in that direction?

Well, we have the opportunity to do so. Did you know that 20% of the people in our city are living below the poverty level? That's not a statistic that applies to a far-away place, such as New York City, or Chicago, or even Charlotte. But right here, almost one-quarter of our people have incomes below the poverty level. Do you think that would have bothered Jesus? If he were to come here, do you think he would seek those people out? It seems, from the way he spent his time, that those were the only people he felt comfortable with!

If Jesus were to return to earth and could visit one church in our city, which one do you think he'd visit? We can't say for sure, of course; but I'd be willing to bet that he would visit the most ramshackle black Baptist church that he could find. Not because their theology is necessarily the most complete. Not because other people, too, are not in need of his healing and renewing presence. But because "they hurtin'" the most! Whatever problems we may have, they are not psychological and economic and political and societal -- and certainly not to the point where our survival is almost at stake!

Or maybe Jesus would visit our city's Rescue Mission. Did you see that feature article in the Sunday newspaper two weeks ago? Their work is with the last, and the least, and the lost. That sounds very much like what Jesus' own ministry was about.

But there's no reason why Jesus should have to visit a church at all. And given his past pattern of behavior, he'd probably wander over to some streets whose names most of us don't even know, where the bums hang out -- those who, by our standards, are degenerates. But they know the love that they'd like to receive. And they know they're not getting that kind of love. And they've had plenty of experiences of not getting it. And from their point of view, there must be another kind of degenerate, worse even then those in the first verse read in today's epistle lesson (I John 3:17): one who doesn't even look to see whether his brother is in need, and in that way closes his heart against him. Jesus, on the other hand, has been called "the man for others." And we? How is it with us?

III.

Martin Luther said that we meet Christ in our neighbor. And really any neighbor will suffice to validate that statement at least in part. Any neighbor can confront us with a bit of Jesus' humanity and with Jesus' call for love. But the Christ, the Messiah of Israel, is the one who turns everything upside down, so that when he's finished, even the lion and the lamb are friends! Our next-door neighbor is probably too much like us to be that kind of Christ for us. Only someone totally unlike us can fully be Christ for us: can fully confront us with a way of seeing things and a series of problems and a means of coping that we never even imagined. In other words, only a neighbor who is unlike us, from among what our society may consider to be the least of Christ's brothers and sisters, can make us whole people, can fill in the gaps in our own humanity, and can draw us fully into the human race. That's what Christ came to do, you know. We read in Ephesians, chapter 2, that "now in Christ Jesus you who once were far off have been brought near. For he has made us both one, and has broken down the dividing wall of hostility." As Christ works through people and can be found in people, so he is with us in our unlike and unlikely neighbor; and we are in <u>full</u> fellowship with him, <u>only</u> when we are in full fellowship with people who are most unlike us. It turns out that <u>they</u> are the vine and branches of Christ, and if we remain separated from them, we are likely to be cast forth as a branch and to wither.

So for our own sakes, we would do well to get in touch with some people who are unlike us. If you were a Protestant in Northern Ireland, that would mean a Catholic. If you were a Kikuyu in Kenya, that would mean a Masai or an Asian. If you were a German, that would mean a foreign laborer, probably from Turkey or Spain. If you lived in South Dakota, that might mean a Sioux Indian. But here, what else could that mean (for most of us) than a black person? And if the black comes too much from your own economic class, then that might not meet the need, either. But one step at a time.

We do this for our own sakes, and also because, as Christians, we have a vision of all people loving one another. And we want to be part of that vision. But we can't love what we don't know. So the first step is to get to know those people who are most strange to us and who, because of their strangeness, are perhaps a little frightening to us.

That step is so important. There are so many problems in the world created simply by fear of the unknown -- usually accompanied by misinformation about that unknown. We cling to what we're familiar with, and we distrust everything and everybody else. We see examples of that in the inter-tribal wars and animosities within the same country in Africa. But my wife and I experienced it in an even more ludicrous form in Southwestern Germany, where someone who married a local resident and moved in from two towns away was treated with utmost suspicion, as though she had just been sent to them from a terrorist cell. You see, town loyalty is so strong in that part of the country that you hardly ever marry someone outside your own town. We once heard one of the townspeople say, "I'm a Münzinger; I'd never marry a Nürtringer!" -- which seemed really funny to us, because they were all Germans, and not only that, they even were all Swabians, sharing the same dialect of German! How much more similar could they be?! And yet they found reasons to keep separate and to foster distrust. And that was occurring in the technologically most advanced country in Europe! Christ calls us not to perpetuate that pattern. Christ calls us to get acquainted with people who are different from us.

That is easier said than done, of course. People tend to associate with others who are like them. It may not be easy to break into their circle of friends. They may be suspicious of your motives. But, who knows, you might get an affirmative response, as well. In any case, it will take a while to really become friendly. Genuine relationships take a long time to develop. But that's why something like this almost has to become a project for us. If we don't consciously set out to reach across these barriers and to try to bridge the gaps created by traditional social patterns, the change will never take place. It's just easier not to bother. We can talk in church all we want about Christ making us one, but if _we_ don't act, we shall not become one, and God's will, will not be done on earth.

IV.

But we have strayed, a bit, from our concern with following in the footsteps of the Master. Because it is quite unlikely that the blacks that most of us will have a chance to meet will be the kind of people that Jesus ministered to. Most of the people that _we_ rub shoulders with are probably much more _similar_ to us than dissimilar, in spite of some superficial differences. Perhaps we need to discover that. Certainly the _last_ thing that I want to be suggesting is that all blacks automatically are poor, uncultured, and powerless. But what about those at the bottom of the totem pole, the least of Christ's sisters and brothers: those who still don't believe that an education will really help _them_, and who therefore still are poor, and, as a result, powerless, badgered by whatever wind of bigotry happens to blow their way?

Let me tell you of the experience of Walter Wink, as I draw this sermon to a close. Walter Wink was a professor of New Testament at the

Hartford Seminary Foundation, and in the early 1970s he wrote a good, short book entitled *The Bible in Human Transformation*. It is essentially a psychologically-oriented book about how we can be guided by the Bible into becoming more complete individuals, more fully part of God's new creation. He used this book successfully with study groups in various churches, but he discovered a problem with it and with its emphasis; because the early '70s were still times of social and structural change in the United States, when people's concerns with the problems of the poor and the oppressed were much greater than they are today. And he found that, although he was dealing with politically liberal congregations, he was having no success in getting them concerned with the problems of people outside their group. Once they found ways to focus their attention on their own problems, by using his book, those problems and methods for dealing with them became so fascinating that they didn't want to deal with anyone else. As a result, they couldn't enter fully into the new creation, because that is a creation of community, in which those "who once were far off have been brought near." In it, it isn't only the lion and the lamb that eat together.

If we contrast a study group on personal growth with what Jesus was doing, we can't help but be struck by the difference. What does that contrast say about our understanding of what it means to be a disciple of Jesus? What does it mean, for us, to walk where Christ walked? Can we possibly be indifferent to the problems at the bottom rung of society? Or is Christ himself, who was born as an outcast in a stable and who may well have been part of the lower class, suggesting that God's way of improving society as a whole is to improve -- or to radically change -- the structures that bear upon the least and the last? What can we, as a small congregation, do, to be better Disciples of Christ? Not very much, if we're not thinking about these problems or looking for ways in which we <u>could</u> make a difference. Perhaps that is what a social action committee could focus our attention on. Because then, when the <u>kind</u> of fruit that Christians are to produce is related to the <u>place</u> where it is needed most, God can open whole new dimensions of reality to us, and we may see, in a totally new way, what it means to be loving, and supportive, and meek, and to bear one another's burdens, and to turn the other cheek. We'll certainly be reminded of our need to be branches attached firmly to the vine, and we may discover where other branches are to be found, and even where the vine itself is. Amen.

Let us pray. Breathe on us, breath of God, that we may love <u>all</u> whom

You love and do what You would do, through Jesus Christ, our Lord. Amen.

6 Easter (A)

"Without God or with God"

(Acts 17:23)

As you heard in the first scripture reading, the Apostle Paul found the people of Athens to be very religious. In the polytheism of their day, they worshipped many gods and had separate altars for each of them. Just to be sure they were covering all their bases and weren't leaving any god out, they even had an altar "To an Unknown God." Today, some people might be more likely to have an altar not to an Unknown God but to "No God." But I wonder whether they realize what sort of belief they would be implying, if they had such an altar.

Some time ago, a mother asked me what she could say to her teenage children, who were asking for proof that God exists. This sermon is going to be my response. If you are a father, or a teenager, or anybody else, you may want to listen closely, to see what you think of my response and to see whether you can use any of it in conversations with your own relatives and friends.

First of all, you could say that nothing causes itself; so there must be a first cause of the entire universe, and that first cause is God. For better or worse, a bright eighth grader might ask, "But who caused God?" The standard answer is, "God has always existed." Just because all *material* things have to be caused doesn't mean that "something" spiritual, like God, had to be caused by something else at all. Something spiritual is radically different from something material, isn't it?

But the eighth grader might also ask, "Why couldn't the universe have always existed?" Well, it might have. I personally feel more comfortable with saying that something *im*material, such as God, has always existed, than with saying that the thing that has always existed is something material that can deteriorate, like the universe. But not everyone agrees.

You could point to the intricate design of everything in nature: each leaf on each tree, the complexities of every part of the human body, the unique pattern in each snowflake -- and then argue that they imply that there is a vast and ever-present divine being who designed them all. But when a few thousand people die each year because, as we say, "something went down the wrong pipe" -- and got stuck there -- or because of earthquakes, there is evidence of design flaws that we would not expect to come from an all-knowing, all-powerful, and good God.

The bottom line is: there are no proofs of the existence of God that cannot be challenged. Does that end the discussion? No. If there were incontrovertible proofs, there would be no need for faith; but, as Martin Luther said, "God and faith go together."

What he did not say, but what is worth noticing, however, is that atheism and faith go together, too. That is, you are going to believe *something*; and belief that there is no God is also a belief.

The point is, we all make assumptions about the world that we live in. It is possible, of course, to assume that there is no God. But what other assumptions and what other form of reality do you have to acknowledge, if you decide to believe that God doesn't exist? That is what every teenager and indeed every person must take into consideration, when they contemplate assuming that God doesn't exist. What are they left with, if they do not believe in God?

Let me present nine answers to you. You probably won't remember them all, and different people will be attracted to different answers. That's why my list is so long. If you want the complete list, you may pick up this sermon on the ledge outside my office.

These answers identify the other assumptions that you may not realize you also have to make, if you assume that God doesn't exist. They describe the kind of world that you are left with, if you are serious about not believing in God. The list that I offer can move pretty quickly.

(1) First, if you don't believe in God, you are left with a cold, impersonal universe. There would be no heavenly Father caring for His creation.

(2) If you decide not to believe in God, you close yourself off from whatever spiritual assistance might come from God. The Lord God may be with you wherever you go, but you won't reach out to benefit from God's presence, if you don't believe in God.

(3) If there is no God, there is no realistic basis to hope for anything exceptional. Of course, you can hope for whatever you want, just as I could hope to be a starting player on the Chicago Bulls basketball team. But if, in a purely material and deterministic world, the future can be only the logical consequence of what has gone before, there is no *realistic* reason for having any hope that something unexpectedly good could occur or

that something unexpectedly new might happen, like Saul (or you) having a conversion experience, or the great light of Jesus' birth and ministry occurring for people who walked in darkness. You see, God's future is not determined by the past. God isn't trapped there. God can bring newness of many sorts into existence.

(4) Moreover, if God does not exist, there is no ultimate forgiveness. If you want to be moral and just, you will always have the burden of making amends for all of your past, harmful words and deeds. There would be no such thing as wiping the slate clean.

(5) If God doesn't exist, you may never be loved more than you deserve. Only the God of grace can be relied upon to love you that fully.

(6) If God doesn't exist, you have no sound reason not to be cynical. That is, you almost *have* to believe that all people are interested only in themselves. Sure, they can love others, but only if there's something in it for themselves. Without God, you cannot be sure that there's a force for good at work in the world, a spirit of self-giving love that makes people genuinely concerned for somebody else.

On this topic, I pause with a special note to parents and grandparents. One of the best ways of ensuring that children will believe in God, Who, after all, is Love (according to the First Epistle of John) is to be sure that they have experienced love in action over a long period of time, not only in your treatment of them but also in evident ways in which you are helpful to other people, as well. Without that type of evidence of God's love, all other arguments are likely to fall flat.

(7) Moving on: If God doesn't exist, then the biblical story and its view of reality, along with its high moral standards, could be basically wrong. Do you really want to say that?

The Bible actually provides a number of reasons for believing in God. Let me give you four.

First, I mentioned the Bible's view of reality. The writers of the Bible didn't set out to write a fairy tale about the world's best religion, filled with heroes and perfect people. The Bible presents a very realistic view of the world, filled with sinners and scoundrels, whom God nevertheless uses and works through, in order to make the divine will know and to draw people to "Himself" -- scoundrels such as Jacob, who stole his birthright, that is, the right to inherit his father's wealth, from Esau, and yet whom God converted into Israel, the founder of the nation of chosen people, and sinner David, who connived to have the husband of Bathsheeba killed, but who repented and became a great king.

Second, you've got to wonder why the ancient Israelites had such strong moral sensitivities, when none of the nations around them did, if they didn't get them from God. The god worshipped by the Canaanites wasn't concerned about morality at all. He was just concerned about making the crops grow. The Babylonians had 600 laws, but it was as important to them what coat you wore to visit the king as it was not to steal. Only the Jews were sensitive enough to identify ten really crucial commandments, which have held up even to today. The Greek gods made moral laws, but then they broke them, too. Only the God of Israel was firm and consistent in expecting from them and from us the highest ethical behavior. Where did the Jews get the idea that their God was like that, if not from God directly? How else can you account for their being *so* different from all other societies of their time, as far as moral standards are concerned?

Then, third, consider the prophets, who dared to speak out against the leaders of government and business, and who risked their lives to criticize immoral behavior and unfaithful rulers and religious officials. Where did they get the moral sensibility and the courage to do that, if not from God?

And fourth, there is the life and teachings of Jesus, about which I'll say more, later.

Yes, you don't have to interpret the Bible literally, to see the Hand of God at work in biblical narratives.

(8) If God doesn't exist, there is no source of helpful energy outside yourself (at least not ostensibly) that you can draw on. It will not be said of you, as it has been said of others, that "Those who wait for the Lord shall renew their strength; they shall mount up with wings like eagles; they shall run and not be weary; they shall walk and not faint." (Isaiah 40:31)

(9) And finally, if God doesn't exist, you cannot look forward to the possibility of having a transforming encounter with God, an encounter that brings to you a significantly higher quality of life than you may be currently experiencing. You will not be able to say, with St. Paul, "It is no longer I who live but Christ who lives in me!" (Galatians 2:20) Nor will you be able to speak of knowing Christ "and the power of his resurrection." (Philippians 3:10)

Some time ago we were discussing this topic at a college "Religion Discussion Table," and one of the students said, "The best way to prove that God exists is to introduce the skeptic to lots of people whose lives have been changed by Christ." Yes, apart from direct intervention by God, there is no more effective witness than personal testimony of the power of

God in a person's life.

Well, there you have my response. If, in the absence of airtight proof, you decide to assume that God does not exist, you are left with a cold, impersonal universe, cut off from spiritual assistance, with no realistic basis for hope, no ultimate forgiveness, no reliable reason for believing that you will ever be loved more than you deserve, and no basis for avoiding cynicism. You are left with a Bible that is essentially wrong, and with no source of energy that you can draw on, along with no possibility of being born again.

On the other hand, you can take the risk -- and faith is always a risk -- you can take the risk of believing in the God made clearest to Christians in the life and teachings of Jesus of Nazareth,

- a personal force of Love that changes people's lives,
- brings life out of conditions of death,
- goes where love is needed most, as Jesus did,
- builds inclusive communities of loving and faithful -- albeit flawed -- followers,
- subverts conventional wisdom,
- is gracious and gives, even when we don't deserve it (as Jesus' parable of the workers in the vineyard indicates),
- and makes trees good so that their fruit will be good, that is, makes us good people, so that we will naturally do good deeds.

Surely we would want to say, with Isaac Watts, the hymn-writer, that 'Love so amazing, so divine, demands our soul, our life, our all!' Surely if that God is real, as Christianity has claimed for 2,000 years, we can only, in the words of Luther's catechism, "thank, praise, serve, and obey Him." Amen.

4 Adv (A)

"When Did Jesus Become the Son of God?"

(Romans 1:1-4)

Today's sermon is a teaching sermon, and I begin with the question, When did Jesus become the Son of God?

Well, you say, wasn't Jesus always the Son of God? Our theology says he was. So that just helps me narrow the question down to what I really want to begin with. That is the question, When did it dawn on his disciples that Jesus was the Son of God? Or even more specifically, when and how did the idea that Jesus was the Son of God develop?

What you need to know, right away, is that it is highly unlikely that Jesus called <u>himself</u> the Son of God.

The earliest hint of how Jesus' first followers began to think of him in those terms comes in Paul's letter to the Romans, which was written before any of the Gospels were written, even though the Gospels were placed first in the New Testament, since they deal with the person that the New Testament is all about. Romans 1:4 says that Jesus was "designated [or declared to be] Son of God . . . by his resurrection from the dead." Jesus had been such a perfect person that, at his resurrection, it was plausible that God might have "adopted" him as His Son.

But then perhaps his early followers started asking, How was it possible for Jesus to be such a perfect person, in the first place? Because by the time the first Gospel was written (which was Mark's Gospel), we get an answer to that question. At Jesus' baptism, Mark says that a voice came from heaven saying to Jesus, "You are my beloved Son." So in Mark, Jesus became the Son of God at his baptism.

Matthew and Luke were written next; and their birth-stories point to Jesus being the Son of God right from his birth (Matthew 1:20; Luke 1:35).

But according to John's Gospel, Jesus was God through all eternity. What Jesus taught and his type of life have always been true. John says, "In the beginning was the Word, and the Word was with God, and the Word was God. . . . And the Word became flesh and lived among us, and we have seen his glory, the glory of the Father's only Son, full of grace and truth" (John 1:1, 14).

What do we mean by the words "Son of God," anyway? Eduard Schillebeeckx, a somewhat liberal, Dutch, Catholic, New Testament scholar, must have been a bit too liberal in his writings, because he was called to the Vatican and asked, "Do you believe that Jesus is the Son of God?" He replied, "I'll answer that question, if you will tell me what 'Son' means in this context (normally, a son is what is produced when a male sperm fertilizes a female egg and gives a human baby one X and one Y chromosome), what 'of' means in this context, and what 'God' means in this context." I understand that the inquiry panel moved on to the next question.

In doing so, they helped to make the point that "Son of God" is a metaphor. It was not intended to be understood literally. What is a metaphor? A metaphor often takes two words that don't normally go together and puts them together, so that, as a result, we "see" things differently; we get a different "slant" on the topic. "The ship plowed the sea" is a metaphor. Ships are not normally thought of as plows; but when the two words are joined, the reader or hearer gets a slightly different understanding of a ship moving through water.

In the decades after his death and resurrection, Jesus' first followers were looking for some way to capture the special quality of Jesus. Normal, human descriptions were not adequate. Sure, he was human, but he seemed to be so much better than a normal human being. He seemed to have a divine quality about him. So they hit upon the metaphor "Son of God," joining a human word, "son," with a divine word, "God," in an effort to express their view about his specialness.

As centuries passed, the metaphor turned into a literal title. But it still left the Church with the question of how humanity and divinity (God and man) were together in Jesus. There were major debates about this question. Before I tell you what they eventually decided, let me present three wrong answers, that is, three answers that were (and are) considered heresies. Often we can understand something better by understanding what it is not.

The first wrong answer is that Jesus was merely human. The claim was that Jesus was an ordinary, finite man, who was inspired and used by God, but in a higher degree than Moses and the prophets. He was then adopted as Son of God at his resurrection (following the line of thinking that I've already mentioned).

Concerning how the two natures (a divine nature and a human nature) were related in Jesus, it was said that the Word of God was joined to the individual personality of Jesus. (Envision a black stick and a white stick joined together by superglue). In effect that meant that the Word inspired Jesus and he went around doing good.

The way that Jesus and God were <u>united</u> was through moral will. That is, Jesus agreed with God's standards of what was morally right and he was able to carry them out. He had the will to do God's will. That is the way in which he and God were united.

Another argument for the first wrong answer: You couldn't be completely secure in believing in God unless God were free from risk, harm, and danger. If God were in danger of getting hurt, God wouldn't be fully reliable. God would be in danger if God dwelt in Jesus. God's reaching out and going out of Himself into Jesus would be contrary to God's own best interest and alien to Himself, since it would endanger Himself. So to insure that God would not get hurt by the world, God could not have been <u>in</u> the world in Jesus. That's why Jesus had to be merely human.

Athanasius, Bishop of Alexandria in the fourth century, argued against this argument about keeping God from getting hurt. Final religious security, he said, lies in belief that God was willing to take human form, risking Himself for the world. God was willing to get involved. God risked coming into the world and triumphed over it. God is Love, and love involves risk. So it is consistent with the divine nature that God should have taken such a risk. Humanity is not redeemed or saved unless God is involved with humanity. Athanasius said, 'What God has not been part of cannot have been redeemed or made whole.'

If you believe that Jesus was merely human, as we know humanity, that's not what Christianity teaches.

The second wrong answer is that Jesus was primarily God. That answer came from people labeled "monophysites," meaning "one nature." They believed that Jesus had only one nature, and that was a divine (not a human) nature.

They said that Jesus was God in the flesh. Therefore Jesus had no independent existence as a human being but was the Father made flesh.

Stated another way, Jesus was God in a human envelope. (Envision a black piece surrounded by a white envelope.) His <u>personality</u> was <u>God</u>. (Jesus wasn't really tempted and didn't really suffer. God suffered. But if you say that, then you have God compromising His ultimate transcendence [although you also have God fully experiencing the human condition].)

If you believe that Jesus had just one nature, a divine nature, that's not what Christianity teaches, either.

A third approach was to say that the two natures were mixed in Jesus, so that the human nature became more divine, and attributes of the flesh affected God's nature. (Envision a checkerboard with black and white squares.) That formulation was deemed to be incorrect, also.

Finally at the Council of Chalcedon in the year 451, they came up with the "official" answer, which we still endorse today. They came up with the doctrine of the <u>union</u> of the two natures, the divine and the human. They said there is "one and the same Jesus Christ acknowledged in two natures," without confusing (or mixing) them, without changing them, without dividing them, and without separating them. In other words, they said that all of the three answers that I just described were wrong. And then they went home.

Well, actually, before they went home they made their point, which was that how the human and the divine are together in Jesus is a mystery, and we shouldn't be expected to be able to explain the mystery.

But many people, today, would say that the paradox of two natures in one person (Jesus) is inadequate. Certainly, to explain something by saying "it's a mystery that we can't explain" is not very satisfying. So let me conclude by telling you about three modern approaches to this question.

The first approach goes like this: If God is perfect, then it would not be inappropriate to say that perfection is a manifestation of God. God is present wherever there is perfection. <u>That's</u> how divinity and humanity were together in Jesus. Not because there were two <u>natures</u> in him (if so, we must ask how they could be together), but because he was a perfect and fully human being. The human nature was his humanity; the divine presence was his <u>perfect</u> humanity. Accordingly, he made use of all of his potential and was related to everyone in the most appropriate way, so that, in comparison with everyone else, he certainly was extra-ordinary.

But his extraordinariness is, at least theoretically, one that <u>we</u> can <u>share</u>, through the mysterious power -- i.e., the power of God -- that enables <u>us</u> to <u>do</u> what is appropriate and to <u>trust</u> in an ultimacy that is outside our grasp, and therefore to love as fully and as widely as Jesus loved. When that is the case, then God will be in all of us, as St. Paul envisioned when he spoke of God being All in all. Until then, Christians believe that the divine incarnation has taken place <u>fully</u> only in Jesus.

Dietrich Bonhoeffer offered another approach. He said that an appropriate understanding of Jesus is not based on explanation but on relationship. Instead of asking <u>how</u> humanity and divinity can be together in Jesus, you should ask <u>who</u>. Who is Jesus for you? What is your relationship to him? Granted that Jesus was human, he becomes God when he is God for you: not when you decide to ascribe divinity to him, but when something about him "grabs" you in such a way that you accept <u>his</u> standards and values and his way of living, and when you yield your <u>life</u> to <u>him</u>.

Finally, Albert Schweitzer provided a third approach, in the last paragraph of his book *The Quest of the Historical Jesus*. Speaking about Jesus, it says, "He comes to us as One unknown, without a name, as of old by the lakeside he came to those people who knew him not. He speaks to us the same word: 'Follow me!' and sets us to the tasks which he has to fulfil for our time. He commands. And to those who obey him, whether they be wise or simple, he will reveal himself in the toils, the conflicts, the sufferings which they shall pass through in his fellowship, and, as an ineffable mystery, they shall learn in their own experience who he is." We know who Jesus is by following him. Amen.

Let us pray. Dear Lord, of thee three things we pray: to see thee more clearly, love thee more dearly, and follow thee more nearly, day by day. Amen.

13 Pent (A)

"Transformed Sacrifices"

(Romans 12:1-2)

In the first part of today's scripture lesson, St. Paul considers two topics in a way that might give us some new ideas. The first topic deals with sacrifice, and the second deals with what it means to be a human being.

Let's look at sacrifice first. One of the most universal religious practices is the performance of sacrifices. People through the ages have been willing to sacrifice their possessions, their comforts, and even their loved ones to their gods.

Generally, sacrifice is understood as being a bargain with God. If a person is willing to give a present to God, then the divine being is believed to be ready to give some sort of reward back to that person. So Agamemnon, the Greek king who was unable to move his ships out of the harbor because of unfavorable winds, was willing to sacrifice his daughter to the gods in order to get the weather to change.

Even the Bible reflects this understanding of sacrifice. We are told that Jephthah, a military leader of the Hebrews, promised a present to God in order to obtain victory. The present would be "whoever comes forth from the doors of my house to meet me when I return victorious from the Ammonites" (Judges 11:31). It was his young daughter who came to meet him, and she eventually had to be sacrificed.

While this is probably one of the most heart-rendering stories of sacrifice in the Old Testament, the Bible is full of sacrificial thinking, from the story of Abraham almost sacrificing Isaac to Jesus' death on the Cross.

This is the background that we have to be aware of, in order to see what a different view of sacrifice Paul is taking, in our scripture lesson this morning. In the old view, a person who made a sacrifice killed and burned something of value and presented the sacrifice to God. Paul believes that the death of Christ has established an entirely new situation with regard to sacrifice. The old sacrificial system of offering dead animals--or even dead people--is abolished. Instead, Paul calls on all Christians to present their "bodies as a <u>living</u> <u>sacrifice</u>, holy and acceptable to God."

And the sacrifice that we present, which now lets us come alive, isn't offered as a gift to God so that God will do something for us. Rather, it is offered in gratitude for Jesus and for all that God has already done for us through him. Our sacrifice is simply our response to the good news of God's grace and love.

But Paul adds five words to what I've been quoting which seem strange. He says," present your bodies as a living sacrifice, holy and acceptable to God, which is your spiritual worship." Why is presenting our bodies described as our "spiritual worship"? Aren't body and spirit separate? How is the action of the body something spiritual? This brings us to our second question: What constitutes a human being?

Do you think that each of us has a body, a mind, and a soul?

If you think that body, mind, and spirit are separate things, it's because you've been influenced by the ancient Greek way of thinking about human beings. That is different from the Hebrew view, found in the Bible. The Greeks were very analytical. When they asked themselves what a person is, they decided that a person consists of a body, and a mind, and a spirit or soul.

That's alright in the abstract, as labels for the three features that are always present in a human being. The problem comes when you start thinking that body, mind, and spirit really are separate from each other. They're not. Psychosomatic medicine is telling us that, nowadays.

You can't have an alive person without all three--body, mind, and spirit--being present. And you can't have them separately, either. A body without mind and spirit is just a corpse, not a person. And what does it mean to be a mind detached from a body? We have no evidence that there is such a thing.

Wait a minute, you may say, Isn't there some sort of "real me" deep down inside, which would be the same no matter what body I had? No, the biblical view is that our bodies are not just shells to house what you might call your "soul." Think about it for a moment. Imagine that you were the opposite sex, and a different race, and a different height. If you are a short, white woman, would you be the same person if you were a tall, black man? Your life-experience would be totally different. How could we possibly say that our bodies don't matter?

And just as we can't find the mind detached from the body, the same thing applies to the soul. That means we do not have an immortal soul. We got that idea from the Greeks, as a result of their chopping up the person into three parts. But if the soul can't be separated from the rest of us, that means we have no spiritual engine that keeps chugging along, on its own, after our body dies. Remember, the Creed says we believe in the resurrection <u>of</u> <u>the</u> <u>body</u>! If there is resurrection, it is because <u>God</u> resurrects us, not because we have the built-in capacity to continue living after our body dies. Christians believe in resurrection by God and not in an immortal soul.

That has not always been true. Christian theology, in the past, was fully influenced by the Greek way of thinking. But what I have just said fits the biblical Hebrew understanding of what a person is. The Hebrews did not separate a person into body, mind, and spirit/soul. The only distinction they made was between an alive person and a corpse. For them, an alive person is a psychosomatic totality. A human being is body, mind, and spirit interwoven and working together, so that, for example, the mind is aware, because the body has the sense of touch or can feel humidity. A mind, all by itself, wouldn't be aware of humidity.

So when Paul and the Bible use the word "body," they intend it to represent the whole person, the self. In that way, we can't get the erroneous idea that we can give our soul to God but can keep our body and its lusts and self-centered concerns to ourselves.

We had asked what Paul means when he spoke of presenting our bodies as a form of "spiritual worship." What is our spiritual worship, according to Paul? Answer: It is behaving acceptably to God, as our body, mind, and spirit interact to perform in that way. Our spiritual worship is behaving acceptably to God. We are called to see our entire life, our entire self, our daily existence, as a gift that we can present, in gratitude, to God.

But we can do this only "by the mercies of God." Because only by God's mercy--that is, by God's willingness to forgive our sinful rebellion and to accept us back--can we direct ourselves as God would have us be. Only by God's willingness to love and care for those who surrender their lives to Him can we use ourselves for God's purposes.

So Paul adds, "Do not be conformed to this world, but be transformed by the renewing of your minds, so that you may discern what is the will of God--what is good and acceptable and perfect." J. B. Phillips, in a loose translation, presents the problem more clearly. His translation reads: "Don't let the world around you squeeze you into its own mold."

That's easier said than done. Isn't it? We are conformed to the world in all sorts of ways. We all have clothing on, for example--and a certain limited type of clothing, too. People here have not filed their teeth to make them pointy. That's the way our part of the world behaves. We probably agree with much of what TV, radio, movies, and various forms of music tell us about what it's like to be in the mold of an American in this decade. That can make it difficult for us to discern what the will of God is, when God's will is different from the values of the world in which we are living.

Many types of conformity are perfectly OK. But when it comes to values and religious faith and moral behavior, that's a different matter, because God works to improve the world through His people, who are in the world. And if we, God's people, are so much like our secular society that we can't reflect God's distinctive will for the world, then God's will is less likely to be done on earth, and we will be failing in our calling to be Christ's disciples.

But with pressures from all sides to be like everybody else, how can we resist? How can we even know when we should resist? The answer is, we can't--on our own. Left to our own devices, we will be fully conformed to the world and squeezed into its mold.

But God has not left us to our own devices. God has come to the world through the founders of Israel, through Moses, through the prophets, and supremely in Jesus. Through their followers, God has given us the Bible, with more than a few clues as to what God's will is. (It may not be clear, from the Bible, whether it is more important to reduce the Federal deficit or to reduce taxes, but we may be sure that God is concerned about how we as a society deal with the poorest and weakest of our sisters and brothers.) God has brought us into the Church, where the Holy Spirit can be at work, guiding us as we influence one another. And God has given us faith, faith in God and in God's purposes, faith that transforms us by renewing our minds, allowing God to remold our minds from within us.

But what if that doesn't seem to be happening? What if we know that there are ways in which we are not holy and acceptable to God? What if we know that we are more conformed to the standards of the world than even we agree that we should be? How do we get a transformed mind?

I was told of a nurse at a certain hospital who was a Christian, who always seemed to have a glow about her. She always had a smile on her face and always was cheerful and helpful. And one day a patient said, "I'd give the world to be like you!" And the nurse replied, "That's what it takes, giving up the world." "Do not be conformed to this world," says St. Paul. "Be transformed by the renewing of your mind."

Jesus said, "Those who lose their life for my sake [--those who are not conformed to the world--] will find it." (Matthew 16:25) Finding new life from God is called "being born again." And that's why St. Paul said, "If anyone is in Christ, that person is a new creation or a new creature. [That person's mind has been renewed.] The old has passed away; behold, the new has come" (II Corinthians 5:17)

Only you and God know how much you need to be transformed by the renewing of your mind. Only you and God know how much you need to recommit your life to Christ. Take the opportunity to let God renew you fully, this morning, as we sing our next hymn.

"The Strange Wisdom of God"

(I Corinthians 1:17-31)

According to verse 17 of the Revised Standard Version of chapter one of Paul's First Letter to the Corinthians, Christ sent Paul to preach the gospel, "and not with eloquent wisdom, lest the cross of Christ be emptied of its power. For the <u>word</u> of the cross is folly to those who are perishing." The newer translation speaks of the "message about" the cross, rather than the "word of the cross." But I think that that translation misses an important point, which is that the cross can speak for itself. If the cross <u>can</u> speak for itself, what is it saying?

As a crucifix, it depicts an innocent man hanging in a painful execution. The crucifixion makes the point that the most highly developed legal system of Jesus' day, the Roman legal system, was not able to keep that innocent man from being executed. The cross also makes the point that the most highly developed religious system of Jesus' day, the Jewish religion, believing in only one God and endorsing high moral standards, was not flexible enough to accommodate the newness that Jesus brought.

This was the wisdom of the world, and it didn't work. It was a wisdom based on self-centered ambition. (The chief priest wanted to get Jesus out of the way.) It was a wisdom based on pride, the pride reflected in people who say, "We know what's right. We have nothing new to learn." It was a wisdom based on pretensions that our own wisdom and the wisdom of our society can always be relied upon. It can't. It was a wisdom that reflected fear of change. It was a wisdom based on avoidance of pain and avoidance of the death of what we're comfortable with. It is a human wisdom that encourages us to manage our lives only for ourselves and only for our own good. And here's the shocker: It's the wisdom which, most of the time, makes perfect sense to us! That's the wisdom that would be shown to be foolish and that God would destroy.

And "the word of the cross is foolishness," not to us who are saved (as in the King James translation) but to us who are <u>being</u> saved. When we see the folly of the world's wisdom, we are allowing God to nudge us in a different direction, and as a result, the power of God is saving us.

The world did not come to know God through its own wisdom and efforts: neither through the Greek wisdom of Plato nor through the Hebrew wisdom of Proverbs.

So "God decided, through the foolishness of our proclamation, to save those who believe." (v. 21) The foolishness that Paul proclaimed was that God took the initiative to save us. God is not a Judge waiting for us to prove our worth; nor is God waiting to be found, through prayer and meditation. No, Christ died for our sins, showing that God loves us in spite of ourselves. We please God only when we respond to God's love, which God already showers on us. We do good not to get on God's good side but because we already are on God's good side. We do not have to prove that we are worthy. That is the Gospel. We can believe it or not. If we believe it, there is nothing to stop us from behaving as though we were worthy.

"Jews demand signs," said St. Paul. But Jesus wants us to be attracted to his teachings and behavior for their own sake, not because he does some trick or gives some impressive sign which causes us to think, "Well, I guess if he could do that, then I should follow him." No, we are to follow Jesus because we think his teachings and actions are worth following.

Now we come to the next shocking statement, in verse 23: "We proclaim Christ crucified." That seems normal enough to us now, because we've adopted it as our theology. But in Paul's day, "Christ" and "crucified" did not go together. One view of the Messiah was that he was supposed to come on the clouds of glory and bring in the Kingdom of God. He was not expected to be crucified. So that was a stumbling block to Jews. And it made no sense, to Gentiles, that Christians should follow a leader who had been executed. What kind of a leader is that? Sure sounds like a loser.

But faith in Christ saves us, because it keeps us from having to be concerned about earning our own salvation and so it frees us to be concerned for others. So God's foolishness (by God coming to us) proves to be wiser than human wisdom, and God's weakness--even on a cross--is stronger than human strength.

But God doesn't work only through the weak Christ on the Cross. Look at what verses 26-28 say. "Consider your own call, brothers and sisters: not many of you were wise by human standards; not many were powerful; not many were of noble birth. But God chose what is foolish in the world to shame the wise; God chose what is weak in the world to shame the strong; God chose what is low and despised in the world, things that are not, to reduce to nothing things that are."

God chose to work through these "no accounts:" those whom Greek society looked down on, those who weren't having much of an impact on society, who aren't at the top of their class in every respect: Jesus, the country bumpkin from Nazareth; the peasants in the French Revolution; Rosa Parks; the United Farm Workers' Union of a few decades ago; the slow forces of evolution--and soil erosion--to reduce to nothing things that are.

Let me tell you about an experience I had in a hospital. One day when I was a chaplain at a hospital, I was standing beside the bed of a somewhat heavy, not-particularly-attractive woman in her 50s. Something had suddenly gone wrong with her, and she was probably not going to live to see the next day. All of a sudden, the door of the room opened and a short, somewhat heavy, balding man came rushing up to the bed. He said, "It's all right. I'm here now, honey. Everything's going to be all right," as he bent over and hugged her. Here was a homely, no-account man, coming to his homely, no-account wife, bringing all the love, care, and compassion that he could muster.

And I became furious, as I thought of the magazine ads and TV ads that portray nothing but beautiful people and that imply that if you are not beautiful and handsome and well-dressed, you aren't worth anything. How dare they place so much emphasis on superficial beauty and external appearance, and totally ignore love, care, compassion, and relationship, such as was taking place in that hospital room!?

If, guys, you really cannot tell a book by its cover, and if there are many more important features of a person than external appearance, then the wisdom of the world is wrong, and we had better not get sucked into it any more than we already are.

Unfortunately, many teenage girls have been sucked in, don't feel that they can possibly compete with the pretty teenage models, and therefore think that they will never be able to attract a boyfriend. They feel miserable and often fall into deep depression. The fact that, through baptism, they are daughters of the King of the universe does not mean much, as long as they believe that the world's wisdom is right. That's a topic for another sermon.

Why does God shame the wise, strong, and beautiful? We find the answer in verse 29: "so that no one might boast in the presence of God."

Any natural talents and beauty you may have are gifts from God. Even worldly success can be a gift from God. Apart from God's grace, none of it might have come your way. And none of it will last. The adage from the late 60s, "if you have it, flaunt it," is totally wrong. If you have it, be humble and thankful, because if you think you can take credit for it, remember that you can always lose it.

For all of us who are less than perfect and less than totally superior, we need to remember that we have the gospel of God's love, and presence, and power that we can draw on, and we must not accept the world's wisdom, which might judge our circumstances and, using its standards, make us feel inferior. Rather, the word of the Cross invites us to put our faith and hope in another Reality, not a reality that lies outside the world, but a Reality that is something other than the hopes, aspirations, and goals we project for ourselves or allow society to project for us.

In today's epistle lesson, Paul says that God takes the strange step of working through the weak and of challenging conventional wisdom. So Paul is asking, "On what basis will you order your life?" Will God's grace and God's standards be your new life, continually, ever anew? Or will you again, in some way, fall prey to the false wisdom of the world? Just remember, "God's foolishness is wiser than human wisdom, and God's weakness is stronger than human strength." And we all are called to see things God's way.

"Repeatable Salvation"

(I Corinthians 1:18)

Sisters and brothers, are you saved? Raise your hand if you've ever heard someone ask that question. Well, how did you answer it? You might have said, "I donno. I grew up in the Church; I went to Sunday School; I was baptized and confirmed." "Yes, yes," the speaker might have said, "but are you saved? Have you given your life to Christ?" Well, have you?

St. Paul was asked, "What must I do to be saved?" His answer was, "Believe in the Lord Jesus Christ."

Now, there's a difference between believing in Jesus and being committed to Jesus. Believing is easier. Depending upon how deeply you delve into the matter, it is possible to be nudged by others into agreeing with them about traditional Christian doctrine, without giving it too much thought ourselves.

But there is another problem with the way Paul phrases his answer. "What must I do to be saved? Believe in the Lord Jesus Christ." The problem with that answer is that it seems to be too mechanical. Put a mental coin into the slot and out comes salvation. Believe this and you get that. Isn't life more complex than that? Let's see.

What Paul's answer does do is move you toward becoming committed. By believing in Christ you are saved, in that you at least know where to look for guidance. You aren't floundering in a sea of relativity and uncertainty, but you believe there are answers. With regard to the ultimate questions of life, questions like "Who am I?" "Why am I here?" and "What might the future be like?" faith in Jesus Christ means you're not lost. Not everyone can say that. When you think about your future and ask questions about the meaning of life, it is no little matter to believe that Jesus Christ is Lord. Even though your life doesn't automatically become perfect as a result, you're at least on the right track. You're not following a path that will lead to destruction. Not everyone can make that statement.

And a relation to the Lord Jesus can provide the power and the wisdom to live-out the answers that Jesus provides. But when we talk about relationships--especially when we talk about meaningful relationships--we are beginning to talk about commitment. For since the power and wisdom to do God's will come from God, we would normally expect them to come to people who are committed to God and thereby open to God's power and presence.

"But you can't have any fun if you're Christian." I've heard college students say that, and I guess the answer depends on what you consider to be fun. I personally don't consider waking up the next morning with a hangover or with an incurable sexually transmitted disease -- and AIDS isn't the only one -- to be fun. And as one of my students once said, "You've always got to be thinking nine months ahead." This is where responsibility, and standards, and judgment, and reasoning, and faith come into the life that we actually live.

But if faith in Christ is a commitment to Jesus and his way, and if Jesus' way is God's way, and if God's way is what is best -- which it is by definition (Christians don't worship the Devil; we believe that what God is is what is ultimately right) -- if God's way is what is best, why does it make sense to follow what is less than best? Besides, if belief is not just accepting doctrine but involves a relationship and, indeed, a relationship with a God Who changes people's lives, a Christian can be a person who <u>feels</u> like doing what is actually worthwhile doing.

Even if you should embark on a new relationship with God in a way where you experience the difference, however, sin is never completely banished from your life, as we all know. But a <u>faithful</u> relationship with God can mean that, throughout your lifetime, the Holy Spirit will be engaged with you, enabling you more and more to become the same kind of full and complete human being that Jesus was.

The Greek and Russian Orthodox call this process "divinization." In their view -- and I find it somewhat appealing -- it's the whole point of the Christian religion. "God became human," they say, "so that people can become divine." That doesn't mean that people become indistinguishable from God, but it does mean that we can radiate a joy in living, sensing and exhibiting the very best way of dealing with other people and the world around us, that constitutes life at its best. But this is a kind of salvation that doesn't pertain just to behavior. It affects your whole being. It determines what the core of you will be like. It enables you to <u>feel</u> that your life is at its best. It gives you, as Paul said, "everything" that matters. (II Corinthians 6:10)

Martin Luther, that sixteenth century reformer of the Church, may have had something similar in mind when <u>he</u> described the Christian life. Listen to what he said. "This life is not godliness but the process of becoming godly, not health but getting well, not being but becoming, not rest but exercise. We are not now what we shall be, but we are on the way. The process is not finished, but it is actively going on. This is not the goal, but it is the right road. At present, everything does not gleam and sparkle, but everything is being cleansed."

The Christian life is a process, a process of walking with God, a process of following Christ's way. The first Christians, you know, were called "followers of the Way."

The Christian life is also a process of returning to its source. The source of Christian life is the Spirit that was present at baptism. Everyone who is a Christian became a member of the Church when he or she was baptized. Whether we remember that event or not, it was the time when we were taken from the world at large and initiated into that special community of people who dare to claim that what is ultimately real and true was uniquely evident in the life and teaching of Jesus, and that the way to true life is to be his disciple. The Apostle Paul says that "We were buried with Christ by baptism into death, so that as Christ was raised from the dead by the glory of the Father, we, too, might walk in newness of life!" (Romans 6:4) What relevance does this statement have for our life today? Let me spend a little time answering that question.

You probably don't have to be told about the temptations to stray from the straight and narrow path that leads to life at its best. Short-term pleasures or the easy way out often loom large for the moment. Peer pressure, by itself -- i.e., what everyone else is doing -- can nudge us toward behaving immorally. To the extent that we are not yet fully godly, our temperament and emotions can irrupt in ways that we later regret. As we explore new ways of relating to people, we sometimes find that we have made a mistake. At other times, we simply do the wrong thing.

That's why Luther talked about dying daily to sin. Each morning we can cut ourselves off from the evils and failures of our past by remembering our baptism. For just as in baptism we were symbolically buried in water and then resurrected again, so each morning we can figuratively die to our past and rise again to new life with Christ. It's never too late to start again. Daily dying to selfishness and renewing our relationship with God is the way that we grow up into him who is our lord and head.

And all of this ongoing process is completely dominated by the initiative of God. Let me explain this interesting theological claim. Some denominations believe that when people resist temptation, they do it solely by their own effort. Lutherans, along with Catholics, Episcopalians, and Presbyterians, take a different view. They hold that any time we are doing good, it is because the Holy Spirit of God is at work within us. It's an interesting distinction, because you cannot tell which view is correct. When you choose to do something good or to resist temptation, you can't feel the Holy Spirit within you. The Spirit doesn't have molecules that you can feel. But the Lutheran view, following St. Augustine, gives God the glory and also expresses a certain amount of awe and humility at the fact that yesterday you weren't making the good decision but today you are. Why are you behaving that way today? It is because God is at work in you. Besides, this view also says that you're not alone. God can be with you.

But notice this way of understanding "salvation." It's a salvation that doesn't occur just once. For many people, this is a new way of thinking. Let me explain where the rationale for this new way comes from. In the old King James translation of the Bible, Paul says that the preaching of the Cross is the power of God to us who are <u>saved</u> (I Corinthians 1:18). Modern linguistic scholars and more recent translations have looked carefully at the verb "saved," in the Greek, and have seen that it really talks not about us who <u>are</u> saved but about us who are <u>being</u> saved, in situation after situation. And that's the way the Holy Spirit really works. Each time you have to make a decision dealing in some way with morality, i.e., with how you deal with other people and the environment, people in the world around you can check on whether or not you are saved, on whether the Holy Spirit has saved you that time. Or, that time, were you lured in the wrong direction? They can check on whether you're saved, because your actual decision in the particular circumstance will provide the answer. So salvation occurs again and again, for those who live in the real world, since the real world is a mixture of good and evil, and the struggle between the two seems to be unending. In that struggle, salvation occurs again and again for Christians who want to be the best kind of human beings that they can be. It occurs every time they show, by their actions -- and the beliefs from which they stem -- that God has guided them to make the right decision.

Our initial response to the call of Christ puts us on the right road. Our initial response to Christ puts us on the right road; but there are many intersections, detours, and traffic circles on the road of life. We can go astray. But here is the point of the sermon. The God of love is faithful and can save us again and again from actual and potential folly. Beyond that [repeat], the power of God can draw those who are faithful into God's higher realm of existence, with the result that problems and temptations of the past simply vanish away. A Christian <u>can</u> be a person who <u>feels</u> like doing what is actually worthwhile doing.

Let me close with words from a hymn from the nineteenth century, which we'll sing in a minute. It describes the Christian life, in part, as "finding, following, keeping, struggling" and then asks whether the Christian life is "sure to bless." Does it pay off? Drawing on 2,000 years of history, the hymn finds that "saints, apostles, prophets, martyrs answer 'Yes!'"

"Whom Do We Think We're Fooling?"

(I Corinthians 13:1-13)

Whom do we think we're fooling? As far as the secular world is concerned, we Christians can believe whatever we want about God and Christ and Communion and anything else, but if our lives don't reflect the kind of love that Paul talks about in our epistle lesson, we might as well close the church down.

Interestingly, that's the kind of standard the secular world had at the very beginning of Christianity, too; and Christians met that standard. The pagans back then were known to have said about the Christians: "See how they love one another!"

Jesus had a similar standard: "By their fruits you shall know them." (Matthew 7:16) Whether "they're" worth following or joining will be determined by the result of what they do and how they behave, because, as St. James said, "Faith without works is dead." (2:26b) "I by my works" -- i.e., by what I do and how I behave -- "will show you my faith." (3:18bβ)

Let's take a look at the kind of love that St. Paul said can result in good works.

But first, let's get that first verse out of the way, where Paul talks about speaking in tongues.

Who here has ever spoken in tongues? Raise your hand if you have ever spoken in tongues, in this biblical sense.

Here's a way of understanding what speaking in tongues is all about. It goes back to the fact that God is not just an idea. God is real, a reality that can overwhelm you with its presence and fill you with such a surging of energy that your whole body tingles. God's presence can make you absolutely ecstatic! And in those moments of ecstasy, you may want to praise God. But you don't want to pull yourself out of the ecstatic experience in order to think rationally about what the subject of your sentence is going to be and what the verb is and which words will come first. Instead, you just open your mouth and let flow whatever syllables just happen to come out. Sometimes you can't even keep yourself from doing that. That's ecstatic utterance, the experience of speaking "in the tongues of mortals and of angels." And I daresay it's wonderful! It's the work of the Holy Spirit of God.

But some churches turn this grace and gift of God into a law. They make a rule that requires people to speak in tongues in order to become a member of their church. They shouldn't do that; because you can't demand that the Holy Spirit act at your bidding or conform to your requirements.

Apparently (and unfortunately), according to St. Paul, speaking in tongues does not automatically make you a loving person. Yet being loving may be even more important than having faith.

Now, what kind of love are we talking about? Well, our New Testament text was written in Greek. Greek has five words for love. Let me distinguish between the three most popular ones.

One Greek word for "love" is *philia*. It basically means " friendship." It works its way into the name of one of our cities, Philadelphia, meaning the "city of brotherly love."

Another Greek word for "love" is *eros*, from which we get the word "erotic," a lustful reaching out to someone because of what you will get from that person. That's not the word that Paul uses for "love."

The Greek word that Paul uses is *agápē*. It's spelled a-g-a-p-e and it's pronounced not "ay [as in "say"]-gape" but "ah-gah-pay." It is not the common form of love. It's God's type of love: self-giving love; sacrificial love; reaching out and giving, even if you don't get anything in return. It is concern for the other person and for the well-being of the other. It acknowledges the intrinsic value of the other, not just their value for your use. It is love of the unlovely and the undeserving.

When Paul talks about specific features of love, he presents one that is so basic. He says that love is kind: helpful in little ways, because it is concerned for the well-being of the other. So it's also not rude.

Now that you know the meaning of *agápē*, we can understand why Paul says what he does about love.

Love does not insist on its own way. Of course not, if we're concerned for the well-being of others and don't expect anything in return. Consider how this would apply to congregational governing council meetings. This is surely a call for a willingness to compromise, as we recognize the value of the other person's concerns. That doesn't mean you have to be a doormat to be walked all over: your concerns have value, too -- but not exclusively. And it may well make sense to apply this understanding of love differently when you're dealing with children than when you're dealing with people with mature judgment.

A person who is loving is <u>patient</u>. Of course, because love does not insist on its own way or timing, and others are so valuable that we never give up on them. That's also why love <u>hopes</u> all things. Because others are so valuable that you never give up on them, love never considers someone to be hopeless. That's also why love endures all things.

And agape-love is not envious, because it wants the best for the other and is not preoccupied with itself.

It's interesting to notice that, in all his discussion of love, Paul doesn't talk about what to do when the flame of love dies down. That's because, in Christian theology, love is not a feeling or an emotion but an act of the will. When we are called to love God, it is not expected that our heart will flutter because God is a real living doll. Love of God is more like self-giving devotion to God. It's not an emotion; it is a commitment that we, by the power of the Holy Spirit, decide to make.

So when we are patient, or kind, or treating the undeserving in some other loving way, we are carrying out an act of will. We are doing it because we have decided to do it, whether or not we feel like doing it. (Parents frequently behave this way toward their children. Right?) We may do the loving thing because we believe that God loves us and has given us the power to do it. We may even have prayed for God to make us more loving. And if we haven't, we <u>could</u> pray for God to make us more loving. After all, that's what God is for, since God is the source and power of love at its fullest. But in any case, our actions that result are not based on our feelings.

Paul concludes the 13th chapter of I Corinthians by saying, "And now faith, hope, and love abide, these three; and the greatest of these is love."

<u>Faith</u>, of course, is very important. It keeps us from falling into despair. It doesn't let us give up. It orients us toward God, our source of strength. So it saves us in the present. It's the first, and basic, and really indispensable step.

Faith makes it possible for us to <u>hope</u>, to look to the future and to look optimistically.

Faith and hope apply only to the individual, however. But <u>love</u> takes an important final step. It relates us to other people. It reaches out and <u>does</u> something. It does lots of things --often excitedly and creatively. As a philosopher said: one day, after mastering the winds, the waves, the tides, and gravity, after all the scientific and technological achievements, we shall harness for God the energies of love. And then, for the second time in the history of the world, we will have discovered fire. Love gives to those in need. It loves the unlovable. And it does those things in ways that show the patience of Job and the kindness of Christ. It is the greatest and most excellent way.

12 Pent (B)

"Sacrifice"

(Ephesians 5:1-2)

Our Gospel and Epistle lessons this morning come from a lectionary. A lectionary is a list of prescribed Bible readings for every Sunday and holiday in the church year. Many denominations are using the same lectionary, nowadays, which means that, on at least some Sundays, all over the world in Orthodox, Roman Catholic, Episcopal, Lutheran, Presbyterian, and Methodist churches, the people are directing their attention to the same biblical passages. The lectionary follows the sequence of the major events of Jesus' life, and it keeps the minister from preaching on just what he or she is interested in.

When we look at the tail end of our Epistle lesson, today, we see a strange command. Ephesians 5:1 tells us to "be imitators of God." Puny us?! Why should we be able to imitate God?! Well, the answer is, God can give us the power to do so. God gives what God commands. If we're serious about following God's way, the same Power that makes us serious can also make us successful. God's way is what's best, and we function best when we do it God's way. Indeed, if God is the Ultimate Truth of the universe and the power behind the way things operate at their best, it would seem only prudent not to go against that tide but to get in gear with it.

But Paul wants us to imitate <u>God</u>! What's that? If God is Spirit, just what is it that we're supposed to imitate? We can't even prove that God exists. If there is God, how do we learn anything about God? Should we just guess? Should we make up what <u>we'd</u> like God to be or what <u>we</u> think is ultimate, or most basic, or most worthwhile? If we do, how will we know whether or not we're right? No, if God exists, then God knows what God is like; every other guess or preference is likely to be wrong; and we will know what God is like only through God's own Self-revelation.

Christians believe that God <u>has</u> been revealed, most fully in the actions and teachings of Jesus of Nazareth. So we look to Jesus, if we want clues as to what God is like.

"Therefore be imitators of God . . . and live in love, as Christ loved us and gave himself up a sacrifice to God."

Karl Barth, one of the greatest theologians of the twentieth century, said a good preacher will prepare a sermon with a Bible in one hand and a newspaper in the other. Why? Because if, as Jesus said, God "knows," so to speak, even the number of hairs on your head, then God is concerned not only with what goes on in your daily life but also with the major events taking place in the world, as well. Sometimes Christians limit God's concern to their own personal lives, and they don't think about what God's will is with regard to the major issues of the day.

Today, I want to take a look at one such issue. The issue is affirmative action, possibly a euphemism for preferential treatment of minorities. Preferential treatment, in general, takes place all the time. We treat better those whom we prefer.

At the end of the 1800s and the beginning of the twentieth century, hundreds of thousands of immigrants from non-English-speaking countries came to New York City. Perhaps some of your ancestors were among them. Immediately, they needed jobs to support themselves and their families. But how could they find work if they couldn't even speak English? Well, what they would do is ask someone of their own nationality what factories had foremen who spoke their language, and they would apply for work there and be hired. If you were German, there was no point of applying for a job where the foreman was Italian, because all of the other workers spoke only Italian. Now there's preferential treatment! And there are probably millions of Americans today who are well established financially, because their forebears had been given that kind of preferential treatment.

When the children of former black slaves would apply for work, they would be handed a broom and be happy that they had a steady -- if small -- income. If their children showed some manual dexterity and wanted to improve their lot by working as a plumber, or an electrician, or a carpenter, they found that they couldn't get those jobs, because in order to get them, they had to be members of a union, and you could only be a member of a crafts union by the invitation of someone who already was a member. And those who were members preferred to work with people who were like themselves.

The problem applies to all sorts of other jobs, too. Even though many applicants may be qualified, we prefer to hire people who will fit in and work well with our existing work force, and that means it's only reasonable that we should hire people who are like the ones who are already working for us. Well, what if you're not like the ones who are already working there? What if you're a member of a minority group? How do you break into a world that is always dominated by the majority?

A member of the National Urban League once suggested this analogy. He said it's like a race between two men who start at the same point, but one is in a T-shirt and track shoes and is running on a cinder track, and the other one is in a football uniform and is running on sand. It doesn't take many seconds before the one on the cinder track is far ahead, and everyone agrees that the race is unfair. So the two runners are told to stop right where they are, and the one in the football uniform takes off that uniform and puts on track clothes and gets onto the cinder track. Now, if the race is resumed from that point, will the race now be fair? The other runner is still far ahead.

Most people would say the race would not be fair; and what affirmative action is doing is providing a way for the person or the group who is behind to catch up.

If a quota keeps a majority member from getting a job, that person still is in a better position to get another job than a minority member would be who had to face the natural preference of majority employers. Besides, if blacks are the minority, blacks constitute only 12% of our population. Even if every one of them had a job, they couldn't begin to fill all of the jobs or places in graduate school that there are in this country.

But some poor whites or minimally qualified white males may be forced to suffer. That's true. It would be nice if the majority could remain comfortable while also helping minorities. But if, in the real world, that is not always possible, can we at least see some fairness in the pendulum swinging the other way? Can whites, and especially while males, find a basis for accepting the possibility that it's their group's turn to be dumped on?

There is a truth that the Christian religion knows which, even if you don't think it applies to this situation, is worth considering. The third word from the end of our epistle lesson is the word "sacrifice." At the end of our gospel lesson, Jesus is depicted as saying, "the bread that I will give for the life of the world is my flesh" (John 6:51b). The statement refers, basically, to Jesus' sacrificial death.

When Christians interpret Jesus as dying for the sins of the world, they are doing more than just appreciating what Jesus did. They also are acknowledging that there are times when sacrifice is necessary, in order for something worthwhile to be accomplished. Parents often recognize this truth and act on it in ways that their children don't even begin to imagine.

Even more strongly, when Christians say that Jesus is the Son of God who sacrificed himself, they are saying that sacrifice is part of God's own nature, part of the ultimate truth of the universe. Sacrifice can be the best thing to occur. Sacrifice is not outside God but is part of the divine reality. God can be present in sacrifice.

We would prefer to hear that part of the epistle that tells us not to steal but to work honestly, because we do that. We would prefer to hear the epistle tell us to tell the truth, because we mostly do that. So that is not the Word of God to us.

Ephesians 4:31 says, "Put away from you all bitterness." Are you bitter? Supreme Court Justice Clarence Thomas once said this in an interview: "There is nothing you can do to get past black skin. I don't care how educated you are, how good you are at what you do -- [if you are black] you'll never have the same contacts or opportunities, you'll never be seen as equal to whites." Verse 31 about putting away bitterness may apply more to a black congregation than to a white one.

"Therefore be imitators of God.... [L]ive in love... Love does not insist on its own way."

The Greeks have at least three words for "love," and the word that Paul uses here is *agápē*, self-giving love, love directed toward the needs of the other, love that loves even the unlovely, even those who we might feel don't deserve it. It is the word that describes God's love for us. And we are called to be imitators of God, by the power of that same love.

Of course, almost anyone can love in the abstract, but God loves in the concrete. God's love was evident in the actions and teachings of Jesus. But the concrete Jesus is no longer here. If God's love is to take concrete form in the present, there's a good chance that it will have to do that through us. As members of the Church, we are the body of Christ in the present day.

To whom did Jesus show love? Well, he spent most of his time with the halt, the maimed, the blind; with tax collectors and prostitutes, people on the fringes of society, the poor, and the powerless. That's saying something important about where God's primary concerns are, where God's love is needed most. If we are to be disciples of Jesus, it would seem to urge us to be biased on behalf of what today we would simply term "minorities."

Christ's love, which trusted God and thereby freed him to be concerned for others, clearly showed itself to be a sacrificial love. If in our comfortable circumstances we don't think of sacrifice too often; if our immediate instinct -- and not an unhealthy one -- is to stick up for "our rights;" perhaps the Word of God to <u>us</u> is "sacrifice."

"Judgment Day"

(Hebrews 9:24-28)

What do we have to do to get God to like us? Answer: Nothing. God already does.

But how can that be, since we are sinners? True, but our sins have been paid for by Christ's death on the Cross. So when we are sorry for our sins and repent of them, that is, resolve not to do them again if we can possibly help it, we are covered by the penalty-payment that Christ made and our sins are blotted out.

Why do we say this? Well, this part of Christian theology comes out of the Hebrew sacrificial system, which saw sin as an affront to God. Sin wasn't just a form of disobedience or of separating ourselves from God, it was a kind of thumbing our nose at God. And it is. As the psalmist said, referring to God, "Against you, you alone, have I sinned and done what is evil in your sight." (Psalm 51:4)

To make amends for this insult to God -- to get back on God's good side, as we might say today -- the ancient Hebrews felt that they had to offer different kinds of sacrifices, depending upon how serious the sin had been. But God is perfect and God's Law is perfect; and since all animals and birds that were sacrificed were blemished and therefore in some way imperfect -- or, even if they were unblemished and perfect, they were being offered by a sinful and therefore imperfect person -- no sacrifice could be good enough to wipe away the stain of sin completely. So, as the Second Reading said, the high priest had to enter the Holy Place in the Temple year after year, to offer sacrifices for the sins of the people.

Then Jesus was crucified, and his disciples found themselves asking, 'Why would God let a perfect person like Jesus be killed in that way?' And thinking along the lines of the sacrificial system of their Jewish religion, they said, 'Aha! Maybe that was God providing the perfect sacrifice! And since Jesus wasn't paying the penalty for his own sins, since he didn't have any, maybe he was the perfect person paying for the sins of everyone else, so that no more sacrifices would ever need to be made.' And that's what our text says: "He entered into heaven itself . . . to appear in the presence of God on our behalf. . . . He has appeared once for all at the end of the age to remove sin by the sacrifice of himself." In that way, God's justice had finally been met; the gap between humanity and divinity had been closed; and humanity was finally, once again, on God's good side.   Another early Christian theologian said it slightly differently, without making reference to sacrifices. He said that when Adam sinned, he brought sin into the world, thereby pulling all of humanity away from God. Jesus was the Second Adam, the human being who finally lived in perfect harmony with God again, thereby providing a basis for believing that God could be predisposed to view us favorably.

These views pave the way for saying that, nowadays, we believe that God loves us in spite of our waywardness, just as a parent loves a child in spite of its misbehavior. In fact, God may treat us even more like grandchildren, as you may know, if you are inclined to be more lenient with your grandchildren than their parents are.

It isn't that God doesn't care about how we behave. In our Gospel lesson, God urges us to give sacrificially. In our psalm, God sets the example: The Lord cares for the stranger; he sustains the orphan and widow. The story is told of an Episcopal bishop who would quiz Confirmation classes before confirming them. But instead of asking them questions about the Creed and about their beliefs, he would ask them what they were doing to help the poor and the needy.

And if we do less than we really can, or if we actually break God's laws, what is the point of divine punishment? It doesn't obliterate our sinful tendencies. Besides, sometimes we get the only punishment we need, and that is the absence of feeling good as a result of not having done good. God's way is to forgive and to say, 'O.K., put that mess behind you and start again, trying to do better next time.'

Mortals die once. That is what our text says and that is the teaching of Judaism, Christianity, and Islam. We are not trapped in the cycle of death and rebirth that is called "reincarnation." Some people use reincarnation to explain certain personal or personality traits. 'Oh, she's like that,' they say, 'because of what she did in a previous lifetime.' Or they use it to explain why bad things happen to us. 'That's his karma at work,' they say. Karma is the moral law of cause and effect. For every good thing you do, you will get a reward -- if not during your present life, then in a future lifetime. And for every bad thing you do, you will get an appropriate punishment, either in this lifetime or a future one. There is no escape; and there is no forgiveness. There is no forgiveness. You pay for every misstep. This view certainly is just. It also shows that the Christian God is just in a different way: in a way that reflects the fact that God is Love. And whatever its merits, reincarnation is experienced as a real albatross around the neck of those who believe it. For Hindus and Buddhists, salvation consists of getting <u>out</u> of the continuous cycle of death and rebirth.

Our text speaks of judgment. Notice that there is a difference between judgment and condemnation. Judgment is just about making a decision about something or forming an evaluation of something. (He's handsome. That's the right height. That's sweet enough.) Condemnation is a <u>negative</u> decision about something or someone.

Because we repent of our sins, we keep in touch with God. Every time we repent, the gap between us and God closes. We say we want to do things God's way, even if we don't always succeed. So when God judges us, God looks at us through Jesus, who "appears in the presence of God on our behalf," as though Christ were standing between us and God, and God sees only the perfect Jesus, instead of our sinfulness and shortcomings. So, as Paul says, there is now "no condemnation for those who are in Christ Jesus." (Romans 8:1)

The author of our epistle expects Christ to return, but this time not to deal with sin but to save those who are looking for the new life that he can bring. There is a story of a Sunday School teacher who asked her class where God is. One boy answered with assurance, "In the bathroom in my house." The teacher asked why he was so sure of that. The boy replied, "Because every morning when I'm in the bathroom, my father bangs on the door and says, 'My Lord, are you still in there?'" Well, God may not have arrived in our bathrooms, but many people are impatient for what they understand to be the Second Coming.

Yet there is an important sense in which Judgment Day and the Second Coming occur frequently. After all, is the Almighty God restricted by time, so that God can judge and come to us only at the Last Day, at the end of time? Or is it more likely that every time we make a decision, God is present and judges us. That is why we have confession every week: to repent and be forgiven for what we know God would have judged us to have done wrong -- and for our more basic sin of separation from God which has not been fully overcome.

Similarly, Christ does not wait until the end to come to save us. Christ speaks to us through the insights we get from sermons. Christ comes to us in response to prayer. Christ comes to us in Holy Communion. And

Christ can overwhelm us and transform us by his power in this life, when we least expect it.

14 Pent (B)

"Can Faith Save You?"

(James 2:1-17)

James, chapter 2, really gets us, because we do tend to treat the rich better than the poor; and when we do so, according to verse 4[b], we are expressing evil thoughts through our actions.

Indeed, we are showing that we don't really believe in Jesus Christ (v. 1). Wow! What an accusation!

The poor, however, also are rich, because "God has chosen the poor in the world to be rich in faith" (v. 5a). The poor, of course, need to have faith, because they can't rely on their meager material goods. And because they don't have many material goods, they appreciate the problems of those who are in need and so, perhaps paradoxically, they often are good at sharing. They are heirs of the kingdom that God has promised. And if God uses us to bring in the kingdom, then we can't ignore them and their needs.

Listen to verses 15 and 16 (TEV/CEV). "Suppose there are brothers and sisters who need clothes and don't have enough to eat. What good is there in your saying to them, 'I hope all goes well for you. I hope you will be warm and have plenty to eat' -- if you don't give them the necessities of life?"

Interestingly, James doesn't hesitate to identify class distinctions and even to say that it is the rich who are oppressing the poor. And sometimes the rich oppress the poor without even knowing it, because they are so far removed from experiencing the life that the poor are forced to lead. I don't remember which Frenchman pointed out that the law, in its equanimity, forbids the rich as well as the poor to sleep under bridges. How many rich people do you think are affected by that law? Laws tend to help the rich. Well, not surprisingly. The rich make the laws. But if money is needed -- in large quantity -- to provide effective assistance to the poor, in a variety of areas (as a means of bringing the kingdom of God to earth), then a way that the rich might oppress the poor, today, would be by not making sufficient money available. And to those who would say that the poor don't deserve assistance, because they're just lazy and won't work, James responds with the words, "mercy triumphs over judgment." (v. 13b)

Then James asks (v. 14), "What good is it if you say you have faith but do not have works? Can faith save you?" Here we encounter an apparent discrepancy between Paul, who says we are saved by grace, not by works, and James (v. 17) who teaches that faith without works is dead.

Even James supports Paul, however, when James says (v. 10), "whoever keeps the whole law but fails in one point has become accountable for all of it." That sounds a lot like Paul saying (Galatians 3:10-11a), "All who rely on the works of the law are under a curse; for it is written, 'Cursed is everyone who does not observe and obey all the things written in the book of the law.' Now it is evident that no one is justified before God by the law." But then Paul goes on to say that "since all have sinned and fall short of the glory of God, they are now justified by His grace as a gift." (Romans 3:23-24a) "We hold that a person is justified by faith, apart from works prescribed by the law." (Romans 3:28)

Remember that James asked, "What good is it if you say you have faith but do not have works? Can faith save you?" Paul says you're saved by faith, while James questions whether faith alone can save you.

One way to understand this discrepancy is to learn that Paul and James understand "faith" differently. For Paul, "faith" means trust, trust in God and a committed relationship with God. Understanding "faith" as trust, can faith save you? Of course it can. It can save you from giving up. It can enable you to dare to go through difficult times. It can enable you to dare to take risks that lead to benefiting yourself -- and others. Trust leads to a relationship in which we feel loved, a relationship to which we respond by loving others, which then generates good works. Such good works are not done to get God to accept you or save you; they're done <u>because</u> God accepts you (which means you're not saved by them).

James understands "faith" quite differently. For James, "faith" means intellectually accepting Christian doctrine, believing "The Faith." You have faith when you agree with the teachings of the Church. James' view does not emphasize a relationship with God.

That view of faith, as accepting doctrine, didn't result in people being motivated to do good, so James had to call for works. He had to require that good works also be done.

Now, common sense leads you to know that Christian faith is not limited to believing doctrine. It also affects how you behave. Skeptics, of course, demand good behavior from us. They're all too ready to find hypocrites, whose actions contradict what they say they believe. And Jesus endorsed their concern, when he said, "by their fruits you shall know them." Perhaps that's why non-believers eventually could say about the early Christians: "See how they love one another!"

If you're worried about getting into God's good graces, if you're worried about doing enough to please God, Paul says, 'Forget about it. You're free already. Faith in Christ liberates you from worrying about whether God accepts you, and that means that it frees you to be concerned about others, since you don't have to be concerned about yourself.'

With that faith, knowing that God accepts you in spite of yourself, you will not <u>want</u> to look down on the poor. You will think about whether there is some sense in which you are oppressing the poor and will take appropriate action if you are. And with that faith in the present power of Christ you <u>can</u> do the good things that James wants you to do, because you know that faith without works is dead.

5 Easter (C)

"I Am Making All Things New"

(Revelation 21:1-5)

Today's Second Reading deals with one of the most important themes of the Christian Faith, namely, the belief that God is making all things new. That theme was inaugurated when Jeremiah looked forward to God making a new covenant with the people of Israel. It was continued in the new humanity that people glimpsed in the behavior and teachings of Jesus. It was picked up by the most ancient version of Christianity, namely the Greek Orthodox Church, with its doctrine of "divinization," the teaching that the purpose of Christianity is to make each of us as perfectly human and as divine -- or at least as fully in touch with God -- as Jesus was. And it extends to our vision of a time in the future when God will make <u>all</u> things new.

Since this vision comes from the Book of Revelation, I'd like to say a few things about that book, before looking more closely at the Second Lesson.

It is important to notice that the first verse of the first chapter of that book says that someone named John, on the island of Patmos, had a vision of "what must soon take place." Well, you know about some of the strange and horrifying things that this book talks about: bowls of wrath being poured onto the earth, and a beast with seven horns, and angels opening seals and blowing trumpets, resulting, among other things, in one-third of the earth burning up and the sea turning to blood. Have those things taken place? No, they haven't. And since they did not soon take place, that fact provides an excellent reason for suspecting that they will never take place -- at least, not in any of the details that you can find described in the book.

Look, John was writing at a time when the early Christians were being severely persecuted. He was writing to comfort them and to urge them to hold fast to their faith, assuring them that there was light at the end of the tunnel. What sense would it make for him to be consciously saying, "I know you're miserable now, but wait till I tell you what's gonna happen in the year 2010!" Would that be taking their misery seriously? No, it would not. Rather, as Adele Collins, Professor of New Testament at the University of Chicago, has suggested, if John came back to earth 100 years later and was asked about his predictions, he'd probably say, "I guess I got it wrong" -- unless he would say, "Oh, I never intended what I wrote to be taken literally!"

The great traditional denominations of Christianity have never placed much emphasis on the Book of Revelation. And when you read the history of those people who have, you see that they just make fools of themselves, as their proposals for what the different images and symbols in the book mean turn out to be wrong, time and time again.

A favorite image is the beast with the number 666 on its forehead. Some early Protestants said it was the Pope. After them, people said it was Napoleon, then Franklin Delano Roosevelt, then Hitler, after each of whom the world was supposed to end. Nowadays, the "mark of the beast" is supposed to be the International Product Code, since it often consists of three sets of six vertical lines.

Actually, we don't have to make such wild guesses. We know who the beast was. In order to know how we know, you need to understand three things. First, the Book of Revelation was speaking out against the Roman government. For that reason, it was written in code language, so if Roman soldiers found the text, they couldn't charge the Christians with sedition.

The second thing you need to know is that some Aramaic and Hebrew letters stand for numbers, just as in Latin, where I stands for 1, V stands for 5, X stands for 10, etc.

Thirdly, if you write the title "Nero Caesar" in Aramaic and add up the value of the letters contained therein, you get 666. We know who John had in mind when he wrote about the beast. It was the current Roman emperor.

But people can make a lot of money writing books that apply the symbols found in the Book of Revelation to the present day. It makes them seem very smart, since they appear to know what is going to happen in the near future, even though Jesus said no one can know. He said that he didn't. Nor did he try to frighten people into believing in him. Yet in chaotic times, people crave a glimpse of certainty. They forget that St. Paul said, "We walk by faith, not by sight." (II Corinthians 5:7)

Revelation was the last book admitted to the Bible. It was not widely endorsed and read by Christian congregations. That's probably because it is full of vengeance. It's rather un-Christian, when you think about it; it's quite unlike the teachings of Jesus. It became part of the Bible because people thought the Apostle John wrote it. There are several reasons why biblical scholars say that the fisherman John did not write it, which I won't take time to go into here. But there is one argument that should be easy to accept. It totally eliminates the theme of "Love" that permeates both the Gospel and the epistles of John.

Another reason why the book was eventually accepted was that it contained passages like chapter 21, which enunciate themes that the Christian community did endorse. Let's take a closer look at that chapter.

"Then I saw a new heaven and a new earth; for the first heaven and the first earth had passed away, and the sea was no more." Why a "new heaven"? I can see why we might need a new earth. The earth is old and crumbling. People have fallen away from God and are corrupted. They are dragging the earth down. But why would we need a new heaven?

Scholarly commentaries say this verse is talking about radical discontinuity. Its wording is a symbolic way of saying God will change everything. That idea fits the Hebrew way of saying "everything," which is to speak of extremes, thereby implying everything between those extremes. So when the Hebrews wanted to say "everything," they would say "from the River to the Great Sea," meaning the Euphrates River and the Mediterranean Sea, which included all of the land that they knew about. Or they'd say, "from East to West, or "good and evil," or "heaven and earth." God will change everything.

Or perhaps the word for heaven was intended to be plural, "heavens," meaning "sky." Then the verse in Revelation would fit with Isaiah 65:17, where God says, "For behold, I create new heavens and a new earth."

II Peter 3 says "the heavens will pass away" (v. 10), "But according to [God's] promise we wait for new heavens and a new earth in which righteousness dwells (v. 13)." This view of "a new earth in which righteousness dwells" fits perfectly with what comes next in Revelation.

"And I saw the holy city, new Jerusalem, coming down out of heaven from God, prepared as a bride adorned for her husband; and I heard a great voice from the throne saying, 'Behold, the dwelling of God is with mortals. He will dwell with them as their God, and they shall be his people, and God himself will be with them.'" Jerusalem was the symbol of God's presence. The Temple had been there, the Temple where God dwelt. But now there was a need for a new Temple, since the old one had been destroyed in the year 70. The Revelation to John was written in 90, so the author knew of the need for a new place for God to dwell.

Notice that these verses are not about our going to heaven but about God coming to earth. It is a vision of a transformed earth, which is totally consistent with the vision found in the Hebrew Bible.

And notice that the passage does not say that people finally discovered that they had been little gods all along. That view, which is found in some New Age religions, is not what Christianity teaches. Even in this paradise, God is still distinct from the people.

Continuing with the text: "God will wipe away every tear from their eyes, and death shall be no more, neither shall there be mourning nor crying nor pain any more, for the former things have passed away." The New English Bible says, "the old order has passed away."

How do we know the Christians were being persecuted? The answer is found in the reference the verse makes to tears and to pain. Reading this text is like listening to one side of a telephone conversation. So when the text says, "God will wipe away every tear," the implication is that there were tears that needed to be wiped away. The fact that the text chooses to talk about the eradication of crying and pain suggests that there was much crying and pain among the Christians at that time.

"And the one who was seated on the throne said, 'See, I am making all things new.'" Here we arrive at the core of the Christian Faith. Whether it be resurrection, or being born again, or new life in Christ, or divinization, or a transformed world, Christian hope is based on belief in the power of God to make all things new.

We see one version of that newness in today's Gospel lesson. Jesus said, "I give you a new commandment, that you love one another, even as I have loved you." How is that a "new" commandment? Well, the earlier standard of excellence was that we were to love our neighbor as ourself. So the degree to which you loved your neighbor and the amount of love to be shown to your neighbor depended upon how much you loved yourself. The new standard presented by Jesus was for us to love others as much as Jesus loved us. And Jesus died for us. So Jesus here calls us to love others self-givingly and without conditions.

And God works through the love of Christ's disciples to bring newness and improvement to the world. Certainly that applies to the self-giving love of mothers, as they influence the experiences and behavior of their children, thereby molding them in new ways. It applies to fathers, too. Unfortunately, the fathers who need to be reminded of it are usually not in church. It applies to those human efforts that have resulted in polluted rivers becoming clean again, so that fish willingly swim in them. It applies to the fact that some endangered species can now be taken off the "endangered species" list. And God works through more people than just Jesus' disciples, as we saw when Mikhael Gorbachev decided that Soviet communism should move in a new direction.

But in all these instances, you might ask, Are we talking about something radically new, or are we just talking about renewal?

I suspect that we wouldn't be talking about God making all things new at all, if, over the centuries, millions of Christians did not endorse St. Paul's claim that "if anyone is in Christ, that person is a new creation or a new creature; everything old has passed away; behold, the new has come." (II Corinthians 5:17) We're talking here about the new birth experience, about a thorough commitment to Christ, about such a surrender to God and to doing God's will that moral behavior becomes simply second nature. Depending upon a person's state before such a conversion, that change could really have been radical. Would it be accurate to say that such a person was merely "improved"? And yet we look the same. I would argue, appearances to the contrary, that the power of God to transform people's lives can produce radical change indeed, and it is the strongest argument, from a Christian perspective, for opposing the death penalty. While a person is alive, the Holy Spirit still has the opportunity to make that person new.

It certainly seemed to make a difference in St. Paul's life, and the world hasn't been the same ever since. In spite of "affliction, hardships, calamities, beatings, imprisonments, [and] hunger," he could still say, using the editorial mode, "We are treated as impostors, and yet are true; . . . as dying, and behold we live; . . . as sorrowful, yet always rejoicing; as poor, yet making many rich; as having nothing, and yet possessing everything" -- that matters. (II Corinthians 6:4d-5, 8c-10)

That's what God's newness can look like in an individual person. What would it look like in the world at large?

The biblical vision is of society at peace. But not a superficial peace. Not just the absence of war. Not the kind of peace where people smile on the outside but are seething with rage on the inside. Rather, a universally harmonious peace, which in Hebrew is denoted *shalom*, where everyone gets along with everyone else -- and with nature, and where everything in nature is in harmony, as well; where "the wolf and the lamb shall feed together, and the lion shall eat straw like the ox," as Isaiah (65:25) said; where children are raised so well that there is no reason for them to commit antisocial acts; where there are no oppressors, not even among us; and where "they shall not hurt or destroy," where everyone feels safe and secure.

That's why, incidentally, "the sea was no more." But this vision of a new earth doesn't mean we wouldn't be able to go swimming in the ocean. No, once again we're dealing with symbolism. The Old Testament sea was where Leviathan, the dragon, dwelt. It was a place of chaos and a source of threat and danger. But in the Old Testament, God tamed the sea. God brought order out of chaos at the time of creation, just as God can bring order and calm into the chaos of our lives. The absence of the ocean means that, in the new earth, when we all behave like God's people, there will be no longer any source of danger.

A final point. We shouldn't let our sophisticated awareness of our own responsibility and of the impact that we and other people can have on the world deceive us into thinking that we can be fairly certain about what the future holds. If the world is in God's hands, then the future is not simply the logical extension of everything that has happened in the past. Rather, the future is like advent, in which God comes to the world. And when God comes, God brings something really new, since God is not like us. God has done that in the past, and God continues to do that. And that can be quite comforting, especially when we've done all we can, and the results aren't what we had hoped for. The Bible says God is involved and "is making" all things new. Indeed, "eye has not seen . . . what God has prepared." We and our world are in the care of a power that can make and has made and will make all things new. So may it be.

"A Last Sermon"

(Micah 6:8)

As I started preparing my final sermon, here, I found myself thinking about a famous last lecture and a last sermon that I've heard about.

One was a speech Winston Churchill gave after World War II at Eaton, the English public school (which means, in our language, the private school) that he attended as a boy. The students were honored that this former Prime Minister, at the end of his career, had come to speak to them, and many of them brought notebooks to jot down bits of the wisdom they anticipated. But when Churchill stepped to the podium, all he said was, "Never give in. Never give in! Never. Never! Never! Never!" And then he sat down. How's that for a speech? If you like short ones, it has a lot to commend itself. There are times, of course, when we should not take it too seriously. When we're heading in the wrong direction or when we want the wrong things, it is not a virtue to be persistent. At other times, however, Churchill's speech may be the only speech we need to hear.

Legend has it that John the Elder, the writer of the last book of the Bible, also gave a talk that was easy to remember. At the end of his life, he left the island of Patmos and went to the mainland in present-day Turkey to give his final sermon. The house was packed. It was literally a house. They didn't have church buildings then, because there weren't that many Christians yet.

He began by saying, "Little children, love one another." And people thought, "Ah, that's a good way to begin. Let's see how he develops it." But all he did was keep saying, "Little children, love one another. Little children, love one another."

(Paul Engle, founder of the University of Iowa writers' program, at age 74 wrote, "I come to the end of my life convinced that love is not only possible, in a basically unlovely world, but it is the ultimate reason for life on earth.")

There are times when filling the air with words is not what is needed.

And perhaps you have just heard the most important part of my sermon already.

We older ones know how tenuous our hold on life is; and that thought can sometimes make us ask what our life is all about.

I'm reminded of a cartoon I saw in *The New Yorker* magazine of a scene looking down upon many businesspeople standing in long lines in front of ticket windows in Grand Central Station. At the end of one line was a man in a long, black coat and a long, black beard, saying, "What does it all mean in the infinite scheme of things?" Well, what does it all mean? What is the point of our busy-ness? What, after all, is the purpose of life? What are we here for?

One answer is found in our First Reading. The prophet Micah asked, "What does the Lord require ... but to act justly, to love loyalty (as the New English Bible says), and to walk humbly with your God?"

"What does the Lord require?" If you don't like the idea of being required to do anything, think of this statement as suggesting, instead, what the best way of life is. After all, what God wants would be what the best is, wouldn't it be? So even for a person who doesn't believe in God, here is a proposal that the best way of life is to behave justly, to be loyal, and to have an appropriate sense of humility. Let's look at each of those features.

"Do justice." When we consider what justice is, we immediately run into some difficulties. Because for Christians, our standard of justice comes from God. And God's ways are not like our sinful ways. God's justice is the kind that gives even to people who don't deserve it. You'll remember Jesus' parable of the laborers in the vineyard, where everyone got paid the same, even though they didn't work the same number of hours. It seems that God's justice is a form of love, which shouldn't be so surprising, if, as the First Epistle of John says, God is love. God loves us even when we don't deserve it. That type of love is called "unconditional love."

Unconditional love was a central feature in a series of adult forum discussions at a church I used to belong to. The topic was "Helping Teenagers to Grow Morally." It was clear, first of all, that we don't dare wait until kids are teenagers, before we start teaching them morals.

Morals that "sink in" will of course we morals that children learn at home. And two of the most important traits to inculcate in youngsters, so that those traits are already present when it is time to consider teenage sexual morality, is respect for others and responsibility: respect especially for people of other races and cultures and for members of the opposite sex. That kind of respect will be learned from the way parents deal with each other and from the jokes they tell and from the comments they make. And responsibility for one's actions will come when children have to face the consequences of what they do and are not bailed out too readily by their parents.

Underlying that kind of training, however, must be the kind of parental love that takes the kid back, even when he or she doesn't deserve it. If you say to the child or the teenager, "If you don't make the choices that I think are best, don't come running to me when things go wrong"--that's not unconditional love. And unconditional love may be the only setting in which teenagers will talk seriously with their parents.

St. Paul said, "Love does not insist on its own way." That's worth thinking about and applying to more than just children. Love cuts the other person some slack. I've never said it like that before, but I think that that's right. So if a parked car straddles a line and takes up two parking spaces, and if you leave a note on the windshield pointing that out, a loving gesture would not include calling the campus police, as well. Cut them some slack. When dealing with children, of course, this approach gets tricky, because a loving parent doesn't let children do whatever they want. But there is a need to distinguish between what you know is best--especially for a child--and simply insisting on doing things your way.

Now for the second feature of the best kind of life. "Love loyalty." The Hebrew word translated as "loyalty"--or "mercy" or "kindness"--is hesed. It can also be translated "steadfast love." You can see how that can be taken to mean "loyalty." Hesed is the word used in the Bible when talking about the power that guaranteed the covenant between God and Israel. Now that relationship was worth maintaining. And now we see why Micah used the word and what he had in mind when talking about loyalty. We are called first and foremost to be loyal to God: to be committed to the highest and the best.

That loyalty transcends more limited loyalties, and it can keep our interests and commitments from being focused too narrowly. Because it is possible to be loyal to relationships and causes that are harmful or wrong. That's why the Hindus have the god Shiva, the Destroyer. Sometimes we find ourselves heading down a wrong path, or being in a rut, or being loyal for neurotic or self-destructive reasons. We sense that we ought to stop and go no further. But we sometimes feel that we've invested so much up to this point that perhaps we ought to stick with it. That's when Shiva can help us to break with the past and head in a new direction. The transforming, mind-changing power of the Holy Spirit can do the same thing.

It is never too late to start again. And if our basic loyalty is to what is best, that will give us permission to turn away from what is less-than-best.

Now to the third feature. Micah tells us to walk humbly. That doesn't mean you have to be a doormat and let everyone walk all over you. But one thing humility brings is an admission that you don't know it all. Someone who knows it all isn't automatically open to something new: isn't alert to learning more--especially if what you could learn could come from someone whom you consider to be inferior. So there's at least that value in humility.

But Micah actually says, "Walk humbly with your God." Minimally, that tells us to subordinate ourselves to what we consider to be the best. Follow the truth at least as <u>you</u> see it.

Be true to the highest values that you are able to acknowledge at present. Sometimes we don't even do <u>that</u>!

But, of course, Micah was speaking to the people of Judah, and their God was the God of the Bible. It would never have occurred to Micah that the people he was speaking to were free to choose whatever God or whatever values they wanted or to understand the Ultimate in whatever way their limited minds could conceive it. If there truly is God, we are not dealing with something we've made up. God establishes the criteria for who or what God is. God also sets the standard of what is highest and best. Indeed, God possibly even <u>is</u> that highest state or best condition. Micah is telling us that there is a standard and a power outside us that "knows," so to speak, what is best. Our task is to get into harmony with it. Devotion to anything else is devotion to an idol.

That leaves some people in this country, nowadays--possibly some whom you know--with a problem that Micah didn't have. The problem is to decide whether there really is God at all. Is there an Ultimate that we might get into sync with?

Let me conclude by saying three things about that question, briefly. First, if there is God, then it is only logical to do things God's way, since presumably God is in a better position than you are to know what is best.

Second, if we <u>are</u> out of touch with God, then we may not be able to rely on our own sensibilities to recognize the divine will, let alone to follow it. We may need to listen to what the Church has said over the centuries. And the risk of a more thorough commitment may also be called for. It's what the Muslim religion calls "*al Islam*," the surrender to God. It's what Jesus and St. Paul call dying to the old way of life, so that a new life in the power of God can emerge--in this lifetime.

And third, Jesus had a suggestion. He said, "Try following what I say and see whether your own experience of doing so doesn't cause you to conclude that my teachings come from God" (John 7:17). The best way of living comes from following the will of God. There's another answer to the question of what it all means in the infinite scheme of things.

Appendix I

WHO WROTE THE BIBLE?

Introduction

Nobody claims that the Bible dropped down from Heaven fully written. So the question becomes, Who wrote the Bible? Or phrased a little more carefully, How did the Bible develop into its present form?

Inspiration?

One of the later epistles in the New Testament says, in some translations, that all scripture is inspired (II Tim. 3:16). Another late epistle says, "men of God spoke as they were moved by the Holy Spirit" (II Pet. 1:21). There are three features of these quotations that need to be considered.

The first is the fact that at the time those statements were made, the only scriptures that existed were the Old Testament. The New Testament had not been put together yet. Could that fact mean that only the Old Testament was inspired? (If not, does the claim also apply to the Koran?)

The second question to consider is what it means to be inspired. Does "inspiration" mean that God dictated the Bible word for word, following the fundamentalist claim that the Holy Spirit "gave the writers the words to use"? Could the Bible count as being inspired if it captures divine truth or spiritual insights, while at the same time getting some of the historical facts wrong? Could "biblical inspiration" mean about the same as saying that a sermon was "inspired," if it was a particularly good sermon?

Thirdly, the entirety of II Timothy 3:16 makes clear that the purpose of inspired scripture is religious teaching, correction, and training in righteous living. This verse does not claim that the Bible provides reliable information about science or history.

Not Literally Accurate

One thing is clear: most recognized biblical scholars (those who know the ancient languages and know how to evaluate literary changes and historical and cultural influences on the Bible) would say that there is overwhelming evidence that the Bible is not literally accurate in all respects. That would mean that the Bible was not dictated by God word for word. Presumably, God would have gotten all of the facts right.

Seeing God

Consider three pieces of evidence that the Bible is not 100% accurate, when interpreted literally. In the book of Exodus, around the time that Moses received the Ten Commandments at Mt. Sinai, a group of elders went up to Mt. Sinai with Moses and had a meeting with God. The Bible says, "they saw the God of Israel" (Ex. 24:10). In John's Gospel the Bible says, "No one has ever seen God" (Jn.1:18). At a literal level, one of those statements has to be wrong. (John's statement is supported by Ex. 33:20.)

Sun Standing Still

There is a claim that Joshua made the sun stand still. If you think about that claim from a scientific point of view, you will realize that it could not possibly be correct. When we talk about the sun standing still, what we mean, of course, is that the earth stops spinning on its axis. For the earth to stop spinning would be like someone driving down a highway at 90 miles per hour and suddenly jamming on the brakes. Everyone in the car would fly through the windshield. If the earth suddenly stood still, we all would go shooting off into space, and the friction caused by the earth suddenly stopping would probably result is everything burning up or turning into massive molten lumps.

When the Bible writer said the sun stood still until a particular battle had been completed, it was like Casey Stengle saying, "It ain't over 'til it's over." The Hebrews were fighting against enormous odds, but by golly– their faith caused them to say "by God"–there was enough sunlight so that the battle didn't end until the Hebrews had won!

Sequence of Jesus' Life

In the New Testament, take the four Gospels and compare the sequence of events in Jesus' life. You will find that the events do not follow the same sequence. To cite one example, Jesus heals Peter's mother-in-law <u>before</u> he calls his disciples, according to Luke; in Mark, the healing is the second event <u>after</u> he calls his disciples; and in Matthew's Gospel it comes five events and four chapters later. (John does not mention it at all.) The Gospels simply do not follow the same chronological sequence.

Process of Development

Rather than saying that God dictated the Bible word for word, biblical scholars say that the Bible underwent a long developmental process, starting with people reporting their interpretation of events as they experienced them, and with others then repeating those reports orally until at some point the reports were written down. The written material was later pulled together by editors, who found meaning in arranging the material one particular way rather than another way and who even occasionally changed the material or added to it to make it more relevant to the time when it was being compiled. Let us consider some sample passages as examples of why scholars say the Bible developed in the way that has just been outlined.

HEBREW BIBLE

Pentateuch

Creation Stories

Genesis 1 contains the seven-day creation story. In Genesis 2:4b, another creation story begins. In this second creation story, human beings are created before plants are created. In the first creation story, plants come first and human beings are created at the very end of the sequence. How could there be two creation stories?

Remember that there were twelve tribes of Israel. It might not be impossible for the different tribes to have had different accounts of the origins of their tribe and of the history of the Hebrew people in general, including different myths to explain how the world began. An explanation for two creation stories is simply that Genesis 1 contains material from one particular group or source, and Genesis 2 contains a different creation story from a different tribe.

God's Name

As a way of confirming the claim that we are dealing with two stories generated by two different groups, notice that God is given different names in these two stories. The ancient Hebrews had many names for God. They called God "Elohim," "Yahweh." "El Shaddai," "El Elyon." "the Fear of Isaac," and others. In Genesis 1 the word for God is "Elohim;" in Genesis 2 God is given two names in Hebrew: "Yahweh Elohim." When they are translated into English, the fact that God is given two names does not appear strange to us, because the names are translated as "the Lord God." But if you know that each Hebrew word is really a different name for God, what you see this particular passage saying is "God God." The passage takes two names for God and puts them together, and that fact will jump out at a person reading the Scriptures in Hebrew, whereas it will not be noticed by someone reading an English translation.

As an explanation of the fact that different names for God were written side by side, we should remember that eventually all of the tribes of Israel came to worship one God, named "Yahweh." But prior to that time, scholars theorize, more than one group of tribal traditions had already been written down with just "Elohim" as the name for God. It is very possible that at a later date, an editor went through that written material and said, "We must make it clear which particular elohim–which particular god–we worship." So every time he saw "Elohim" he inserted the word "Yahweh" in front of it, to make clear that it was <u>Yahweh</u> Elohim that the Israelites worshipped. The editor never did get his hands on the material in Genesis 1.

Interwoven Sources

Eventually, the stories of the first "tribe" (in this case, probably some priests), the stories of the second group of tribes, and accounts from other sources were interwoven into what has become the first five books of the Bible, called the "Pentateuch." When you understand that some parts of the Bible have several different strands of stories that have been woven together, you are in a position to explain some passages in the Old Testament that otherwise are very puzzling, such as contradictions that seem to occur, and the same story being repeated, as the accounts from different tribes are placed side by side, so as not to offend a particular tribe.

Here are a few examples. Also in connection with the Exodus, at one point the Pharoah decides to let the Hebrew slaves go. In another passage shortly thereafter, people are all excited because the slaves have escaped. Did the Pharoah let them go or did they escape? It is probable that one tradition says they escaped and another tradition says they were permitted to leave, in response to the miracles that Moses was supposed to have performed. In each traditions' account, the story makes perfect sense. But when the accounts are interwoven, you have what looks like a contradiction.

It is also likely that there was more than one exodus. The accounts of the routes that the Hebrews took as they were leaving Egypt depict some of the former slaves taking various routes along the northern part of the Sinai peninsula, while others swooped down to the southern part of the peninsula where Mt. Sinai may have been.

J and E Sources

Scholars have been able to sort out these combinations of stories, partly by identifying those that talk about "Yahweh Elohim" and those that talk only about "Elohim." One source of written material they label "J," for the group that calls God "Yahweh." The letter J is used because German scholars decided on the labels, and in German a "Y" sound is spelled with a "J." This material comes from the two tribes that stayed in the southern part of Israel. Their stories can be contrasted to another source that is labeled "E," because its stories refer to God as "Elohim," and they seem to come from the ten tribes that remained in the northern part of Israel after Solomon's kingdom was divided.

As you examine the content of these two groupings of stories, you find other recurring features that show that the sources reflect two different types of societies. The J source is much more authoritarian than the E source, for example. When governmental and religious leaders act, in the J material, they act autocratically. In the E source, there is much more democracy. Whereas in J, <u>God</u> makes Moses the mediator, the <u>people</u> make Moses the mediator in the E source. In E, God's covenant is made with all the people (Ex. 19:2b-6; 24:3-8), whereas in J the ceremony sealing the covenant is only for a select group (Ex. 24:1-2, 9-11).

In J, God is considered to be very near, and there is reference to seeing God. God is given human features. E, on the other hand, posits a great distance between God and the world; it speaks only about hearing God. Its God is more spiritualized, less concrete.

According to J, the Covenant will last forever. In E it is conditional, depending upon the behavior of the people.

In J, people obey God by obeying the <u>ritual</u>-laws of the priests, with whom God made the Covenant. In E, Covenant obligations are moral: E contains the Ten Commandments.

Retrojective Commandments

Another interesting observation that scholars have made is that all of the commandments that God gave to the Hebrew people were given only to Moses. During the time of the judges, after the Hebrew tribes had entered the Promised Land, God gave no new commandments. When the new kingdom of Israel was being developed under Saul, David, and Solomon, God didn't give any new commandments. When the Temple was being built and questions arose concerning how big it should be and what kind of sacrifices should be offered and when, none of the answers to those questions can be found in accounts of the days of Solomon. The answers, when they were provided, were given by God to Moses while he was in the wilderness.

In the wilderness the Hebrews were nomads. They were leading sheep and wandering around, presumably for forty years, and yet it is at that time that God gives them laws on how to arrange their agricultural affairs: what crops not to grow next to other crops, how to divide up plots of land, and when to let the crops lie fallow—matters that seem totally irrelevant to nomads.

In the story of the Exodus, Moses gets everybody ready to go, and there is a feeling that the Egyptians are going to be breathing down their necks at any minute. Then he stops, and for two chapters he tells his people how to celebrate the Exodus after they have arrived safely in the Promised Land, many years later. Doesn't that seem odd?

The conclusion that scholars have come to is that all of these commandments actually originated much later than Moses' time. They were developed at a time when they were needed: when the Israelites needed agricultural laws and when they needed some decisions about sacrifice in the Temple and about how to celebrate the Exodus. But as a way of authenticating the commandments, to get the people to treat them seriously, the claim was made that God had given the commandments to Moses, way back in the times of their ancestors, and now was the time when they were expected to carry out God's ancient laws.

Of course, this view does contradict the tradition that Moses wrote the first five books of the Bible. But that is only a tradition. There is nothing in the Bible that says Moses wrote the first five books. If he did, then he described his own death (in Deuteronomy).

Deuteronomy

Deuteronomy has its own story. That book seems to have been an ancient scroll that was found in the Temple sometime after the reign of Solomon. King Josiah was cleaning out the Temple, wanting to purify the religion of Israel, and found a scroll which seems to be the core of what is currently Deuteronomy. Later, some sections were added at the beginning and end; but with regard to the issue of sources, Deuteronomy provides its own source.

Priestly Source

There was one other spurt of writing that probably began during the Exile, after the Babylonian army destroyed the Temple for the first time, in the year 587 B.C.E., and moved large numbers of people from Jerusalem to Babylonia, in what is now southwestern Iraq. Priests from the Temple were included among the exiles. In exile, they came to understand their nation's history and theology differently than they did when they were in Palestine. They came to believe, for example, that God was not restricted to the Temple but had moved with them into Babylon. Ezekiel's vision of the wheel in the middle of the air was a psychological symbol of God on the move with the Israelites.

They also came to believe that Yahweh was more than just a tribal God. And it was probably then that the first creation story in the Bible was written, because they began to conceive of Yahweh as the God of the entire world. They probably made use of a number of the features of the Babylonian creation story when writing the one that we find in Genesis; but they modified those features to portray what they believed about God.

Scholars have given the label "P" to the writing that these priests did. We have now looked briefly at "J," "E," "D" (for Deuteronomy), and "P," which all seminarians in the seminaries of all of the major mainline denominations in this country learn routinely. The information presented here is not new. It has existed for over one hundred years, although it has not always filtered down to local congregations.

Psalms

Let us look quickly at other parts of the Bible. Many of the Psalms came from songs developed around campfires, where people would gather in the evening. We still find this occurring in sections of Saudi Arabia today. People would add verses to the songs they would sing each night. The verses that were popular were repeated and consequently were propelled into the future. Verses that were not popular were dropped. The Israelites were religious people, so many of their campfire songs could easily have been religious in nature.

Some of the psalms come from very personal meditations about how God had behaved toward individuals and about their feelings about God. Still other psalms were developed in connection with festivals in Jerusalem.

Prophets

For simplicity's sake, we may say that the books dealing with the prophets probably came from the prophets, although it is important to notice that the prophets were not primarily writers of books. They were preachers, often standing on soapboxes and saying, in effect, "Repent, because you are breaking God's moral laws; and if you don't repent, God will punish you."

Some of the prophets really did have scribes. We know that Baruch was the scribe of Jeremiah.

The book of Isaiah probably came from three prophets. Scholars think so, because of the kinds of things that are said in that book. In the early part of Isaiah, the words come from someone living in Jerusalem and predicting the destruction of that city if the people do not obey God's laws. Later parts of the book look forward to the time when the people will be able to <u>return</u> to Jerusalem, as though those statements were coming from a totally different time period.

There is probably even a third grouping of chapters that comes from the very beginning of the time when people <u>had returned</u> from the Exile to Jerusalem. All of these different sources were sewn together to make a scroll of a particular size, and that scroll was labeled "Isaiah," which is why we had assumed that only one prophet wrote it.

Establishing the Hebrew Bible

The books of the Pentateuch were probably combined into a single document when the Second Temple was built, as described by Ezra and Nehemiah. Many other religious writings existed, but the Jews did not have to decide whether to count them as Scripture until Christians came on the scene. People then started calling Jesus the "Messiah" and started to treat as Scripture the letters that Paul wrote and some gospels that had been written. Also, the Temple was destroyed for the second time. So around the year 90, the successors to the Pharisees met in the town of Jamnia or Javneh, on the Mediterranean coast, and finally decided which writings would be Holy Scripture for them. It was then that they decided which prophets they would revere, which psalms they would use, and which pieces of wisdom literature, such as Proverbs and Ecclesiastes, they would include in their Bible. In other words, it was only then that they decided the content of what Christians traditionally have called the "Old Testament" (but what people who are more respectful of Judaism nowadays are calling "the Hebrew Bible").

Apocrypha

But the story does not even end there, because other writings existed. There were I and II Maccabees and I and II Esdras; there was Tobit; there were stories that relate to the book of Daniel. These and others had been written in Greek, and the Jews never officially counted them as Scripture.

But the early Church treated them as Scripture. So when the Roman Catholic and Eastern Orthodox churches were compiling their Bible, they included those books. They eventually included at least nine (either books or parts of books) that are not in the Protestant Bible. Protestants call those books the "Apocrypha." During the Protestant Reformation, Luther and Calvin followed the standards used by the Jews when deciding what to treat as holy writ, so they did not include the Apocrypha. Within Christianity, therefore, there is a larger Old Testament among Catholics and the Eastern Orthodox than among Protestants.

NEW TESTAMENT

Now let us take a look at the New Testament. For the sake of simplicity, we shall deal only with the Gospels and Epistles.

Gospels

The Gospels of Matthew, Mark, and Luke are called "Synoptics." They see Jesus' life in a similar way. John's Gospel is very different. When the Synoptics describe Jesus cleansing the Temple (turning over tables and driving out money-changers), that event occurs very near the end of his ministry. In John it occurs in Chapter 2. John's writing is much more symbolic. He wants to depict Jesus as a "new broom that sweeps clean," so he places the event of Jesus cleansing the Temple right at the beginning of his Gospel, as if to say, "Here is somebody who is going to make a really big change in the Jewish religion." John does not seem to be at all concerned about being historically accurate. At least, he certainly places the cleansing of the Temple at a different chronological point in Jesus' ministry than where Matthew, Mark, and Luke put it.

Synoptics

The Synoptics are not exactly the same, but there <u>are</u> large portions of them with the same wording. Fifty-one percent of the verses in Mark are repeated exactly in Matthew and Luke. That tells us that all three Gospels were not firsthand accounts. It is highly unlikely that people who saw the same event would describe it in exactly the ssame words.

So the question becomes, Who copied from whom? Copying is not automatically bad. If you want the message to be passed on accurately, copying could be better than changing the words every time the message is repeated.

Eventually we find ourselves asking, "Who was the first of the Gospel writers?" There is some renewed interest in this question nowadays, but at the moment the scholarly consensus is that Mark was the first Gospel writer. Here are some reasons why.

It seems as though Mark provided the chronological sequence of events that Matthew and Luke followed. The latter two do not follow Mark in every instance, but when Matthew deviates from the series of events in Jesus' life that Mark reports, Luke follows it; and when Luke deviates from that series, Matthew follows it. They seem to hold Mark's sequence in common, suggesting that they were using his Gospel as the basis for their own.

Mark's Greek is worse that Matthew's and Luke's, and it makes more sense to think that when Matthew and Luke were copying from Mark, they cleaned up his grammar, rather than to suppose Mark was copying from perfectly good grammar and make it worse.

Mark is more redundant than Matthew and Luke. In their versions of similar stories in Mark, they leave out his unnecessary wording.

Mark's Gospel includes some Aramaic phrases, although it is written in Greek. It is likely that Jesus spoke Aramaic. The gospel closest to the time when Jesus lived might have remembered phrases that Jesus actually used, whereas later gospels would be less likely to. Matthew and Luke do not use those phrases.

Mark also contains some errors. In one instance in his Gospel when Jesus lists the Ten Commandments, Jesus includes a commandment that is not one of the Ten Commandments. He says, "Do not defraud." When Matthew and Luke report this event, they simply leave out "Do not defraud."

In another place, Mark quotes from a prophet but gives him the wrong name. He says he is quoting from Isaiah, but the quotation comes from Malachi. When Matthew and Luke deal with that passage, they identify the prophet correctly. In all of these examples, it seems likely that Matthew and Luke were working with Mark's material and improving it as they did so, thereby indicating that Mark wrote first.

Moving to another topic, there are some passages which are the same in Matthew and Luke but which are not mentioned in Mark at all. Certainly in these instances Matthew and Luke could not have been copying from Mark. Scholars propose—and this is only a hypothesis—that there may have been another document, filled with sayings of Jesus (not reports of healings, not narrative), which Matthew and Luke took material from, when they were writing, but which was not available to Mark. Scholars call this document "Q," from the German word "Quelle," which means "source."

Matthew also has some special material that none of the other Gospel writers had. For example, Matthew is the only one who talks about the three wise men finding Jesus at his birth. Matthew also is the only one who talks about the holy family going into Egypt after Jesus is born. None of the other Gospels reports those events.

Luke, too, has special material not found in the other Gospels. Luke is the only place where there is an account of angels and shepherds at Jesus' birth. Luke's is the only Gospel that has the Good Samaritan parable and the parable of the Prodigal Son.

That fact helps to make the point that probably all of the stories, accounts, narratives, sayings, and teachings in the Gospels once circulated as independent units. Somebody saw Jesus heal someone; that person remembered that event. Another person heard Jesus say something particularly insightful; that person remembered that. And these recollections persisted, often unrelated to any other occurrences for long periods of time, as different people who were with Jesus at different times remembered different events. The person who saw Jesus heal Peter's mother-in-law may not have known whether that event came before Jesus said, "Turn the other cheek" or afterward. He or she may not even have been present when Jesus said, "Turn the other cheek." There is no way to coordinate all of this material so as to make it chronologically accurate.

Eventually, it probably was Mark who pulled those reports together and wrote them down, but we have no way of knowing the chronological order of the events in Jesus' life. What Mark seems to have done was to depict Jesus as starting out in Galilee, getting a group of followers there, and only at the end of his life going to Jerusalem. And to the extent that Matthew and Luke follow Mark, they follow basically the same course of events. John, on the other hand, has Jesus go to Jerusalem for at least three Passover festivals. So we are not even sure whether Jesus' ministry lasted a year (as it could have, in Mark's chronology) or as long as three years. The fact that we do not know the chronological order of Jesus' life, however, does not automatically mean that particular events that were reported had not actually occurred.

Scholars think that Mark was written around the year 68. If Jesus was 30 or 33 when he died, about forty years passed before anything about him was reduced to writing. Matthew and Luke were written around the year 85, give or take ten years.

The Gospels probably were not written earlier, because the disciples expected the world as they knew it to end. Jesus spoke about the coming of the Kingdom of God. When it did not come during his lifetime, his disciples expected that, since he had risen from the dead, he would return very shortly and bring the Kingdom. But time passed and that did not happen. Meanwhile, the original witnesses to Jesus' ministry started to die. Then the Second Temple was destroyed by the Romans, and Christians thought, "Certainly now the Kingdom of God will come." But it didn't. So they thought, "We had better write down some of these traditions about Jesus, while there are still some live witnesses to tell us about him;" and that is probably when the first Gospel was written.

Another surprising thing to notice is that the writers were not eyewitnesses. Mark is not listed as one of the twelve apostles. Tradition says that Mark learned about Jesus from Peter. Luke is not listed among the twelve apostles. Luke was a traveling companion of Paul. Matthew is sometimes listed as an apostle, but not in all of the Gospels. Yet if it is the case that Matthew copied from Mark, then the writer of Matthew's Gospel probably was not an eyewitness. If you were an eyewitness, you would not have to copy from someone else.

John

John also is listed as an apostle, but John's Gospel reflects all sorts of non-Jewish ways of looking at the world. Scholars do not think that John the apostle wrote John's Gospel, partly because it reflects a typically Greek—not Hebrew—way of looking at things. The ancient Hebrews tended to be very concrete in the way they viewed reality. The Greeks were much more willing to be abstract and symbolic. As already noted, John's Gospel is filled with symbols. You do not find that in Matthew, Mark, and Luke. Only in John's Gospel do you find such abstract phrases as being "of the truth" and "children of light." That is hardly the language of a Jewish fisherman, which John was.

Matthew, Mark, and Luke contain many pithy sayings of Jesus and short parables. You find none of that in John's Gospel. Instead, in John's Gospel Jesus engages in long discourses. Jesus talks for three chapters in a row, very unlike the Jesus depicted in the Synoptics.

The healings that the Synoptics report are not found in John's Gospel.

Scholars think that John was written last, after the early Church had a chance to start thinking extensively about who Jesus was. John's Gospel reflects much more theological development than the others. For example, Jesus talks about himself, in John, in ways that are very different from the Synoptics. In John he says, "the Father and I are one" and "I am the Vine, you are the branches" (another example of a very abstract way of speaking).

Epistles

With regard to the Epistles, not all of them that have been attributed to Paul were written by Paul. There are seven that are considered to have been genuinely written by him. They are Romans, I and II Corinthians, Galatians, Philippians, I Thessalonians, and Philemon. There are others whose authorship is disputed. And there are others which, even though they say they come from Paul, probably do not. They are I and II Timothy and Titus.

You might be surprised that anyone would dare to write a letter saying it was coming from Paul when it really was not written by him. But if you were to look at the practices being followed in the Roman Empire in the centuries surrounding the time of Christ, you would find that it was very common for people in a "school" of philosophy founded by a leader one or two hundred years earlier to write new material in that philosophical way of thinking and to attribute it to the school's founder. It was a way of honoring their dead leader. It was a way of saying, "If our leader were still present, this is the way he would think about current affairs." So it was not a matter of plagiarism or of pretending that somebody else was doing the writing; it was a standard means of honoring somebody whose way of thinking you endorsed. Scholars suspect that that practice was being followed in the case of the "Pastoral Epistles," those letters written to Timothy and Titus, who were new pastors in the Church at that time.

Scholars make this claim, because they find stark contrasts between those epistles and the ones that they think genuinely come from Paul. Paul's epistles reflect the expectation that Christ will return soon. In I and II Timothy and Titus, there is no expectation of Christ returning soon. Instead, there is reference to passing on the tradition to the next generation. The Church has settled into its new role as an organization, and in order to avoid false teachings, what it emphasizes is passing on the tradition about Jesus and passing it on accurately.

Another contrast: "Faith," in Paul's view, was personal trust in God, living with God minute by minute. "Faith" in the Pastoral Epistles is referred to as "the Faith" and treated as though it meant "the doctrine." You have faith when you believe the doctrinal formulations that had not yet developed when Paul was writing.

In Paul's time, the Church was governed by charismatic leaders, people filled with the Holy Spirit, who, because of that fact, took charge of local congregations. By the time of Timothy and Titus, there were presbyters and bishops who were ordained by the laying-on of hands. Ecclesiastical affairs were getting much more organized and settled. And since these contrasts are so great, scholars are inclined to say the Pastoral Epistles were probably not written by Paul.

Another way of checking authorship is by comparing the language used. There are many words that Paul uses over and over in his genuine epistles that are not used at all in the Pastoral Epistles. And there are words that are characteristic of the Pastorals that do not appear at all in Paul's genuine epistles.

Establishing the New Testament

Many people are surprised to learn that other gospels and epistles were written that were not included in the Bible, such as the Gospel of Thomas, the Gospel of Peter, and the Epistle of Barnabas.

The question then becomes, How was it decided which ones to include? It is interesting to note that, although the Church in the first four centuries held a number of ecumenical councils, where bishops from all over the Roman Empire convened to make decisions about important matters, there was never a council held to decide which books to include in the New Testament.

The books that eventually got into the New Testament had three characteristics. First, they were the ones used most often in the churches. What counts as Christian Scripture? Answer: the writings that Christians read and take seriously. Especially in the very early years, church meetings on Sundays would consist, in part, of reading the mailbag. The small and scattered bands of Christians drew encouragement from letters they received from churches in other parts of the Empire, especially if the letters came from Paul or other important leaders. We find in the epistles themselves wording that says, essentially, "after you have read this letter, pass it on to another church" (Col. 4:16). So the Bible itself gives us the clue that that is what was happening. The epistles that were read over and over again and the gospels that were used frequently were the ones that eventually became official parts of the New Testament.

The early Church also thought that any work in the New Testament had to be written by an apostle or by the scribe of an apostle, since the apostles were eyewitnesses. Nowadays, scholars would challenge the claim that the writers of the Gospels actually were apostles, but back then people thought they were. The works of Paul were included, because Paul had a conversion experience in which he felt he was an eyewitness of the Risen Lord. His writings were taken seriously for that reason.

Another interesting point is that a writing did not have to claim to be inspired, in order to get into the Bible. Some early Christian writers, such as Clement, Polycarp, and Irenaeus, claimed to be inspired, but that claim was not sufficient to justify including their writings in the New Testament. So inspiration was not a criterion for admission.

The third characteristic of any writing included in the New Testament was that it had to agree with Christian teachings, i.e., with what Christians, as a group, said they believed.

Over the decades–indeed, over the centuries–different bishops in different locations made lists of books that they considered to be authentic Scripture for churches in their diocese. It was not until the year 367, however, that Athanasius, the bishop of Alexandria, in Egypt, came up with a list of New Testament books corresponding exactly to the list of books in the New Testament today. So for 300 years, what counted as the New Testament was very fluid. But eventually everyone accepted Athanasius' list, and that is why we have the particular books in the New Testament that we do have.

IMPLICATIONS

As a final consideration, notice that nothing presented here destroys the truth of the Christian message. What has been dealt with is not the content of the Christian faith but its container. Occasionally, when people encounter the possibility that the Bible is not accurate in every way, or that it was pieced together and modified over time, they swing to the conclusion that it must not be of any value at all. There is no reason to adopt that view, however. The spiritual truths, the insights, and the religious teachings of the Bible can all be true, even if we do not know the order of events in Jesus' life and even if other parts of the Bible are more poetic than historically factual.

For people who believe that God dictated the Bible, the material presented here does provide reasons for modifying their thinking. But that modification just requires that they see that God works in more subtle and complex ways than perhaps they had thought. God seems to work that way today, and it is likely that God also worked that way during the centuries when the Bible was being formed.

Appendix II

"GODSPELL:" A MODERN VIEW OF JESUS

At a time when many people have developed a new enthusiasm for Jesus, while others have dropped out of the church, because its traditional doctrines seem to be out of touch with the world as they actually experience it, we look with interest at the portrait of Jesus presented by a modern popular musical such as "Godspell." ("Godspell" means "good tale." It is the Old English spelling of "gospel.") What is it that John-Michael Tebelak and composer-lyricist Stephen Schwarz see in him who has been called "Son of God" and "Savior"?

The answer to that question is not as clear as it might be. Godspell does not include the confession at Caesarea Philippi (Mt. 16:13-23). Instead, its most famous song, "Day by Day," reflects the fact that people are attracted to Jesus but have trouble understanding him. Nevertheless, they want to see him more clearly, love him more dearly, and follow him more nearly.

Although the play claims that it is based on the Gospel According to Matthew, it does not portray all of that Gospel; and eighteen percent of it deals with passages from the other Gospels.

Signs of Jesus' Significance

At the beginning of the musical, much confusion results from arguments about personal identity and about meaning and purpose in life. Into this confusion comes John the Baptist, blowing a ram's horn (in the original production) and saying, "Prepare ye the way of the Lord!" The implication is that the answer to the ultimate question is about to be given. The fact that the ram's horn is blown on the Jewish New Year may be an additional hint that the author is pointing to something new. Later in the show, he expresses the expectation that "the birth pangs of a new age will begin."

The conventional title of "Christ" is not used, except as a squelched curse-word. It is replaced by the more ancient Hebrew word "Messiah." The author may be purposely not utilizing the title around which extensive doctrine has developed, in order to encourage his audience to view Jesus afresh.

Although the reasons for Jesus' death are not presented clearly, the play seems to suggest that he is crucified for being anti-establishment. John the Baptist's diatribe against respectable people (the Pharisees and Sadducees) sets the tone. The chief priests and elders question Jesus' authority; Jesus inveighs against the Pharisees; and Judas betrays him. On the other hand, rather than presenting a clear reason, Tebelak may simply be portraying what often happens to a person like Jesus, in accordance with John 3:19 ("light has come into the world, but people loved darkness rather than light").

The musical contains only a few signs of an atonement motif. (The fact that the ram's horn is blown also on the Day of Atonement provides one sign.) Dressed in blood red, Jesus pronounces the traditional Hebrew blessing (translated) before each part of the words of institution at the Last Supper, thereby clearly tying that event to the Passover meal, with its celebration of liberation from bondage. And, of course, Jesus is crucified.

In different garb, he narrates the angel's announcement of the Resurrection; and the show ends as the disciples sing "Long live God!" and "Prepare ye the way of the Lord," thereby implying a continuation by divine agency of what Jesus taught and did, and of what he was in touch with.

Jesus as Threatening Moral Teacher

Tebelak's most evident picture of Jesus is that of a moral teacher who encourages belief in God and who warns of punishment for not being good. Jesus' first announcement is that he did not come to abolish the law. Forty-eight percent of the play deals with his teachings concerning morality and behavior, compared with only twenty percent of Matthew's actual Gospel. As though this emphasis were not sufficient, the play makes use of fifty-one verses stressing morality and judgment from other Gospels.

The teaching function of Jesus is reinforced in a song which speaks of "studyin' the good Lord's rules" and of "learnin' every line in every last commandment." The first half of the play centers around the Sermon on the Mount, with enactments of its moral teachings interspersed with parables which often are illustrative.

Jesus' teachings emphasize love and self-giving, but some teachings are of the more harsh, "thou shalt not" variety. Jesus, himself, is cheerful but serious in his presentation. His disciples tend to respond to him warmly, even though his teachings are not always what they want to hear. This response could stem from their realization that his critical judgments are made in the spirit of love. His disciples also may intuit that he is right. His teachings could be viewed as the real truth breaking through to us.

But what should our motive be for being moral? And how is the truly moral life carried out in practice? Tebelak's answers to these questions overlook Jesus' most profound insights.

In the play, Jesus' disciples are told to learn their lessons well, in order to save their souls and—as something mentioned in passing—to avoid going to Hell. If the disciples are miserable being good, that doesn't matter, because they will go to Heaven. "Job had nothing on you." "It's all for the best." "You gotta stay pretty in the city of God." Also, "you gotta live right."

The play does not depict moral behavior as resulting from a relationship of essential trust in God, whereby the individual is freed to take the risk of determining the most morally appropriate action in each different circumstance, as Jesus himself did. In other words, the moral life is not depicted as loving God and then doing as you please, as St. Augustine suggested it could be. Nor is it depicted as a response to God's love of us. Neither is there a hint of the power of God to transform lives, so as to make moral behavior our natural behavior. Rather, morality is depicted as a matter of scrupulously following commandments. Yet many people today realize that the most winsome personalities, the most genuine and even the most fundamentally moral people, often do not "live right" in terms of the scruples of rule-following.

One-third of the musical deals with judgment and related warnings. So intense is this motif at one point in the play that Tebelak reaches for the John 8:3-11 story of the woman caught in adultery, to introduce a tempering note of mercy. But the motif is resumed again with the separation of the sheep from the goats, with the goats being sent to eternal fire. At this point the play seems to cry out for the disciples to plead "come sing about love," which they do in a song of penitence entitled "We Beseech Thee, Hear Us."

Faith and Grace

Although almost three times as much attention is paid in the play to moral behavior as is paid to faith, the value of faith is by no means ignored. Fairly early in Act I, Luke 18:1-14 is used to depict the vindicated faith of a persistent widow and the faith of the publican compared with that of the Pharisee. The need for and the appropriateness of faith also occur in such teachings as taking no thought for the morrow, the Parable of the Sower, the father giving his son bread instead of a stone, the Great Commandment, and the Temptation in the Wilderness.

Indeed, many segments of the play may be viewed as an acting out of the doctrine of justification by grace through faith. (The words of one song run, "No gifts have we to offer for all Thy love imparts." Another acknowledges sharing "man's guilt and fall" and sings of "love that draws us lovingly ... and ... longs to bless.") The disciples feel liberated by Jesus' acceptance of them, even though they don't always live up to his moral standards.

The musical numbers are divided equally between those stressing the Law and those reflecting the Gospel. "Learn Your Lessons Well" ("You can reach [the promised land] if you keep alert") is followed by "Bless the Lord" ("The Lord to thee is kind / He will not always chide / He will with patience wait / His wrath is ever slow to rise / And ready to abate / He pardons all thy sins"). "All Good Gifts" ("...are sent from heaven above") nevertheless is followed by "Light of the World" ("You can't have that fault and be the salt of the earth"). Do "goodness" and "light" come from "heaven" or from one's faultlessness? Is salvation by God's grace or by moral perfection? The play does not offer a clear answer to these questions.

Completing the Picture

But neither the New Testament Church nor John-Michael Tebelak sees in Jesus simply an itinerant preacher of morality. The Gospel writers may have reflected their faith that Jesus was more than just a teacher by attributing additional miracles to him. Tebelak's "more than" does not take that form. His other dimension takes the form of joy. The production bubbles with colorful costumes, upbeat music, and joy. It asks that "songs be heard instead of sighs." A significant portion of the show's theology may be stated in its musical score alone. The happiness of the performance must be considered, along with the words of Jesus, to get a complete picture of the play's view of Christ.

In addition, the author connects Jesus with all people, not just a few. Tebelak may purposely intend to present Jesus as the embodiment of true humanity, to whom all are related (and who is related to all). Following his baptism, for example, Jesus identifies with the general dejection of the people by leading them in singing "God Save the People." In the play, Jesus predicts that all–not just Peter–will betray him before the cock crows. Jesus is related to each person personally, and their response is "take me with you" and to sing of his being "By My Side."

Theological Reflections

The show provides support for two significant and related statements that can be made about Jesus. The first deals with Jesus himself. The second deals with the relationship between Jesus and us.

1. Although Jesus clearly is human, he possess a quality of life that we do not have. This is his uniqueness. There is a "qualitative distance" between him and us, between his commitment to the truth and ours, between his ability to love and ours, between his sensibility to Ultimate Reality–his perception of what is significant–and ours. He evidences the joy, profundity of purpose, sensitivity to the downtrodden, and inner serenity that we would like to have. In his own life, he is in control of many of the things that dominate our lives against our will. He is in touch with things which don't die. He shows what it means to be fully alive. Since we are not fully and abundantly alive, he personifies "new life" breaking through to us. He is concerned for our "eternal" well-being: for the depth and quality of our existence. He does not seek it with us, because he already has it.

2. Since much of what is true of Jesus is not true of us, he throws into bold relief the evil in us and in our society which we don't want to acknowledge. Through him, we are confronted with an impact from outside our realm of existence. Jesus qualifies, therefore, as a messiah, the coming of whom changes things and makes them as they should be. Christians over the centuries have found his "otherness" to be peerless and have therefore acknowledged him as the Messiah. He brings a "cosmic consciousness" which we do not want to ignore, one which draws us outside ourselves and which keeps us from being overwhelmed by the purely mundane. It also thereby enables us to develop wider horizons and a deeper sense of community. Through our interaction with him, he "imparts," generates, or at least points to a state of existence which enables us to be loving and self-giving. Through a relationship with him, our behavior and outlook change, because we admit that he embodies a superior quality of life, a life that has an impact on us. For those who choose it, his way of being has authority, and his love and newness offer forgiveness, a chance to start again.

Jesus is like us, so he can communicate with us. He also is not like us, and consequently he can bring a new "dimension" to our existence. In traditional language, he is both human and divine.

INDEX OF BIBLICAL REFERENCES